Michael Dames

Mythic Ireland

with 152 illustrations

Thames and Hudson

To Ériu, forgive my trespasses

(Frontispiece) *People in a landscape, gathering for Christian prayer on a pagan cairn, somewhere in Ireland*

Designed by Liz Rudderham

© 1992 Thames and Hudson Ltd, London

First published in the United States of America in 1992 by
Thames and Hudson Inc., 500 Fifth Avenue, New York,
New York 10110

First paperback edition with corrections 1996

Library of Congress Catalog Card Number 91-67303
ISBN 0-500-27872-5

Printed and bound in Slovenia

Contents

The oldest of the old follows behind us in our thinking, and yet it comes to meet us.

MARTIN HEIDEGGER

Introduction
Setting out

Ireland and Myth

It is often said that the Age of Myth is over, and that the gods of humanity's childhood have been supplanted, first by the *real* Christian god, and then by the reality of scientific reason. The assumption is made that only as rapidly fading superstition, and in old-fashioned places like Ireland, does the shadow of myth still fall.

In this book it will be argued that Irish mythology is far from dead. Instead, it springs to enjoyable and valuable life through the interplay of language with place-names, medieval manuscripts, contemporary folklore, and modern Irish literature. Together these words are found to complement Ireland's landscapes, and her ancient monuments, art, and objects of common use, to tell stories of deities presumed lost. They return to illuminate contemporary life in Ireland, and help to define future prospects for the world in general.

Irish myths offer an insight into the original nature of human dwelling on earth, and now that the estrangement of our own civilization from a previously deified natural order is recognized as a self-destructive aberration, it may be that Ireland's archaic legacy begins to assume a new relevance.

Ireland, scholars affirm, has preserved the richest store of mythological traditions of any country north of the Alps. This legacy sometimes caused bewilderment to those trained exclusively in the Christian tradition. For example, a medieval Irish monk wrote, in a colophon to his copy of the *Táin Bó Cualgne* myth:

I do not accept as matter of belief certain things in this history, or rather fiction; for some things are diabolical superstitions, some are poetical inventions, some have the semblence of truth, some have not; and some are meant to be the entertainment of fools.[1]

Every civilization tends to assume that *it* is 'fact', and others are 'fiction', but in Ireland the myths of previous ages are inclined to hang on and on, till eventually (with or without permission), they become embedded in the consciousness of subsequent eras. It is as though each

(Opposite) Map of Ireland showing provinces, counties, and locations of places and features discussed in the text

successive wave of Irish culture is half-mesmerized by the myths it has rejected, and in some form acts out the vanquished beliefs, so imparting to the country a compound psychic charge both subtle and strong. In this process of accumulation little is discarded and everything is modified.

Over six millennia, Ireland has evolved an ecology of interdependent 'myth species', a pluralism that might serve as an antidote to over-reliance on an isolated technological outlook, or priestly dogma.

Since the first human communities settled in Ireland nine thousand years ago, the country has received and developed at least four major canons of myth. They are: first, 7000–2000 BC, the myths of the Mesolithic hunter-gatherers and of the New Stone Age (Neolithic) farmers. The latter were 'present throughout most of the island by about 3200 BC, with evidence of their arrival from 3700 BC onwards'.[2] The myth of this era, termed 'Old European' by the prehistorian Gimbutas,[3] revolved around the figure of a female goddess of birth, death and regeneration, matched by a matrilineal human order.

Second were the myths of Indo-European warriors which emphasized a male sky god, reflected in a patriarchal human society. (Present in the Irish Bronze Age, c. 2000–800 BC, this mythic wave is most clearly represented by the Celtic-speaking invaders of the Iron Age, beginning c. 800 BC.)

Third, from AD 500, Christian mythology introduced concepts of Original Sin, and a dualistic division between body and soul, world and spirit, previously unknown in Ireland. The subdivision of the Christian myth between Catholic and Calvinist followed the seventeenth-century settlement of Ulster by an Anglo-Scottish population.

Fourth, 1700–2000, came Scientific Rationalism, introduced by English and Anglo-Irish urban populations. At first glance this is not a mythology, since it rejects all supernatural accounts of reality, preferring to describe the cosmos through an ostensibly objective language of numerical abstraction (mathematics) – an entirely subjective choice.

The recent appreciation by Popper and others that 'scientific discovery is akin to explanatory story-telling, to myth-making, and to the poetic imagination'[4] places science in the broad mythic field where, in any case, it was born and nurtured. There, the idea of objectivity appears as one among many story-telling techniques. The nineteenth-century conviction that the modern world had entered a post-mythic state now appears to be a delusion. Instead (and especially in Ireland), we inhabit a commonwealth of interacting mythic states which includes modern science among its number.

In present-day Ireland, four seemingly incompatible mythologies interact. Each in turn has claimed an exclusive grasp of the truth, before merging with its rivals to create new hybrids that are gradually accepted as authentic. As a result, evidence of the very oldest mythic layer can still be recognized at the contemporary surface of Irish life, offering hospitality to later inputs.

Archaeology suggests that between 4500 and 2000 BC, waves of Indo-European peoples spread from an area of South Russia towards India and Ireland, carrying a patriarchal, horse-mounted warrior culture and the group of languages to which Irish and Sanskrit both belong. Today, Ireland is one of the principal repositories of Indo-European culture

Marija Gimbutas, visiting Ireland in 1989, commented:

Old European monuments stand here in all their majesty. In its legends and rituals, this country has preserved many elements which in other parts of Europe vanished long ago. Much that stems from pre-Indo-European times . . . is still very much alive in Ireland. I would say that the ancient spirit of Ireland is closer to the Old European [fourth millennium BC], despite the rather early appearance of Indo-European peoples here.[5]

In Ireland, the oldest is not necessarily the faintest, or most distant, so instead of attempting a chronological account of Irish mythic sequences, this book accepts that the layers are now thoroughly intermingled, and they are described accordingly.

Ireland and Otherworld

The co-existence of the archaic within the modern makes Ireland a complex place, and its power to fascinate stems partly from its endemic ambiguities. These are now reflected by the multi-faceted reality presented to the entire world by modern physics, where ghostly interlacings are inferred at the sub-atomic level. In its old habits, Irish life may be said to epitomize this emergent sensibility. Thus a markedly conservative culture coincides with the latest view of nature, and archaic practices are supported at a fundamental level by today's theory. Traditional Irish attitudes may literally be said to offer prescience or foreknowledge of recent science at its most kaleidoscopic.

There are numerous senses in which Ireland is a multiple world. On the political level, the current division between the Irish Republic and Ulster (declared to be part of the United Kingdom in 1921), means that on both sides of the border people are aware that there is another version of island reality, a fact emphasized further by divisions within Ulster. These outward disparities stem from different ways of imagining, embodied in two languages, Gaelic and English. Even when, as now, Gaelic is little spoken, its supernatural assumptions infiltrate and affect the use of English in the Republic, contrasting with Ulster's Anglo-Scottish employment of the same words. In Ulster, pre-Christian mythic layers tend to be suppressed, whereas in Eire even the primary Neolithic stratum continues to impinge on the collective imagination.

This amazing continuity of myth can be explained in part by the fact that Ireland is still a mainly rural country, where agriculture has been regarded as a sacred art for at least five thousand years. Recent mechanization has yet to dismantle this attitude completely. Nor has it totally eradicated those traces of the original Neolithic deities who lived on as *aes síde* – the fairies, or people of the mounds. These lesser spirits of the land remained fearfully vivid through the first half of the twentieth century. As intermediaries, they enabled people to stay in touch with their ancestral gods, who had taken refuge in the *síd*. Such magic halls were located inside mountain or monument, or in an 'Otherworld' beneath a lake, or 'somewhere' in the western ocean. Foolhardy or adventurous mortals could hope to enter these places.

'Otherworld', so defined, has long since waned, but another version is waxing strong. To most Irish people currently alive, their land is a place across the sea, rarely if ever visited. Forty millions of Irish descent live in North America, and millions more in Britain and Australia. For them Ireland is a point of ancestral reference – an island hidden in cloud, whose profile looms the larger the less it is seen.

With the Irish population scattered across the world, Ireland's position is elusive, both in space, and (as this book tries to show) in time. Ireland lies here *and* there, now *and* then. The Other is often heard knocking on both sides of her door.

Word of Myth

Those who prepare for a mythological journey in Ireland by looking for a definition of myth in almost any English dictionary will receive a discouraging shock. Myth, it appears, has a very bad name.

The 1989 Oxford Dictionary defines it as 'a purely fictitious narrative usually involving supernatural persons, actions or events, and embodying some popular idea concerning natural or historical phenomena; in generalized use, an untrue or popular tale, a rumour'. Longman's says: 'Myth is a false story or idea, something or someone invented, not real'. Collins' Cobuild adds: 'An untrue idea or explanation; the word is often used to show disapproval'. 'A widespread but false idea', contributes Penguin, whilst Scribner-Bantam emphasizes the degrading consequences: 'A false belief held by a people to justify social institutions, such as slavery'.

Fortunately, some obsolete Scottish usages of the word take us nearer the role played by myth in contemporary Ireland. They include, 'To show, to mark, to notice, to measure', and 'the marrow of a bone'. With that we come to the archaic pith of the word.

Current pejorative meanings of the word *myth* were not invented by the language priests of the Anglo-American scientific rationalism, but derive from an attack launched in Greece during the late fifth century BC by the Sophist philosophers. The existing Greek word *muthos*, meaning 'word', or 'speech', derived from an Indo-European root, *mudh*, meaning 'to reflect, to think over, to consider', did not suit the Sophists' purpose, since *muthos* implied the sacred, with its 'words' coming directly from, and about, the gods. Myths told how they created the universe by, and in the sound of, their words. This art was both tangible and divine – a direct revelation of the truth, syllable by syllable, in definitive acts of speech, from which all else followed, as the great *Chi-rho* page of the Book of Kells, illuminated by Irish monks in AD 800, continues to demonstrate.

The Sophists sought to oust *muthos* from this central position, and to put in its place a new concept of 'word', named *logos*. *Logos* would convert 'word' into the transparent vehicle for their abstract thought, rational argument and logical discourse.

With the passage of time the academics spread their preference for *logos* over *muthos* throughout the Graeco-Roman world. (So great was the prestige of *logos* in the eastern Mediterranean during the first century AD that St John and interpreters of his writings misapplied Logos as a title for Christ, though plainly his words are those of Muthos, the divine revelation of a god.)

Following the victory of *logos* in Anglo-America, the very meaning of *muthos* has been largely converted into a term of intellectual abuse, despite the efforts led by Eliade, Campbell, and others to redress the balance.

Sacred Word in Ireland

The Romans never invaded Ireland, and so the cult of Greek *logos* which they had spread through much of Western Europe did not take root there.

By the time the first Christian missionaries arrived from Britain, the Roman Empire had collapsed and the tide of *logos* had temporarily ebbed. Thus the fledgling Christian Church in Ireland faced a community untouched by *logos*, united by an enthusiasm for myth, and led by a powerful body of literati-poet-priests, who employed the technique of writing, not in abstract speculation, nor chiefly in disseminating Christian texts, but primarily to set down in the Irish language the vast corpus of pre-Christian mythology by means of which the oral tradition continued to provide Irish society with its spiritual and social coherence. Working directly from this oral mainstream, from the sixth century onwards, they described the deeds of gods, and the associated ritual and imagery (human and divine), with an authenticity practically unmodified by ecclesiastical control until AD 1000 – a situation unique in Christian Europe.[6] These authors had in view an audience from all over Ireland, and connected local and provincial specifics to an island-wide whole. A thousand years after they put down their pens, their achievement is still available and relevant.

By the tenth century the ravages of the pagan Vikings caused the Church to take a more rigorous attitude towards pre-Christian myth of every kind, including stories native to Ireland. Pressure was then applied to squeeze the old gods from future writings by attempting to disguise them as invented historical personages – a procedure known as eheumerization. Yet this mask, donned for the sake of both rational and Christian propriety, largely failed to conceal either the deities or the continuing mythic orientation of the Irish people.

Language shows this to be the case. Irish language and grammar is a concrete reality and its literature (even when written in Latin or English) 'has a peculiar concreteness of expression and imagery',[7] which may be properly called primitive. It is deliberately and literally non-sophisticated, and survives as an alternative to, and a critique of, an international *logos* regime which may itself be showing signs of internal collapse.

In this century Irish writers have carried an archaic appreciation of myth to the van of the modern movement and into the heartland of logic-obsessed Europe. For example the young Samuel Beckett in Paris attacked the devotees of *logos*: 'You are not satisfied unless form is so strictly divorced from content that you can comprehend the one without bothering to read the other...'[8]

Instead of this fateful gap, he recommended a mythic use of words as found in Joyce's *Finnegans Wake* (called *Work in Progress* in 1929). Beckett explained: 'Here form is content, content *is* form...It is not written at all. It is not to be read – or rather it is not *only* to be read. It is to be looked at and listened to. He is not writing *about* something; he is writing something. When the sense is sleep, the words go to sleep. [See the end of 'Anna Livia'.] When the sense is dancing, the words dance.'[9]

Myth, Rite and Symbol

Myth can be regarded as one of three interrelated aspects of religious expression. Its word and story is re-enacted on the human plane by means of ritual (sacred acts). Myth re-activated by human *rites* also requires a sacred *place*, whether natural, built, or a combination of the two, and tangible sacred objects. These physical symbols can be discovered in landscape features, and are emphasized by enclosure, temple architecture and sacred art.

The word symbol comes from the Greek 'to throw together, to unite', and the symbols employed by myth, whatever their size, represent the visible convergence of the cosmic pattern within the living body of the godhead. The 'walks' undertaken in this book are a movement towards integration of myth with ritual and symbol.

The attempt to join myth, symbol and ritual into one is helped in

Ireland by the *Dindshenchas*. These are collections of sacred stories (Irish, *senchasa*), written down in verse and prose from AD 1160 onwards using archaic oral sources, explaining the origin of noteworthy Irish place-names, or *dind*.[10] *Dind* is cognate with Old Norse *tindr* – a 'spike, tooth, mountain peak'. Both traditions compare mountain peaks with the teeth of the gods,[11] and the Irish stories typically conclude with absolute union between god and place, when the deity dies and is buried at the spot carrying his or her name.

The *Dindshenchas* were arranged to make a clockwise, or rather a sunwise circuit of Ireland, starting in the north-east. They are mythic rather than historic, and bring sacred topographic memories under the scrutiny of solar and lunar 'eyes'. These scripts offer a valuable means of access to a neglected pagan landscape, lying close to Christian or prosaic surfaces.

Step by hesitant step one follows the tracks. Some are still kept open by living pilgrims; most have long since been abandoned.

The Five *Cóiced* (Provinces)

A five-fold structure is fundamental to Irish myth, as Rees and Rees have demonstrated. It follows that the Old Irish word for province is *cóiced*, literally 'a fifth'. MacCana writes of this One-plus-Four arrangement as 'fractions of an all-embracing totality, coterminous with the land of Ireland, involving the cardinal points, . . . an ancient cosmographic schema, with parallels in other great traditions of the world'.[12]

Parts one to four of this book describe journeys into the provinces of Ulster, Munster, Leinster and Connacht. Each of these regions can be shown to have developed its own emphasis, while drawing from the common store of national experience. This is demonstrated by focussing attention on selected sites within each province. These provincial findings are then brought together in the fifth province, *Mide*, from where a web of relationships is seen to run to and from every part of the island, making a mythological web spun by the deities.

The first 'walk', in Ulster, encounters the relationship between Irish Catholicism and the pre-Christian myths which found shelter within the body of the early Church, and have remained therein ever since. This theme is explored at St Patrick's Purgatory on Lough Derg, Co. Donegal, still the scene of annual pilgrimage. This starting place is chosen because Christianity represents the most recent and widespread overt claim to Godhead, and is the gauze through which other deities are largely seen.

The dominant religion at any given time in Ireland usually grants shelter, however reluctantly, to waning pantheons. So the late twentieth century has seen the Church herself move towards the rising temple of materialism, and in the same mood as that of a pagan bard, who, falling on hard times, comes to knock on a monastery door, while the

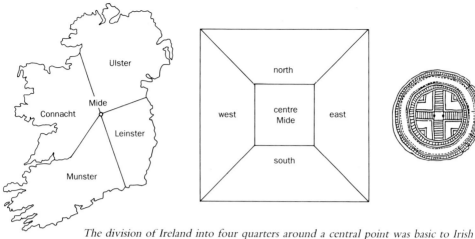

The division of Ireland into four quarters around a central point was basic to Irish myth-making long before the Celts arrived, c. 2,500 years ago. It is reflected in the patterns of Irish gold discs, made c. 2000 BC (right), and in Gaelic sayings such as 'into the five points' and 'the five parts of the world', meaning, in all directions

pre-Christian figures of the Cailleach, or Hag, and of the demi-god Finn McCool, continue their wanderings through the public imagination.

The Munster 'walk' focuses on Cnoc Áine and Lough Gur, where Neolithic and Iron Age myths are seen to combine in twentieth-century folk belief. Here the central figure (befitting the southern province of Ireland's high noon) is the sun goddess Áine. Her cult is traced through the rich assemblage of monuments erected around the lough, where the archaeological evidence is interpreted with the help of oral traditions of equal antiquity. Listening to Mr Tom MacNamara, a Lough Gur inhabitant, running through his repertoire of stories (which he learnt word-for-word from his neighbour, Tom Carroll, who died in 1988 aged 93), one is reminded that these are not illustrations of ideas, but a liturgical evocation of deities who live in monument and landscape.

From the inhabitants of Lough Gur one learns that myth, even in its decline, is best known from the inside. To *wear* the stories makes for an understanding denied to objectivity, and opens the way towards dozens of holy wells and Marian shrines, Finn's seats, and sea coves remembered for supernatural landings. In Munster, the prosaic and the numinous are on good terms.

The third 'walk', in Leinster, concentrates on Dublin as a mythic construct. Prehistoric, neoclassical, and modern attitudes are seen to merge in the internationally renowned achievements of Leinster's poets, novelists and playwrights. Her word artists have revealed the mythic nature of urbanism *per se* by lifting the mundane metropolis into a series of new universes; as Cyril Connolly remarked in 1929.[13] Joyce, Yeats, O'Casey and Beckett have revitalized a tradition whereby 'poets' act as priest-midwives to Leinster. They hint at the re-integration of urban with rural Ireland, in pursuing their visions beyond the constraints of historical time and simple geometric location. In Ireland's capital, thanks to them, we see the archaic turn up on the doorstep of the Here and Now.

Connacht, the western province, is rich in myths of war, honed by the Iron Age enthusiasms of a warrior society, who followed the exploits of their gods. They in turn modelled their behaviour on the elemental play of natural forces. The Slighe Mhór, or great east-west road across Ireland, formed the axis of these rivalries. Where it crossed the Shannon, Connacht's eastern boundary (and a major mystical and physical axis), the qualities of western-ness is developed in the legends of Goll, King Eochaid, and the hags of Keshcorran. Endings and deaths mingle with a new-found desire at the Ess Ruaid Falls in North Connacht, where a Samain or end-of-year love feast was central to a myth of national importance. In Connacht the themes of love and war, life and death, are merged, in a manner which made the province the proverbial seat of wisdom.

The vertiginous grandeur of Mide, the fifth province, is approached in Part Five. Mide gathers together sites from the surrounding provinces, to make a rotation taking a year to complete, and annually repeated. The assembled deities are witnessed engendering an Eternal Instant, endlessly dividing and reuniting, and exchanging animal and human forms. Mide presides over a dynamic pattern, where the entire island is affected by four 'provinces' of Time. These traditionally began at the festivals of *Samain*, or Hallowe'en (1st November), the start of the New Year; *Imbolc* or Oimelg, also called St Brigit's Day or Candlemas (1st February); *Beltaine* (May Day), the start of summer; and *Lughnasa* or Lammas (1st August), the start of harvest and autumn.

Mythic Ireland is centred on the story of a divine space-time cycle in which provinces of time continuously interact with provinces of space, thanks to a mythic narrative which draws them together as the visible life of the gods.

Finally, the mythic narrative is carried across the domestic threshold in sacred attitudes to the house, based around the Fire Goddess (Saint) Brigit. Through her, the dwelling and its ceremonies are seen to flare on the hearthstone of infinity, bringing the furthest lights of divinities within the scope of the family. This possibility, it is suggested, has by no means gone, any more than has our only source of domestic light and heat, the sun. By its light (while the power to wonder remains alive), the inhabitants of a modern bungalow may yet consciously transform their dwelling into the occasional fulcrum of the universe, provided the mythic words (whether of liturgical or spontaneous utterance) are sounded.

The art of synthesis, upon which myth-making depends, is still commonly practised in Ireland. It involves skilful use of whatever comes to hand, in adding to the palaces of the gods, and in digging secret tunnels between them.

In Ireland, shoreline boulders were held to embody elemental powers, and myth, as a two-way process, was dialogue with the Other

Midwinter Solstice

Samain
(Hallowe'en)
Celtic New Year
November 1st

WINTER

Midnight

Imbolc or **Oimelg**
(Feast of St Brigit)
February 1st

WINTER
SUMMER

Autumn
Equinox

AUTUMN

Dusk

SPRING

Dawn

Spring
Equinox

HALF
HALF

Lughnasa
(Lammas)
August 1st

Midday

SUMMER

Beltaine
May Day
May 1st

Summer
Solstice
(St John's Eve)
June 23rd

Ireland was traditionally divided into four provinces of Time, initiated by the festivals of the four quarterdays: Samain, marking the start of winter, and a new year; Imbolc, spring; Beltaine, summer; and Lughnasa, harvest. These 'provinces of time' continuously interacted with the provinces of space

18

But far from offering an escape from the real world, myth proclaims reality's hidden essence, and inspires social structure to arise from the heart of the narration.

However, it could be argued that the dominant myth in modern Ireland is provided by the anti-mythic rationalism, imported into the country, and developed at an accelerating rate since 1700. Notably intolerant of other forms, rationalism often believes that it has eradicated them.

Yet no sooner have the old deities 'disappeared' than they have acquired fresh relevance as metaphors of cyclical renewal lacking in the positivistic world view of the last three centuries, which is currently being devoured by its own short-sighted greed.

The time has come to look again at earlier myths, if only because they are less lethal than the brittle certainties of recent materialism.

Ireland, the emerald isle, is a jewel no longer. She may be green at the core, but black and grey spots are spreading rapidly over her skin in the shape of lifeless loughs, deadened by silage effluent, the slurry of intensive cattle rearing and the residues of chemical fertilizers. Her Sea fills with Britain's radioactive waste, and her sky is often darkened by the fumes of industrial Europe.

In the midst of a tale of fast-accumulating ecological misfortune, some eyes cannot help straying towards the green knoll, to scan slopes half shorn of sacred words. Considering this depletion, can one speak of the possibility of recovery?

Given time, the Green movement may eventually mould a new tongue in the *logos*-vacuum without reference to ancestral voices; but there *is* no time. The need is immediate, and since, in any case, the intention of Green consciousness is to develop root-systems, the poetic turf of Ireland may now come in useful. The mulch of Irish mythology is nutritious, not least because it combines semi-decayed fragments mixed together from Iberia, France, Britain, the Baltic, and from as far away as India, on the opposite shore of the Indo-European cultural sea.

After millennia of rain-soaked opportunities to mature this combined international heritage in comparative seclusion, Ireland is in a position to offer its mythic, flame-filled peat to a world in need of sacred meaning, by a metaphorical extraction that would not leave a hole behind.

Given present conditions, these mythological walks in Ireland are not an exercise in nostalgia. Instead, they take roads where the oldest of the old follows behind us in our thinking, and yet comes to meet us.

Part One ULSTER
St Patrick and the Hag

St Patrick's Purgatory

The Road to Ferry House

Mythological walks are bound to follow the tracks of the gods, and the revelatory journeys of the first carriers of a new god's name. In the northern province of Ulster this leads us straight to St Patrick's Purgatory, where, by the manipulation of hope and terror, the dominant Irish deity of the present millennium achieved and sustained his supremacy, with the help of the patron saint.

To Catholics, Lough Derg is by far the most sacred lake in Ireland. It lies broad and grey, five kilometres wide, among unpopulated, heathery hills, in Co. Donegal. The placid surface is dotted with woody islands, and when the wind drops the whole scene sustains an intense silence, as if the universe is holding its breath in preparation for a fresh start.

Today, the believers have come and gone, leaving their cars and mini-buses behind, parked in rows on the lakeside.

Beyond the cars are a clutch of single-storey buildings, in the style of a country railway station of the last century, known as the Ferry House. Inside there is a stout deal table, some benches arranged around the walls, and a black empty grate at one end. The drivers and passengers have all departed for the other world of Station Island. Like a battleship it lies moored in mist, a mile offshore. Capped by the octagonal cone of its basilica roof, the first officer can peer through clerestory windows in all directions over the tops of dormitories whose grey walls fall sheer as a hull into the water on all sides.

This stone ship is designed for the transportation of human souls to Purgatory. Although from a distance no passengers are visible, the vessel is crowded with the devout, reliving the agony of the early Middle Ages in complete mythic identification. This is no place for tourists, which is why none come. Lough Derg is for pilgrims. A pamphlet on the waiting room table explains:

Lough Derg has been Ireland's national shrine of pilgrimage since the time of St Patrick (fifth century). Pilgrims arrive daily and do not need to make

(Previous page) St Patrick, patron saint of Ireland, in a Festival tableau in Stuttgart, 1617, showing the smoking vent of Purgatory at the summit. St Patrick's 'Purgatory' in Co. Donegal became famous throughout Christendom

Pilgrims embarking for St Patrick's Purgatory, July 1990. Every summer, tens of thousands of Christians cross to an encounter with the sacred on Station Island. The tip of its basilica is believed to mark the spot beneath which St Patrick descended into Purgatory

any booking arrangements for their three-day stay. About twenty thousand make the pilgrimage every year.

What to bring

Because many of the Exercises take place in the open air pilgrims should bring warm and waterproof clothing. They may not bring to the island cameras, radios, musical instruments or articles to sell, distribute or for games.

Pilgrims may arrive on any day of the season until 13 August and they must have fasted from all food and drink (except plain water) from the preceding midnight.... When registering at the lake-shore pilgrims pay in advance for accommodation, leaflet of instructions, boat fare, etc. There is no other charge. [In 1989 the rates were £12 Irish currency, or £11 Sterling; many Catholics from Northern Ireland attend.]

When to come

Boats are available from 11.00 am to noon and from 12.45 to 3.00 pm. The crossing to the island takes about five minutes.

Pilgrims must be at least fourteen years of age, and free from disability. The nature of the penances excludes anyone under doctor's care and the very old.

The Exercises

Having arrived on the island the pilgrim goes to the hospice, removes all footware and begins the Stations.

A twenty-four hour vigil, a night of continuous prayer, is the chief Exercise of the pilgrimage. To do this successfully pilgrims need to be well rested before arriving. On the second night they go to bed on the island and leave Lough Derg for home on the following morning at 10.00 am.

Pilgrims are expected to attend all the Exercises of the pilgrimages as approved by the Bishop of Clogher in 1988. Three Stations are to be completed before 9.20 pm. All the prayers of these Stations are to be said silently.

Begin the Station with a visit to the Blessed Sacrament in **St Patrick's Basilica**.

Then go to **St Patrick's Cross**, near the Basilica: kneel and say one *Our Father*, one *Hail Mary*, and one *Creed*. Kiss the Cross.

Go to **St Brigid's Cross**, on the outside wall of the Basilica: kneel, and say three *Our Fathers*, three *Hail Marys* and one *Creed*. Stand with your back to the Cross, and, with arms outstretched, renounce three times the World, the Flesh and the Devil.

Walk slowly, by your right hand, four times around **the Basilica**, while praying SILENTLY seven decades of the Rosary and one *Creed* at the end.

Go to the penitential cell or 'bed' called **St Brigid's Bed** (the one nearest to the bell-tower) but if there is a queue take care to join it before going to the Bed.

At the Bed

(a)   Walk three times around the outside, by your right hand, while saying three *Our Fathers*,[1] three *Hail Marys*[2] and one *Creed*.[3]

(b)   kneel at the entrance to the Bed and repeat these prayers.

(c)   walk three times around the inside and say these prayers again.

(d)   kneel at the Cross in the centre and say these prayers for the fourth time.

The exercises are then repeated at six more 'beds', named after saints Brendan, Catherine, Columba, Patrick, Davog and Molaise.

What is the purpose of these repetitions? The Lord's Prayer (which always comes first) consists of words originally spoken by the Godhead. He *instructs* his followers to repeat them. By doing so, they hope to establish his universal order on earth. Similarly the Virgin Mary is 'encountered' by being hailed, while The Creed lays out the details of the Christian cosmic drama. Said together, the three prayers construct the myth of which they speak. That is why, for believers, they cannot be spoken too often.

During the all-night vigil that follows, the prayers of the four Stations are said aloud, and in common in the Basilica during the night of the Vigil. Between these Stations pilgrims may leave the Basilica, use the night shelter, and walk around the immediate vicinity of the Basilica only, taking care to keep their voices down.

Gradually, the space around the pamphlet fills up with the throb of an outboard motor, and an open boat approaches the mainland jetty.

A young man and woman leap ashore and run between the puddles to one of the cars. Their faces are animated by something more than the pleasure of release. Thoroughly shrived, they make off at speed, like Adam and Eve before the Fall, towards the garden of a new existence. Having secured his vessel, the boatman, dressed in yellow oilskins, plods up the ramp and into the Ferry House. He is old. He has been ferryman here all his life. Once in his youth he had cycled to the Croagh Patrick mountain pilgrimage in County Mayo, 'but that was, oh . . . years ago. Will you be going barefoot?' (meaning on the pilgrimage) he asks.

The Medieval Pilgrimage

One of the earliest surviving accounts of St Patrick's Purgatory is to be found in Giraldus Cambrensis' *Topography of Ireland*, of 1186. He described 'an Island, one part of which is frequented by good spirits, the other by evil spirits'.

There is a lake in Ulster containing an island divided into two parts. In one of these stands a church of especial sanctity, and it is most agreeable and delightful, as well as beyond measure glorious for the visitations of angels and the multitude of the saints who visibly frequent it. The other part, being covered with rugged crags, is reported to be the resort of devils only, and to be almost always the theatre on which crowds of evil spirits visibly perform their rites. This part of the island contains nine pits, and should anyone perchance venture to spend the night in one of them (which has been done, we know, at times, by some rash men), he is immediately seized by the malignant spirits, who so severely torment him during the whole night, inflicting on him such unutterable sufferings by fire and water, and other torments of various kinds, that when morning comes scarcely any spark of life is found left in his wretched body.[4]

Here the incoming tide of Christianity can be seen to split the world into a dualism of Good and Evil, with the newly divided self made visible in the form of a divided island. Previously, light and dark had been accepted as equally necessary and interdependent, like winter and summer, with the horror of 'the Hag' regarded not as wickedness but another aspect of a totality presumed to be good.

Therefore Patrick was required to show the truth of his doctrine. On the island in Lough Derg, he attempted to do so; or rather he prayed there to his God to show him how to demonstrate the truth, and in response God immediately offered the saint a nocturnal trip to Heaven and Hell in the form of a dream. As Roger of Wendover wrote in the late twelfth century:

Whilst the great Patrick was preaching the work of God in Ireland, and gaining much reputation by the miracles which he there performed, he sought to reclaim from the works of the devil the bestial people of that country by fear of the torments of hell and desire of the happiness of heaven, but they told him plainly that they would not be converted to Christ, unless they first saw with their eyes the things of which he told them.[5]

In Geraldus' words, he procured by the efficacy of his prayers an exemplification of both states, even on earth, as a salutory lesson to the stubborn minds of the people.[6]

The modern Catholic Encyclopaedia defines Purgatory as 'the state, place or condition in the next world, which will continue until the Last Judgement, where the souls of those who die in the state of grace, but not yet free from all imperfection, make expiation for unforgiven venial sins, or for the temporal punishment due to venial and mortal sins that they have already been forgiven, and so, by doing, are purified before they enter heaven.'[7]

For Catholics Purgatory was (and is) a kind of vestibule below the level of living, where the souls of the dead worked off their lighter punishments prior to the Last Judgement. At Lough Derg, access to Purgatory could be gained by *the living* through incarceration in an island cave; and from there also glimpses of Heaven and Hell, in repetition of St Patrick's experience, might be had. Roger reported:

The Son of God appearing to him, led him into a desert-place, where he showed him a cave round and dark within and said to him, 'Whosoever in true penitence and constancy of faith shall enter this cave for the space of a day and a night shall be purified therein from all the sins which he has committed against God during all his life, and shall also there not only behold the torments of the wicked, but if he shall persevere steadfastly in the love of god, be a witness also of the joys of the blessed.[8]

Scholars now say that St Patrick never referred to Lough Derg in his writings, never visited the lake, and was wholly unconnected with it until several centuries after his death. This shows that myth can be more important than history, as does the unsubstantiated claim made in the current official Guide that the island has been a national shrine since the fifth century. Belief creates its own truth, as Lithgow discovered in 1619, when travelling in Ireland: 'Hundreds of the better than the common sort have demanded of me if Jerusalem and Christ's sepulchre were in Ireland and if the Holy Land were contiguat with St Patrick's Purgatory.'[9] The implication is clearly that for many Irish people, the islet in the lough *was* the Holy Land. Thus holy centres of a given kind flock together, and become indistinguishable through faith, layer upon layer. Before the advent of cheap air travel it was often the *places* that did the flying. This is not to deny the compulsion that drove so many on the Crusades and brought people from all over medieval Europe to the shore of Lough Derg; but having reached one sacred spot, it was found to contain others, as gifts from the pilgrim's heart.

On arrival at Lough Derg, medieval pilgrims found that 'St Patrick' has 'constructed an Oratory on the spot...enclosing the cave which

Saints Island, Lough Derg (above).
Now deserted, it was the site of the
Purgatory from the twelfth to the
sixteenth century. Then the Purgatory
was 'moved' to its present site on
Station Island (see right).
St Patrick (below) discovers the
entrance, and a penitent, attended by
clerics, follows where Christ and St
Patrick had led (fifteenth-century
woodcuts)

27

is in the burial-ground in front of the church, placed a door there that no-one might enter without his leave. He next appointed here a society of regular Canons and gave the key to the prior...Many persons availed themselves of the privilege [of entering] whilst St Patrick was still alive, and when they came out, they testified that they had seen the torments of the wicked as well as the great and unspeakable happiness of the good,' wrote Roger.

In fact, a group of Celtic anchorites (hermits) *had* settled on Lough Derg by the seventh or eighth century, to lead a quiet life, but on what is now Station Island, and knew nothing of all this.

The death of one of their number, Cillene, is recorded in the *Annals of the Four Masters*. They lived in beehive-shaped cells, whose outlines have been reconstructed to make the 'beds' featuring in the present penitential perambulations. Among the carved stones from the eighth century is a Latin cross slab, now incorporated into the basilica wall, and two worn seventh-century inscriptions to St MacNissi. Despite Viking raids, it is believed that this community of hermits was still there when, in the early twelfth century, St Malachy of Armagh encouraged the canons regular of St Augustine to found a priory on the neighbouring Saints Island in the same Lough.

Observing that their Celtic neighbours incorporated a cave into *their* pattern of worship (which they associated with the name of their founder, St Daveoc), the Anglo-Normans responded by 'finding' a cave on Saints Island, and out-Daveoced Daveoc by announcing that *the* original Christian in Ireland, St Patrick, had been led to this newly dug cave by Christ, where the saint received his vision of Purgatory, Heaven and Hell. This rivalry was part of a wider struggle between the Celtic Church, established in the fifth century, and the more recent Latin Church. At Lough Derg the Celtic community lost, and was disbanded.

One of the most popular and eagerly copied books of the Middle Ages was Henry of Saltrey's description, written in 1185, of how he gained access to the dread cavern:

Patrick and his successors established the custom that nobody may enter without licence from the bishop of the diocese of Clogher in which it lies.

The bishop shall first implore the pilgrim to abandon such an undertaking, saying that many have entered and never emerged, ... and diligently advise the pilgrim to try some other penance. But if he persists the Prior brings him to the [Saints Island] church, where he remains during fifteen days of fast and prayer. Then, fortified with Holy Communion, and sprinkled with Holy Water, he is led to the entrance of the cave, with a procession of clergy singing a Litany. At the door a final warning is given, but if the pilgrim remains firm, the door is opened in the presence of all and the priests give him their blessing, and mark his forehead with the sign of the Cross. He enters, and the Prior closes the door.[10]

If these precautions seem over-elaborate, it must be remembered that holy places had to find ways to be taken seriously. Lough Derg chose the Very Severe route to international publicity, and it worked. People flocked to take the ultimate test, and they have flocked ever since. But St Patrick's Purgatory is more than clever marketing. It is founded on the principle of mythic repetition, running in an unbroken sequence from the Son of God, through St Patrick, to the individual. It was Christ's supernatural journey after Calvary which underlay the pilgrimage. 'He descended into Hell, and on the third day he rose again from the dead; before ascending into Heaven.' The canons announced that Patrick had enjoyed a modified form of this experience: he descended into Purgatory where he glimpsed Heaven and Hell, before re-ascending to mortal life. The medieval visitor, chanting the Apostles Creed, was repeating, at the human level, the journey that Christ made between Good Friday and Easter Sunday, a thousand years before; hence the 'confusion' between Lough Derg and the Holy Land in the popular mind. The intention was to close the gap, and the gap was duly closed.

Saltry's account continues:

Next morning the door is opened by a Prior. If the pilgrim is waiting there he is joyfully conducted to the Church for another fifteen days of vigils and prayer. If however he does *not* make an appearance he is abandoned as lost and the door is locked.

Owen in Purgatory

We can get through the door in Roger's version of 1153, in the company of a certain knight called Owen. Shut in by the Prior, he passed courageously along the cave until he was in total darkness. At last the light again broke upon him and he found himself in a twilit plain entering a pillared enclosure, like a cloister, where fifteen men in white garments warned him of the imminent approach of a multitude of unclean spirits who might destroy him, body and soul, unless he carried himself manfully, and called on the name of the Lord.

Left alone, the knight heard a noise around the building, 'as if all the men in the world with the animals and beasts were making it, and after this noise came a terrible apparition of ugly demons, of which an immense multitude rushed into the hall'. They advised him to return through the door by which he had come, to enjoy all the pleasures of the world and wait for a second meeting with them until he was properly dead. The knight held a contemptuous silence at this suggestion. Indignantly, the demons kindled a large fire and 'seized the knight by his arms and legs, threw him into the midst of it, dragging him with iron hooks, backwards and forwards. When he first felt the torture he called on the name of Jesus Christ saying "Jesus Christ have mercy upon me".' At this name the fire was put out, so that not a spark remained. The demons then dragged the knight

. . . through a wilderness of black and dark, towards the place where the sun rises in summer, and he began now to hear lamentations as if of all the people in the world. Then he was dragged to another plain, filled with woe and calamities . . . full of persons of both sexes every age, naked, and lying with their bellies to the ground, with hot nails of iron driven into the earth. Sometimes in the anguish of their suffering they gnawed the dust, crying and lamenting 'spare us, spare us, have mercy, have mercy upon us!' The demons coursed over these wretched beings, striking them with heavy blows.

In another place . . . the people were pinned on their backs and fiery dragons were sitting on some of them, gnawing them with iron teeth to their inexpressible anguish, . . . whilst fiery serpents coiled around others' necks, arms, . . . and fixed iron fangs into their hearts. Toads, also, of immense size and terrific to behold, sat upon the breasts of some, and tried to tear out their hearts.

From the top of a lofty mountain, the demons showed the knight a violent whirlwind from the north, which swept a large number of naked people into a cold stinking river from which they were unable to escape. All were sitting naked, bent down upon their toes, and turned towards the north, apparently awaiting in terror the approach of death.

Eventually he was shown a stinking fiery well in the south, from which hot naked men were shot forth like sparks, before sinking again into the flaming pit. 'That fiery well is the entrance to hell where we live.' (All the torments he had so far seen were a mere foretaste of the real pains of Hell, lying beyond.)

The knight was then made to cross a narrow slippery bridge, dizzily high, over a flaming river.

At last he was released from demonic persecution and saw before him a high wall of wonderful workmanship, having in it a closed gate adorned with precious stones that shone brilliantly. When he approached it, it opened, and a sweet smell came forth, reviving him.

Then out came a procession of crosses, tapers, banners and branches of golden palms, followed by archbishops, bishops, abbots, monks, priests, and ministers of every ecclesiastical degree, all clad in sacred garments. With pleasing salutations and concerts of unequalled harmony, they led him within the gate in triumph. Two archbishops conducted him through most delightful meadows, adorned with different fruit and flowers and herbs. Darkness never fell in that region. Harmonious human choirs lauded the Creator of all things. No-one felt heat or cold.

The holy pontiffs told him that this was the terrestrial paradise before the Fall, populated by those who had purged their sins by penance, and hoped to reach Heaven. (This concept was eventually rejected by the Catholic church at the Second Council of Lyons.)

Then the prelates led the knight to the sloping side of a mountain and bade him look upwards; and asked him what colour heaven was, from where he stood. He replied:

'Like the colour of gold that is red-hot in the furnace.' 'This', said they, 'which you now see, is the entrance to heaven and the celestial paradise. As

The Inferno, engraving after Orcagna, c. 1460–80. The adult being delivered from the Devil's womb indicates a reversed birth, into hot confinement, while the serpents coiled around the inmates may be seen as negative versions of the foetal umbilical cord. Purgatory and Hell are misogynistic conceptions of delivery into living death

long as we remain here, God feeds us daily on heavenly food.' A ray of light [then] descending from heaven, covered the whole country, and the flame, settling in rays upon the heads of each, entered into the bodies of all. At that, the knight felt such a delicious sweetness pervade his heart and his whole body, that he hardly knew whether he was alive or dead, but this feeling was over in a moment.[11]

The knight was then told he must return to the world, and so reluctantly he did. After a visit to the Holy Land he eventually returned to Ireland, where his vision of Purgatory continues to glow.

Purgatory and Earth

Children attending Roman Catholic Confirmation classes in the mid-twentieth century were aware that the mythic journey described above did not end in the Middle Ages but was everyone's inescapable destiny. On entering the Cave of Death, they would be required to stride into the flames. 'The best that my sisters and our friends could hope for, as we gathered in Mrs Donaghue's front room to learn the truth, was that if we were good the certain terrors of Purgatory *might* not be followed by the eternal agony of Hell. Either way, it would be an unforgettable excursion and probably last longer than the Second World War, of which we could not recall the beginning, nor guess the end.'

31

Today, some Catholic authorities adopt a slightly embarrassed tone regarding Purgatory:

The punishments of purgatory and allied topics are much more obscure than the question of the *existence* of Purgatory. All theologians hold that there will be *some* kind of purifying punishment there (from the very etymology of the word) that will cease with the last judgement, [but] a veil of mystery prevents any accurate assessment of the intensity of the pain [and] certain conceptions... stressing too much the horror and misery of purgatory are to be discouraged.[12]

In the eleventh century, Irish belief in Purgatory was so strong that it was thought that purgatorial fires might rise into the real earthly landscape in an Hiroshima-like event:

To wit, a flame of fire, swifter than a blast of wind, which will cleanse Ireland from the Southwest. And that is the fire which in the twinkling of an eye will burn up more than four fifths of the men of Ireland, men, women, boys and girls, without communion, without confession, without sacrifice... black ashes will be made of their bodies, and the colour of the coal [will be] on their souls therein.

Although attributed to Adamnan, Abbot of Iona, who died in AD 704, this forecast was written in 1096, only a few years before Patrick's Purgatory was instituted. It continues:

...the men of Erin have again followed Heathenism as it was at first, before beliefs and before Patrick's advent... they perpetrate wizardry, dealing in charms, philtres, and enchantments, and *fidlanna* [wooden staves, carved with magic signs used in divination], so that every harm is ripe to come, both *scamach* [cattle mange] and murrain, and blight of fruit, and hunger, and famine, and mortality.[13]

A new link between heathenism and all these perils, especially fire, was provided by the Viking raids on Ireland of the ninth to the eleventh centuries. Up the Irish estuaries and navigable rivers, the Apocalypse became a matter of fact, and the wives of Viking warriors conducted heathen rites on monastery altars, as at Clonmacnoise.

'The sea spewed forth floods of foreigners over Erin,' recorded the Annals of Ulster for 820, 'so that no haven, no landing place, no stronghold, no fort, no castle might be found, but it was submerged by waves of Vikings and pirates.' These newcomers were 'heathens who have never believed, with a devil's nature in [their] body'.[14]

By 840 the most important ecclesiastical centre in the country, Armagh in Ulster, founded by St Patrick, had fallen. Churches and abbeys were turned into temples to Thor, and many Irish soldiers, who became known as *Gall Gaedhil*, or Foreign Gaels, joined forces with the pagan Norse.

The establishment of St Patrick's Purgatory in the twelfth century was a clerical reaction aimed against *all* pagan beliefs, old and new. Another effect was the attempt by monks during and after this period to portray the surviving pagan Irish deities as mere historical characters, so robbing them progressively of mythic power.

In the long run, therefore, it could be said that the Viking onslaught gave the Church another chance to complete a project begun in the fifth century – the eradication of the mother of the gods, Ana, and her replacement by Mary, the virgin mother of a celibate god.

This was to be the key act in the proposed de-sexualization of the Irish landscape. The pagan 'Land of Woman' as an Otherworld ideal and standard of earthly perfection, was to be obliterated by abstinence, and by the concept of Original Sin, while the former life-giving orifice of spring, and the maternally sheltering cave, were to be experienced ideally as the many mouths of Hell's vestibule. That, at least, was the intention.

Purgatory was, in the first instance, a negation of the pre-Christian earth goddess. The new religion from the Middle East had denounced the feminine all the way from Eve in Genesis to the Whore of Babylon in Revelations, while Old Testament railing against the goddess in her many guises permeates the writings spread by a celibate priesthood and came into conflict at every level with native Irish tradition. Denunciation of the feminine was now to be equated with virtue in the struggle against the power of Áine, the Irish *magna mater*, as Cormac called her in the ninth century.

The response of paganism was to attempt a compromise, by admitting the surge of purgatorial fire into Áine's bosom, while removing any suggestion of its punitive function. Thus in the account from the Boyish Exploits of Finn, of the Paps of Anu, Finn sees 'a great fire' inside both her mountain breasts.[15]

Similarly, in a poignant ninth-century poem, the god Midir, occupying his fast-fading Otherworld of Bliss, reflects on his isolation, as the people of Ireland are engulfed by the incoming doctrine of sin, and its consequences for every mortal. The Otherworld of pre-Christian gods, from where he speaks, seems like a lost age of innocence: 'Fine and flawless are the inhabitants of [this] land; conception [here] is without sin or guilt ... We see everyone on every side, and no-one sees us: it is the darkness caused by Adam's sin which hides us from those [on earth] who could count us.'[16] The pagan gods watched impotently as the notion of fornication was introduced to the earth, and the matrimonial bed became hedged about with clerical restrictions:

We prescribe and exhort that there shall be continence in marriage, since marriage without continence is not lawful but sin ... Married people then should mutually abstain during the three forty-day periods in each single year ... that they may be able to have time for prayer for the salvation of their souls, and on Sunday night or Saturday night they shall mutually abstain, and after the wife has conceived he shall not have intercourse with her until she has borne her child.[17]

So says the sixth-century Penance of Finnian, one of several early Irish penitentials, drawn up by Irish bishops and abbots, and dominated by

St Patrick and the Devil at St Patrick's Purgatory, medieval woodcut. The belly-face fixes on the saint's loins, creating a split between body and spirit unknown to pre-Christian Ireland

the fear of female sexuality. It is the woman who leads mankind astray, just as it was the goddess whose worship provided the continuing inspiration for Christianity's most persistent alternative. Consequently, murder and theft are given far less attention in the codes than 'sexual offences', of which the Cummean penitential gives thirty-three categories, including thoughts and dreams:

14   He who for a long time is lured by a thought to commit fornication and resists the thought too half-heartedly, shall do penance for one or more days, according to the duration of the thought.

15   He who is willingly polluted during sleep, shall arise and sing nine psalms in order, kneeling. On the following day he shall fast on bread and water, or he shall sing thirty psalms, kneeling at the end of each.[18]

The Female Glen

Having become obsessed with what he sought to renounce, the unfortunate believer then met the same difficulty on a larger scale in a supernatural female called Ériu, the goddess who personified Ireland.

Ever since the first people arrived on its shores, Ireland in its entirety had been regarded as a female deity, identified by many names, including Banba, Fódla, and Ériu. From Ériu, the modern Eire is a conscious derivation. To pagans and Christians alike, Ériu-the-Island was a living divinity, but whereas *the people* more or less continued to regard her as the source of wonder and the sustainer of human existence, to the clergy she became a hostile erogenous zone, harmful to spiritual health, from which they tried to escape through prayers of renunciation, and by rejecting her proffered fruit.

In clerical writings the new pornography of place became centred on the image of the deep valley, where the natural vulva of the land goddess was redefined as the mouth of Hell. This image was playfully echoed by Joyce, in his decision to re-arrange the place names around the Wicklow Mountains so that the river Anna Livia (Liffey) could be said to rise from Devil's Glen:

'But first of all, worst of all, the wiggly livvly, she side slipped out by a gap in the Devil's glen'.[19]

34

As various folk tales, coloured by Christianity, make clear, it was the Devil's *Mother*, sometimes in the form of a wide-jawed serpentine monster, who was the *genius loci* of such places; for example, at Tullaghan in Co. Sligo, where St Patrick pursued her into a springhead. He alone had the courage to drive her from Glen Tachair in Co. Donegal, as O'Donovan recorded in 1835:

Yesterday we travelled through the deep and romantic valley of Gleann Tachair...to its very head, where is to be seen a stone exhibiting the impression of the Crozier of St Patrick, which remains in it since that Saint destroyed Tachar, the serpent or demon, that presided over the valley.[20]

Similar calls on the mythical St Patrick's attention came from every corner of Ireland except the south-east. He alone had the strength to replace a national goddess, Ériu, with a new god for the whole nation, and the audacity to lie on her thousands of traditional 'beds', the stone mounds and barrows by many a spring, to neutralize their potency, without himself becoming contaminated.

Only a celibate priest could hope to traverse the imaginary 'glen' depicted in 1149 in the 'Vision of Tundale' by an Irish monk called Marcus. The glen was

full of darkness and foetor, and such was its depth that none could discern the bottom of it, though he could hear the sound of streams and smell the stench of ordure, and [hear] the outcry and wailing of the souls that were in torment there, and a mist uprose from it. A plank, 1,000 feet long, stretched between the mountain ridges flanking the glen. The plank was a single foot in breadth, and none would dare tread on it, unless driven there by force.[21]

Tundale saw many souls falling from this bridge, yet a priest passed over unscathed, thanks to the power of his Holy Orders over the feminine.

'The impious and unprofitable host of the children of the curse' are plunged into a similar gulf in *Fis Adamnan*. It describes how the region all around had been 'burnt black, waste, and scorched, by the flames licking out of the glen'. The vision goes on to combine the vulva-glen with a female serpent-as-swallower. (In the Middle Ages, snakes were believed to mate through the mouth.) 'Eight serpents were in [the glen] with eyes like coals of fire'. By a great bridge 'three companies seek to pass over, but some fall...into the throats of those eight red-hot serpents...[yet] the chaste passed over with ease.'[22]

There are several references in early Irish literature to an obscure goddess called Crón, identified as swallower and personification of the pitch-black abyss, *allt na cróine*, and possibly the wife of Crom Dubh, the black god of harvest. The Lays of Finn tell of a journey 'to meet the swarthy one', whom Christians had come to identify with Hell, 'or some dread female resident there'.[23] The poet cries out: 'May the Son of the Great Virgin be between me and Crón's Glen.' A dread of Crón's worm is also mentioned.[24]

A true Old Irish word, derived from a pre-Christian deity of the abyss and associated with pot-holes (like the 75-metre-deep Noone Hole near Boho, Co. Fermanagh), 'Crón' has altered its meaning under Christian influence to become 'crime or fault'.

The Christian *Vision of Laisren*,[25] based on a ninth-century source, shows how completely landscape can be transformed to match the changing outlook of the collective psyche. When the human body is regarded with disgust, the earth belches its assent, and pilgrims gather in the earth's guts at Lough Derg to experience the full horror at first hand.

No wonder that Station Island was treated with awe, for there an entire mythic system was grounded. Yet in *being* grounded, it was compromised from the outset and threatened from within, since the Purgatory cave was inherited from a denigrated goddess.

Drawn to attack the image of her life-giving orifice as a rival to be overthrown, Christianity converted the very threshold of her love into The Crack of Doom, to be used as a punishment hall prior to Last Judgment. That this was a dangerous policy from the Christian viewpoint may be judged by the accounts of some medieval pilgrims, who emerged from incarceration in bewilderment, recounting visions of beautiful women who had proffered invitations to their banquet. Beneath the floor of Purgatory still lay the pagan Land of Women – an alternative buried dream, rising unbidden into the hearts of Christ's pilgrims and expressed in song by the minstrel Tuileagna Mac Torna, who called Lough Derg 'Eire's Pilgrimage...the Paradise of pleasant waters...with its soft-sounding shore...a quiet calm-grey fairy lake...supreme Paradise of Tuathal's Land'.[26]

In 1517, a visiting Papal Nuncio reported that the Purgatory Cave was called The *Well* of St Patrick, and that it was roofed by rock like a millstone, whose echo when struck gave rise to many fables.[27] These features hint at the oracular power and fecundity of an earth mother still in possession, secretly protecting the eternal spring of Nature's holiness from the doctrine of Hell-fire lit around its brim.

Lough Derg in Europe

Between the thirteenth and the nineteenth centuries continental Christian writers referred to St Patrick's Purgatory more often than to any other place in Ireland. So strong was their impulse to focus on the Purgatory that it became synonymous with Ireland in its entirety, which was consequently credited throughout with purgatorial qualities.

'O Ireland! Ireland!, sad and gloomy country,' cries a character in a German play, written in 1815.[28] If this description corresponds imperfectly with the Ireland that people encounter who actually *go* there, it also serves to show how a mythic frame of reference can influence the geography and personality of a country, not least among those who describe it from afar. The remote westerly location of Ireland, on the extreme edge of the medieval world, helped propagate its rise in the continental imagination as a place beyond the sunset, and beyond death, which in Christian terms, *had* to mean Purgatory.

By playing this role for Christendom, Station Isle completed a balanced trio of sacred sites – with the Garden of Eden in the East and Christ's rock-cut Jerusalem tomb in the centre.

Europe can be said to have used Ireland for its own purposes, and in formulating St Patrick's Purgatory the canons of Lough Derg drew on a continental legacy of ideas and imaginings, including the classical underworld of Virgil's *Aeneid*, written in the first century BC in Italy.

For Virgil, the chief glories of human life lay in opposing the soul to Nature and in overpowering Nature – ideas which Christianity would soon develop further. The *Aeneid* also offers a version of the world beyond death as a land of gloom and sorrow. In the Cave of the Sybil of Cumae the hero comes to a place where 'Grief and the Venging Cares have set their couch; There wan Diseases dwell and dolorous Eld, Fear, ill-advising Famine, loathly Want, Dread shapes to look upon – and Death and Toil, Then Death's own brother Sleep, and Evil Joys of mind, and on the threshold full in view Death-dealing Warfare.'[29]

Neither Patrick nor Christ were born when these words were written, which in turn illustrate the indebtedness of Roman literature to the world of the Greeks.

The Co. Donegal Purgatory can be seen as an offshoot of an idea conceived before 400 BC, in the Athens of Socrates and Plato, who introduced a fundamental rift between mind and body. They venerated the mind as the seat of the virtuous spirit or soul, and condemned the body as the Errant Cause, source of evil and misfortune.

Thus Lough Derg holds a mirror to Plato's 'Phaedo' dialogue of Socrates: 'The soul of the philosopher greatly despises the body, and avoids it...' The soul 'thinks best alone by itself,... by avoiding so far as it can, all association or contact with the body'.

'So long as we have a body, and the soul is contaminated by such an evil, we shall never attain completely what we desire, that is, the truth.

'Purification consists... in separating, so far as possible, the soul from the body and teaching the soul the habit of... living so far as it can... alone by itself, freed from the body as from fetters.'[30]

In time, Christianity incorporated this teaching, and so, a thousand years after Plato's death, his Mind-Body division reached Ireland. First Saints Island and then Station Isle echoed the same words with an Irish accent. Far from being uniquely Irish, they articulated a central theme of European civilization during the last two-and-a-half thousand years.

Since in all mythologies (including the Christian) the individual is a cosmos-in-miniature, a person divided in two implies an equivalent split in the macrocosm. Thus the spirit or soul which previously had been united with the body of the world was driven out, leaving behind a soulless mass of gross matter. Animals, plants, rocks, rivers, clouds, stars, sun and moon, were all now denied their share of the divine

(Left) Station Island in 1666, showing a dog-legged Purgatory building, Caoranach's bones (rocks), the saints' 'beds' or hut circles, and the dormitories, one for each province. (Above) Grave-clothes of a medieval man from Tawnamore, Co. Sligo. He wears new shoes for his walk across Magh Mhór (see p.126)

vitality. No longer were they to be regarded as living manifestations of the gods, but as a barrier blocking the view of an abstract and immaterial Godhead. This newly despicable world was repeatedly put to the torch at Lough Derg, and is incinerated again at Hiroshima, and in human-induced global warming. The pilgrimage to Ferry House is an Irish version of a Platonic European walk, where the world, as soulless Thing, is treated with contempt.

Thus we trudge on, flagellating the world out of cultural habit. In this sense, St Patrick's Purgatory re-illuminates the predicament of an entire civilization, reaching far beyond Ireland and the doctrine of the Catholic Church. Among other functions, mythological walks show us who we are and where we are going, for it sometimes takes a vivid experience at a particular place for this to emerge.

Light and Darkness

Under Graeco-Christian influence the habit of dualism went on to cut the spirit into irreconcilable good and evil parts. At Lough Derg this was demonstrated on the ground by the symbolic division of Saints Island into two opposed zones. These were described in 1411 by a knight, Lawrence of Pasztho, one of many Hungarians who made the long pilgrimage. He says that the north-west end was called *Kernagh*, meaning '"Island of Clamour", [and] is clothed in ... acrofolia [bitterly pungent plants], brambles, cornel-wood, elder, and various thorny bushes, and filled with rapacious birds – ravens, kites, hawks and owls, which nest there and emit horrid cries.' This part, he writes, is assigned to Satan and his satellites, including a certain demon, called in Irish *Cornu*, which is like a heron without wings or feathers. It utters 'a cry like blowing of a trumpet, which presages the death of some pilgrim'.[31] In the same year Antonio Mannini also saw the 'corna', as he called it, without 'a single plume or feather on its back, and only four or five on each wing'. It was, he observed, heron-shaped, but larger. The wall defining this part of the island still stands.

In the pre-Christian Irish cycle, the north-west was the dark quarter, where the sun never rises (unlike the north-east, the scene of midsummer sunrise). Lough Derg itself lies in the north-west of Ireland and so Kernagh is doubly well equipped to epitomize darkness.

To set against Kernagh, Pasztho reported the existence of a thirty-yard by five-yard plot in the south-west of the islet, dedicated to the angels and called, in Irish, *Regles*. 'It abounds in oak, yew and other agreeable trees, full of various birds that fill the place with sweet melody.' Here was 'Munster', the sunny province, traditionally associated with music-making.

This provincial subdivision of the ground was repeated on Station Isle, to which the Purgatory migrated in the sixteenth century (the Pope having ordered the closure of Saints Island in 1497 after a Dutch monk had complained of seeing no visions there).[32]

The local response was to re-occupy Station Island, long since abandoned by the Celtic community, and to set up a new 'Purgatory', based on St Daveog's old cave.

Lough Derg and the Reformation

After the Reformation, and the sixteenth-century decline in foreign pilgrims, Station Island came to function as a microcosm of Ireland. Pilgrims were housed according to which of the four provinces they came from, in one of four provincial dormitories. These lay in an arc on either side of the landing place, to correspond to their geographical location in Ireland. This arrangement persisted till at least 1625. Likewise, neat subdivisions of the sky were incorporated into the ritual pattern, for, as Richardson found in 1727, the Stations were repeated daily three times – namely at sunrise, noon, and sunset.[33]

By these means the ideas of heaven and hell were reunited with sensual experience, so immensely strengthening their popularity.

For believers, Station Island was a true microcosm – literally a tiny embodiment of a working cosmology, with foreknowledge of alternative Afterlives, accessible to the normal view of reality held in Catholic Ireland. That is why immigrant Scots Calvinists, in alliance with the English overlords, tried so hard to erase it from existence, in the belief that if denied their Purgatory Isle, the Catholic population would become disorientated, and therefore more easily led into Protestant ways.

On 8th June 1632 the Protestant Bishop Spottiswoode of Clogher 'observed 431 persons doing such fooleries there as is not to be imagined *could* be done among Christians', and then sought the power of the law to eradicate the menace. An Order of the Lord Justices was issued, 'to cause the Chapel, and all the Irish houses now situate on that island called St Patrick's Purgatory, and all the buildings, pavements, walls, works, foundations, circles, caves, cells, and vaults thereof of lime or stones to be thrown in the lough or water'. (A thrifty footnote allowed the proprietor to carry away the chapel masonry for use elsewhere.)[34]

Spottiswoode ignored the written pleas of Henrietta Maria, Queen of Charles I, England and Ireland, who had intervened to protect the island. However, the demolition was delayed for some months because no-one could be found willing to do the work. But on Hallowe'en, 31st October, the bishop landed with an armed party, and found the Purgatory to be 'a poor beggarly hole, made with some stones laid together with men's hands without any great art, and after[wards] covered with earth, such as husbandmen make to keep a few hogs from the rain'. His troop destroyed it, and then 'undermined the chapel, which was well covered with shingles, and brought all down together. Then we brake down the Circles and Saints beds, which were like so many coalpits, and so pulled down some great Irish houses. We effected that for which we came hither...which hath wonderfully displeased them that were bewitched with these fooleries.'

His action launched a sectarian tug-of-war which lasted for two centuries, where the beds and cave were repeatedly reconstructed by Catholics, and as frequently torn down again by the ruling Protestants. (For much of this period Catholicism was a proscribed religion.)

In 1701 Archbishop Hewson described the 'beds' as six circles of stone, above a foot high, and five or six feet diameter, with a gap in the side of each, put together carelessly, and with rocky uneven floors.[35] In this they closely resemble their 1989 appearance. In Hewson's day those shut in the Purgatory, which was by then a dog-legged dark cabin, were given water and tobacco, but denied sleep, on pain of being carried off by the Devil. Richardson (1727) found the cave to measure 22 feet (6.5 metres) long, only 25 inches (63 cm) wide, and 3 feet (89 cm) high. 'It hath a bending within six feet off the far end, where there is a very small window to let in some light and air to the pilgrims. There is little or none of it underground, and it seems never to have been sunk deeper than the rock. It is built of stone and clay, huddled together, covered with broad stones, and all overlaid with earth.'

During periods when access to the island was completely prohibited by the Calvinists, one response of the faithful was to recreate the Purgatory in their own parishes. A microcosm under stress may hop sideways to one of the many other possible locations within the macrocosm.

For example, at the Chapel of Monea in Clogher diocese, 'a large hole was made in the Chapel floor and filled with water as a representation of the holy lake (of Derg), and at Coronea, Co. Cavan, circles were cut in the Chapel floor, and figures chalked on the walls in imitation of the beds and crosses of Station Island. A prompter to the company repeats at each set of prayers: "Now we go round St Bridget's Bed, now we go round St Ann's circle."[36] This was reported with disgust by Philip Dixon in 1836. Disgust was (and is) a common reaction of rationalists to the Lough Derg phenomenon.

With the rise of seventeenth-century reason, even some Catholic clergy, such as Bishop David Rothe, felt it necessary to reappraise the nature of the Station Island cave. In 1624, his solution was to contrast Lough Derg (which he called a *privileged* purgatory, concerned with the living and surviving, but not with the dead), with the *universal* posthumous purgatory, where the sins of the dead are purged. He located the universal purgatory in the 'definite place near Limbo and the edge of the Pit, beside the centre of the Earth'. If this seems to put it a long way from Station Island, it was not his intention, for he continues: 'From a *wayfaring* or 'Precursory' Purgatory (such as that on Station Island) and similar baths, caverns and nooks, the expiating souls in torment in the universal purgatory *can be heard or approached*.'[37] The new logic tells him to separate Station Isle from the *idea* of universal purgatory, while the traditional identity of the two at Lough Derg *almost* persuades him to bring them together again. So located, the particular and the general come within screaming distance of one another.

Perhaps it was to compensate for the small micro-macro gap he had introduced, that he widened the near-access to Absolute Purgatory beyond Station Island, to cover *any* bath, cavern or nook in Ireland. The entire síd level of Ireland could now tune in to the sound of the final torment. (By baths he was probably referring to the subterranean, stone-built sweat houses, a common feature of the landscape in his time.) His concession unwittingly revived memories of multiple entrances to the pre-Christian Otherworld of Tír Na n'Óg, where, as with paired Purgatories, 'Wayfaring' versions merged, at a deeper level, with a universal land of bliss.

Sweat house near Blacklion, Co. Cavan, 1889. Subterranean wood-heated baths were used till 1850. Here Purgatory gives way to the dwelling of the gods – the síd under the hill. Many creation myths attribute the origin of the universe to divine sweat

The last chance any mortal had to enter the Station Island Cave physically was in 1789, for in that year the much disputed bunker was filled in by order of the Catholic prior, because the pilgrims were in danger of suffocation through overcrowding, the medieval discipline having long since broken down. From then on, the extraordinary chamber could work only as a spiritual metaphor, especially after Father Matthew Kelly, having reviewed all the evidence in 1848, reluctantly announced that St Patrick 'probably never visited Lough Derg'.[38] Many priests accepted this verdict, including Father Maguire of Inniskeen. 'God has no need of our lies; neither has St Patrick', he retorted.

Yet, as the 1990s pilgrims demonstrate, it is the mythical, rather than the historical St Patrick whom people follow. (This is fortunate for them, since Baring-Gould, among others, has shown that the historical Patrick was fabricated from the lives of several different men.[39])

As Aristotle remarked, this serves to show that Poetry rather than History is the chief vehicle of enduring truths. By the same token, fiction is preferable to fact, being more resilient before the unpredictable blasts of discovery.

As fiction, 'St Patrick' has achieved a scope that would have been impossible for an individual set in fact, on the narrow heels of a single lifetime.

Similarly, when the Purgatory Cave was lost in fact, it quickly re-incarnated as idea, embodied in a newly substantial thing – the basilica, completed in 1931. Its pinnacle is positioned exactly over the centre of the former cave. In this way, Purgatory was elevated on to the surface as a volume of national prayer, uttered by hungry, exhausted people, who afterwards flop gratefully on to hard bunks, and in the morning drink tea.

The raising of Purgatory to a position on ground level follows the scheme proposed by Dante, c. 1300, in his *Purgatorio*, which he arranged on the tiers of a mountain, with the Garden of Eden defended by a ring of fire on the summit. For Dante, Purgatory was a place where the penitents were reformed in an atmosphere of hope and light.[40] Perhaps the same is true of the Station Isle basilica.

The Water Monster

The Caoranach

In Ireland little is lost; mostly, things get rearranged, in a remarkable conservation of mythic energy. What is not converted hovers on, in an altered yet still recognizable version of its original form. So, at Lough Derg, the guts of a pre-Christian monster, who was called Caoranach, were pointed out to Richardson in 1727. They had been turned to stone, and stood as a heap of large natural boulders at the northernmost tip of Station Isle. As recently as 1932, people were pointing to 'the enormous knot of stone, visible in the rocks off Patrick's Island, as a morsel of the bones of the Caoranach'.[41]

The creature's grip on the pattern of worship was such that her offshore rocky remains, known as The Altar of Confession, were visited at sunrise, noon, and sunset, at the conclusion of every station. 'Here pilgrims go into the water, and go round the stones thrice, saying five Paters, five Aves and one Creed, and then they lean upon the corner of one of the stones'.[42] Finally, they waded to another stone close-by, called *Leac na mbonn*, or footstone.

Lying less than a metre below the lake's surface, this 'flat stone . . . hath a singular virtue of curing bruised and wounded feet of pilgrims'. There they said three prayers. The stone was smooth, and had a hole in the middle of it, in which there was another stone. This suggests the form of a *bullaun*, associated with goddess worship, and especially of Brigid. Bullauns are found throughout Ulster. (They in turn are related to the *yoni* and *lingam*, female-male imagery of the completed cosmos, re-introduced to Britain in the Hindu temples of recent immigrants, but known to the entire Indo-European tradition for at least 4,000 years.)

Of Irish holed stones, Frazer wrote in 1896, 'They are still popularly considered to exemplify that worship of generative power which prevails to the present day in India. In Ireland they are regarded as helpful to women in obtaining successful childbirth, and influence men in securing progeny . . . beliefs which are far from extinct.' Such perforated stones are also considered to cure infantile diseases, and the maladies of cattle – convictions 'firmly accepted in many districts'.[43]

Referring specifically to Ulster *bullauns* – horizontal boulders or rocks with artificial or natural basins – Crozier notes that they are often found by the side of lakes or near megalithic remains, and that they 'played an important role in surviving pre-Christian rites, especially at Beltane and Lammas', when they were sought out by childless women.[44] Wakeman maintains that many Christian churches were erected close to *bullauns*, in order to share in and redirect their potency.[45]

The water that lapped so gently in and out of the *Leac na mbonn* cavity was called The Wine of St Brigid, and drunk by nineteenth-century pilgrims, as hot as they could bear, from a cauldron. They were proud to show off the blisters so received. In the figure of St Brigid, or Brigit, Christian and pre-Christian realities coalesce. She has a foot in both myths.

From her rocky 'chair' on the south shore, she gazes across the lake of her own wine-blood, called Derg (Red), though in her Christian guise her mildness sits incongruously on the visceral coils of the pagan goddess of the lake – the monstrous Caoranach, whose airborn self was heard in the cry of the featherless corra bird.

In Irish, 'Corra' means Female Fiend, and The Devil's Mother. In her pre-Christian role as the Great Swallower she is well-known in Ireland. Flying from Lough Corra in the Galtee Mountains, she swallowed Cliach, while he played on the nearby stream harps, while as chieftainness of the demon birds it was she who had assailed St Patrick on the holy Mountain of Croagh Patrick, in Connacht. There, on her white quartz harvest hill, he had thrown his silver bell at her. She blackened it, and turned it to iron.[46] In the pre-Christian cycle, Croagh Patrick was the supreme expression of the White Goddess-in-harvest, the western peak of the year, after which a rapid decline to the north-west, and winter, was inevitable. Echoing this theme, several oral accounts say that Patrick chased the Corra *from* Croagh Patrick to Lough Derg, a distance of 152 kilometres as the crow flies. The link is strengthened by an alternative name of Lough Derg, namely Lough na Corragh, as Otway discovered from a guide in 1839. At Lough Derg, folk tales say, Patrick killed the Corra, and so turned its waters half red with her blood.

Corra and Caoranach are closely related, etymologically, and as mythic partners. Having struggled with Corra, the pagan energy of the air, it was inevitable that the saint should then confront her submarine equivalent in Caoranach, for as the original advocate of Ireland's first monotheism, 'Patrick' was set the task of destroying all other Gods. Corra is to air, mountain, and island tree, what Caoranach is to lake, and shore. The Irish word *Corr* means 'stork', with childbirth associations, and 'mountain peak', while reaching its long neck downwards, to see its partner, in a third meaning, of 'well or pool'. In a story told in Co. Galway in 1935, the Lough Derg Caoranach features as a gigantic eel which was killing all who passed around the lough, till St Patrick spent two days and nights in the lake fighting her with a sword. At last he found the vulnerable spot in her side, and killed her.[47]

(Above) St Brigit's Stone, Killinagh, Co. Cavan. In cup-shaped depressions on the surface of the stone block or bullaun, *the lesser boulders lie at rest. When they are turned, the human supplicant may ask the saint for help. Bullauns are related to Indian* lingam-yoni *stones (below right), the united essences of male and female deities. A rock-carving on a Neolithic tomb, near Lough Graney, Co. Clare (right), represents the goddess of generation: the affirmation of 'life within death'*

Although the rocks on the north end of Station Island were regarded as her petrified backbone, many believed that Caoranach was not dead, but fastened alive to the bottom of the lough, 'where in times of storm amidst thunder and lightening, the serpent rises, and takes its sport on the surface, and can be seen when men pass that lonely water'. They see her 'riding the waves like a wild horse with a flowing mane, the froth boiling away from its sides, and all is terrible entirely'.[48]

On these occasions her long body, rearing from the water, appeared as islands. Therefore both Station and Saints Island can be claimed as parts of her anatomy. Equally, the whole lough can be regarded as the maw of the female swallower, and all the islands in the lough as morsels sacrificed to her voracious appetite. Some oral beliefs may imply that she also swallowed the sun and moon into her underworld, so converting it into a Realm of light – an event re-enacted by a ritual fire, lit in the sunny southern province of Munster, according to a story from the Arigna valley, Co. Leitrim, which says that before being chased to Lough Derg from the *south* of Ireland, 'she used to have a grand light lit in the mouth of the cave at night, and anyone that saw that light was dead in his grave that time twelvemonths . . . she had a grand place inside this cave and she had a good way of living too, for anything she'd lay her eyes on she brought it by witchery.'[49]

At Lough Derg, set in northern darkness, the Caoranach reached her most ferocious development, in keeping with the winter demands of an annual nation-wide cycle.

This monster [of Lough Derg], called by the natives Caoranach, would suck men and cattle into its mouth at a Miles Distance, and becoming by this attractive quality so very pernicious to the County that no-one durst come near the Lake: at last . . . they obliged themselves to send a certain Number of Cattle to be devoured by it every day, [so that] almost all the cattle in Ulster were destroyed; [then]...they were forced to send *to Leinster and Munster* for supplies.[50]

Thus the tribute in kine of the eastern province of spring and prosperity, and of the southern province of noonday, music, and song, poured down Caoranach's throat, as she sat on Crock na Cunny, a hill 800 metres east of the lough. Cunny, or Cuinn, may mean 'of Conn', thus offering another possible link with Croagh Patrick in Connacht, and so reinforcing a sunwise annual narrative into north-west Ulster. In this drama, due north was (and is) the nadir and the central axis between every sunset and sunrise.

The waters of Lough Derg drain due north, via the river Derg, to Lough Foyle, on Ulster's north coast. The Irish language word *tuaisceart*, 'north', is enmeshed in dangerous qualities. It can also mean 'awkwardness, rudeness, and left-hand side', while *tuais* means 'arrogance, vanity and pride'. *Tuaithe* is 'a negative magic charm or spell'. *Tuairech* means 'forebodings', *tuairse* – 'remnant, remainder'; *tuaicthe* – 'anguished hearts', and *tuaircnige* is 'hammering, beating, smiting'.

Gaelic embodies a mythic view of reality where 'abstract' directions are unknown. Instead they are a vehicle for and an expression of the daily and yearly myth. Language is no neutral bystander. Situated in the northern quarter, the fearful role of Lough Derg is partly the outcome of the verbal associations which make up the fabric of its provincial location.

Finn Conan and the White Worm

In many folk tales it is the 'Gyant Conan' (son of Leinster's sunrise demi-god Finn McCool) who puts the Caoranach into Lough Derg. In one version of the story Conan finds that he has a little white worm stuck between his teeth, which he throws into Lough Derg, and is amazed how it grows. In another account, told by James Ryan of Tamlaght, the worm crawls out of the shin-bones of Finn's mother; these bones were all that remained of her after Finn had carried her across country on his back to the shore of the lough. Seeing the worm, Conan says: 'If that worm could get water enough it would come to something great'. With that, he, or his companion, threw it into the lough, where it soon turned into the monster.[51]

In a story told to O'Donovan in 1835, Finn (alias Fion) predicted its growth after 'sucking his thumb of knowledge', whereas Conan the stolid addressed the maggot, saying: 'Methinks thou hast not got the gums of a big beast – Pity thou shouldst not get enough to drink', and threw it nearly into the middle of the lough, which at that time was called Fion Lough, or Bright Lake.[52]

In pre-Christian terms, the lake was sacred because the phallic worm of the new year, doubling as the necessary maggot that had fed on

Carved sandstone image from Knowth, Co. Meath, 2500 BC. The three-eyed, open-mouthed serpent may be regarded as a Neolithic precursor of Caoranach

the decomposing wreckage of the old year, was weaned in its waters. Originating within the shin-bone of Finn's mother who was a goddess from the *síd* of Almu in Leinster, the word carried the seed of her hidden easterly dawn under the dark waters of Ulster, and illuminates them (Lough Fion) with a hope disguised in horror.

In his naivety, the wise fool Conan is instrumental in reactivating this most perilous sequence of events, and is transfixed in terror as the monster, undulating above and below the water, makes towards him at furious speed.

It is Conan's destiny to be swallowed by the Caoranach. Ancient texts describe the swallowing as his *turas* or pilgrimage.[53] This holy journey took him into the fire of the lost winter sun, deep in the gut of the mother goddess – an alternative 'Purgatory', which by no means died out with the coming of Patrick. O'Donovan reported the belief prevailing in 1835 that the Monster 'still guards a crock of gold [the sun] on the ancient island of Purgatory, and *was seen not many months ago.*'[54] Fed by the sacrificed cattle of every province, the hopes and life of Ireland were digested in Caoranach's body. Humanity watched in awe as the chosen demi-god undertook incarceration within her ghastly passage, as a prelude to the renewal of Heaven on Earth and the restoration of sacred Reality.

Conan was swallowed by Caoranach, and carried in her belly under the lough. Eventually he wounded the monster in the side, cut his way out with his dagger, and swam to shore, having lost his skin and hair by the heat of her entrails, for which reason he was afterwards called Conan Muil, 'Bald Conan'. The monster immediately died, and Conan, having cut off its head, threw it on the shore of Station Isle, where the stones have been coloured red ever since (though Richardson believed this effect to be due rather to a mineral spring). In 1932 Leslie knew of versions where Finn himself was said to have done this heroic deed of finding a way out of Winter's coils, so that all humanity might gratefully follow. It was a Caesarian birth, performed by the infant on its long-suffering mother.

St Patrick in Caoranach

True to the demands of mythic repetition, the folk mind also insisted that *St Patrick* had to repeat Conan's traditional journey into and out of Caoranach. And so he did, according to nineteenth-century folk belief, where the Lough Derg serpent is sometimes called Big Bolaun – 'big as a round tower',[55] in a version told by a Mr O'Connor of Athlone.

St Patrick pursued the beast to Lough Derg, and watched from the main shore as it swam to Station Island, and coiled up there. The two adversaries gazed at each other across the water, till Patrick suddenly stripped off his clothes. Then, crozier in hand, he dived into the lough and thrashed out towards the island. Seeing the saint aproach in a little storm of white water, the serpent opened its great mouth and made at full speed towards him. They met, head to head, and in an instant the holy man was gulped down. (Like any man, a saint would *expect* to take his clothes off when being reborn, just as it was customary for all pilgrims to finish their Station Island obligation by disrobing, and immersing in the lake, paying special attention to washing the head, as people do at Benares, on re-entering the sacred Mother Ganges.)

Mr O'Connor continued: 'Bolan Mor had a great wide stomach, and when the saint found himself shut up there he began striking on every side with his crozier, and Bolan Mor began to throw a flood of blood out of his mouth until the water of the lake was red.'

For St Patrick, there must have been an overwhelming sense of *moral* revulsion at being re-enmeshed in the physicality of the feminine, which might explain why this particular story-teller, out of consideration for the Saint's feelings, refers to Big Bolan as 'he'. Whether it was the Devil or the Devil's Mother, the saint slashed his way out, using his crozier as the sword, grateful to end the nightmarish re-enactment of his nine-month journey as embryo and foetus, from the depths of his own mother.

Embryo and Cosmos

The journeys of Conan and Patrick into the mouth and body of the water serpent are re-enactments of a mythic event, that unites Ulster to a world-wide cosmology. In Borneo, for example, there is a belief in 'the undivided unity preceding the creation of the cosmos, when everything was still, and in the mouth of the coiled water snake'.[56] To plunge into her mouth is to return to the primeval waters. In Lough Derg, as in the *Rig Veda*, the ancient Indian text, 'Caoranach' is the embodiment of 'the indiscriminate flood of lofty waters, which conceive the germ of the Universe, and then generate the fire of the Fire God. These first waters are therefore invoked as 'the most motherly physicians, mothers of all that stands and goes.'[57]

Prior to the division between 'this' and 'that', an embryo materialized in the mouth of the water monster, 'in which all the gods saw each other'.[58] Yet in Indian belief, these same waters beyond heaven and earth are also sheltered *within* the earth, like an Irish lough set between rolling hills, or the tiny spring reputed to lie beneath the Station Island cave, which would make a suitable location for the story.

As to why these ideas have been so widespread, the physical movement of peoples, and the transmission of culture by contact with neighbouring groups, merely serve to confirm the universality of the pre-natal experience, on which every version of the Lough Derg myth, and the Lough Derg rites, are based.

Pagans, Christians, atheists and agnostics are equally imprinted with 'the recordings of non-sensory perception from prenatal life [and] events which have taken place during the pre-natal period which are recorded by the embryo, and can be reproduced in dreams in post-natal life'.[59] Since dreams are the workshop in which myths are designed, the route back and forth, between foetus and folk tale, and between embryo and epic, lies open to all humanity. Indeed, Stricker claims to have found a constant parallelism between embryology and cosmology in all the religions of the Near East and Greece, where the sensitivity of seers matches the findings of embryologists. One Tamil mystic, Manikkavacakar, described the 'memory' of his own fertiliz-ation of the ovum by sperm as 'having gone through the attack of boundless worms'.[60]

One of the purposes of ancient religion was to lead the individual back to his or her pre-natal state, as a means of reintegrating with the lost realm of earliest life experience. Only then (given the micro-macro principle), could the individual hope to recreate the world, in the full consciousness of mythic participation. To repeat a journey previously known only as a compulsory and instinctive happening was one of the greatest of mythic explorations – an appalling prospect, touching on taboos concerning incest with the mother, in a metaphoric, if not a literal mode. But for the human species, blessed and cursed with the power of contemplation, gods or heroes *had* to re-enact this walk to the original egg, because the sacred mystery was contained there. Accordingly, through the teeth-lined cave of the monster's jaws, hero, saint and deity were drawn into the primary ocean, and bobbed around, while waiting for the start of the next cycle of death and resurrection, and the founding of a new cosmos.

At Lough Derg, Ireland re-enacted several versions of a nativity event, where the hero (saint) is both lover-impregnator *and* child of the earth goddess in her aquatic guise.

Brothers sometimes quarrel, and Patrick was certainly jealous of his older 'brother', Finn; yet in the great family of Eurasian civilization, they are recognizably of the same stock, while demonstrating the marvellous diversity of character which can somehow be contained within a small Irish lake.

The 'regaining of the mother' or 'the winning again of the primal situation within the mother' is regarded by the psychologist Otto Rank as the chief task of the hero.[61] Consequently, the church on Station Isle was dedicated to Mary.

The wish to return to the womb has been extensively studied by psychologists and by students of myth and comparative religion, and found to underpin many religious structures and poetic utterances through human history. On one level, *every* mythic 'walk' is an attempt to re-cross the boundary between post-natal and pre-natal worlds – a walk upstream, against the natural current. Instinctively people feel, in Fodor's words, that 'Life is a continuity which does not begin at birth, but is split by birth. The result of this splitting is pre-natal amnesia, but there is also an unconscious persistent effort to re-establish the lost continuity.'[62] However, between the living adult and the lost world of the womb stands the closed gate and dangerous passage, previously experienced at the trauma of birth. To the newborn infant, it involved breaking and draining of the amniotic lake surrounding the foetus, the painful process of labour, sometimes physically injurious to the child, and the first impact on the baby of harsh lights, loud noises, cold air and unyielding surfaces, collectively making an ordeal as severe as dying.

The comparison with death is apt, since most mythologies regard the process of re-entry towards the hidden womb as a form of death. The South American vagina with fangs (*vagina dentata*) is matched in Europe by the toothed Mouth of Hell, or Devil's Mother image. Eliade's world survey of these threshold perils found them portrayed over and over again in the forms encountered in Ireland – a gorge, from which 'victims' fall from a narrow bridge, a crushing between or under millstones (Station Island), extremes of heat, and of course, confrontation with the jaws of whale, dragon or giant water eel.[63] The near-suffocation endured by those incarcerated in the dark of the eighteenth-century 'cave' on Station Isle can be viewed as yet another common form of re-enacting the birth process in a reverse direction.

An additional peril facing a celibate male hero, like St Patrick, stems from the fact that the adult body shares with the new-born infant a phallic relationship to the mother's genitalia, so that every re-enactment of Birth by a Return fantasy stirs up repressed sexual ideas. When St Patrick took off his clothes on the shore of Lough Derg before entering Caoranach his anxieties were profound. In Christian terms, his affair with Caoranach – Eve, the primal mother – was a flagrant and prohibited re-enactment of the original sin, with Eve as serpent, surfacing before his eyes as a terrifying living symbol. He then atoned for his 'sin' by killing the truth of the compulsion to which he had submitted. Off went her head.

By this act, he was also attacking his own Heaven, since, as Fodor maintains, 'all utopian visions reveal a nostalgia for a prenatal bliss, lost on leaving the maternal womb – a happiness in the only perfect form we have ever known it – a Canaan flowing with milk and honey, where we may retrace our steps to the very source of life... and find the answer to the mystery of our existence.'[64]

Humanity is a womb-haunted species. The notion of Eden, like Heaven, is but one of many imaginings derived from pre-natal experience. The Land of Women, as the Irish Otherworld was known, comes from the same source. In human lovemaking, the mutual reward for both partners is the temporary discovery of a comparable sense of all-enveloping space, akin to floating in the amniotic ocean, sometimes combined with the realization of the dream of an androgynous state. This merging of sexes into a primal unity carries resonances of the pre-natal situation. The craving for the androgynous may also amount to an archaic identification with the most primitive forms of animal life, while brief incarceration in Caoranach can be interpreted as an acceptance by humanity of its essential oneness with all organic creation. Perhaps it is more than a coincidence that the abandonment of her myth has coincided with the alienation from Nature which has so recently threatened to wreck the whole pattern of life on earth.

The well-known habit of burying the dead in a flexed or foetal position – common throughout prehistoric Ireland – reiterates the womb image at the far end of an individual's life, making yet another in a series of imaginary and actual returns, and extending the maternal image to the earth itself.

Whatever their form, the desire to construct Otherworlds in the imagination arises from the biological fact, common to all mammals, of having lived in another world, where the static bliss of uterine existence is combined with the surging, positive drama of the foetus's rapid development. Since the system of human reproduction is exactly the same now as it was in remotest antiquity, we stand in an identical situation regarding the source of mythic pilgrimages. While humankind is born of woman, some version of the age-old journey, re-presented in myth, will probably remain central to human culture.

The emphasis on heat in Christian Purgatory and Hell, seen from this position, may derive from the blood heat of the mother's circulation, shared by the foetus, and ritually re-discovered at Lough Derg through imbibing the hot blood or 'lake wine' of the red lough. The Wine Boiler marked on the 1835 Ordnance map at the North End of the isle gave every pilgrim a chance to reabsorb and reconnect with this primal bloodstream, which filled the lough after Conan-Patrick had decapitated the monster. A related purpose of the decapitation was to re-sacralize the wider world from the body of the primal deity. The act was charged with positive meaning. When Caoranach's blood stained the lough red, it signified the rebirth of the whole world as the monster's holy child.

The Caoranach legacy may also enable the fires of Purgatory and Hell to be seen in a positive light, as one fierce offshoot from a very widespread belief in the heat-producing effect of a typical magico-religious experience. In many cultures, the nearer the shaman or hero approached to the bloodstream of the gods, the hotter he generally became. For that reason, shamans in Siberia ate aromatic plants to increase their own body heat, prior to making contact with the divine, while many cosmologies, including the Nordic, regarded the origins of the universe itself as a product of divine sweat. Similarly, when the child-hero Cúchulainn of Ulster first encountered the sacred, his heat became so great that three vats of cold water were needed to bring it under control; the first vat burst its staves and hoops, while the second boiled with bubbles as big as fists.

The concept of Christian Hell was bearable, writes Rank, because 'even the most horrible forms of punishment which man could imagine, to direct against himself, are clothed in the form of the first and strongest pleasure experience of the intra-uterine life'.[65] The womb, scene of the first captivity and binding, gives a weird undercurrent of enjoyment to Owen's agonizings. To this extent, the Christian attempt to split the pre-birth world into Heaven and Hell, as dualistic opposites, is less than wholly successful. Even the overlapping language, whereby the gold and furnace light of Heaven runs perilously close to Hell's description, reveals a common ancestress for the two states. According to Rank, the *real* punishment was originally the expulsion from the womb – that lost Paradise recognized in the parallel Fall of Adam and Eve from their blissful garden.

Daveog

In the minds of the pilgrims who came to Lough Derg after 1150, Conan, Patrick and Caoranach required and received sincere propitiation. If the people's response was 'two-faced', it was because they were confronted by a two-faced reality – two intertwined universes, equally real, derived from a single physiological root. Spiritual and physical survival depended on learning to play a correct part in each.

Polytheistic tolerance came easily to the people, much to the dismay of their priests. Often ridiculed as undiscriminating and muddle-headed, the popular loyalty to the Caoranach stories was the necessary concern of a farming people for the drama of the annual cycle. Today the pluralism of the folk voice gains long-overdue intellectual respectability, since its instinctive chords are now being echoed by the discoveries of cosmologists and nuclear physicists regarding the multiple worlds and parallel structures of physical reality.

A good example of what modern physicists call *superposition* (the existence of two realities co-existing at one point) might be seen at Lough Derg in the figure of St Dabheog, that most obscure personage, venerated by the Celtic community on Station Island, prior to the Augustinian invasion. Christian hagiographies have nothing to say about him – a reliable sign of pre-Christian sanctity granted the token blessing by a new authority. On Station Island, the cult of Dabheog was centred upon the cave, or underground chamber. What pre-Christian significance this had is unknown, but it might have been regarded as a *davoch; dabhoch*, or *dabchach*, variants on a single word which in Gaelic means 'a vat, a mashing vat, a large tub', from Old Irish *dabach*. It also means 'large stomach', as applied to men, and 'a huge lady'. The immense appetite of Caoranach comes into view, along with the possibility that the offerings of cattle made to the lake from Leinster and Munster (where east and south recognized the just claims of north), were symbolically and actually put into the Station Island stomach – the mashing vat of the giantess. Daveog's festival was celebrated on 1st January – the very day on which women in the Hebrides, whose culture was largely Irish, gathered around the Knockin' Stanes for the ritual pounding of barley with wooden mallets. This communal ceremony was focussed on a hollow in the Knockin' Stane boulder. The stane and Daveog's cave were two versions of the fertile interior of the goddess.

Liquor for the vat could have come from the spring reputed to lie beneath the cave. This might also explain why so many claims concerning Caoranach's fossilized bones are associated with Station Island. Her bones naturally lie near her former 'stomach-womb', whose site is now sealed beneath the centre of the basilica.

The '-og' ending of *Daveog* (which as O'Donovan noted in 1835 is always feminine), means that the 'saint' was female, or perhaps a water-monster goddess, access to whose womb could be gained on Station Isle.

Both the ordeal of those incarcerated in the Station Island Purgatory, and the modern Night Vigil in the basilica, evoke the Great Night prior to Creation. Eliade produces massive evidence to show that primordial Chaos is involved in every ritual regression, prior to rebirth. Such chaos is the 'Cosmic Night' of the universal mother, the 'in the beginning' state, where germination and hope of renewal attaches itself to the uterine wall, eventually to emerge, born into appreciation of existence as a sacred gift of the gods. Therefore, this second visit to the womb destroys the 'taken for granted' quality of infant and childhood profanity, and replaces it with adult responsibilities towards sacred truths, previously ignored. Thus the second birth introduces the adult to the solemnity of culture, whereby he or she assumes the need to nurture the cosmos. From now on, Nature is known to be supernatural.

By repeating these adventures in ritual, the pilgrim achieved a similar moment of cosmogonic or macrocosmic identification. That is why, to this day, Lough Derg pilgrims have to *stay awake* throughout the black night of their spiritual rebirth, which has to be known in body and mind, as distinct from the automatic processes which befall a baby prior to parturition.

A good place to watch this happening was 'the Chair of Daveog', a natural rock seat on the mainland overlooking Station Isle. O'Donovan described the chair as lying 'in the townland of Suidhe Dhabheog (Seeavog), where, in the living rock, some impressions of elbows are shown, according to oral tradition, which maintained that Daveog was a woman who died during the *turas*, or pilgrimage walk, and was revived by St Patrick. Then, having reached the rock called her chair, within sight of Station Island, she died again, and was interred on Saints Island.'[66]

In this pattern of birth and resurrection, devotee and deity are happily confused – a right and proper merger, since anyone who chooses to sit on Daveog's Chair with serious intent is shaped by, and so *becomes*, the supportive deity on whose knee he or she rests.

In 1652, Colgan reported that Dabheoc's feast was celebrated on 24th July, as well as on 1st January, suggesting a pattern of harvest-birth veneration to match the midwinter swallowing. To this day, the 'Spa Well' on the lake shore, lying between the Chair and Station Isle, flows all the year round.

On leaving the Lough, as Skelton observed in 1786, each pilgrim was given by the priest as many holy pebbles out of the lake as he cared to take away.[67] Such stone coins were legal tender in the currency of two traditions. They might evoke the Easter Saturday communion host, and the vertebrae of the indestructible beast of the lough. So the pebble in the hand stood for two sacred narratives, both rising from beneath the surface of the mundane, to tell the hidden truth.

Pilgrim on St Brigit's (or St Daveog's)
Chair, Lough Derg, 1830. The natural
throne rises on the lake shore three
hundred paces south of Ferry House

The Cailleach and Bith

The Cailleach at Slieve Gullion

The chief female of the Ulster underworld is the Cailleach, the aged goddess and primal mother of the province. Her body and living presence was, until recently, seen in one of the major third-millennium BC passage graves of Ireland, the south cairn on Slieve Gullion, Co. Armagh.

In 1789, Charlotte Brooke heard that the tomb was locally called Cailleach Birrn's House, or The Old Lady's House, in which it was said Finn McCumhal (McCool) was buried. Thus the solar hero lies timelessly in the womb of the northern province in a stone chamber shaped to evoke the maternal image.[68] The roofing slabs rise in height from entrance passage to main chamber. The surrounding cairn is 29 metres in diameter and 5 metres high.

A well-beaten track joined this Cailleach monument to a circular pool close by, where there was another cairn. In Ulster, there is an interplay between womb-lake and architectural effigies of the mother.

As late as 1938, it was believed that Cally Berry (as she was then called) had thrown a white stone from Slieve Gullion to the Dorsey Ramparts, some kilometres away, where it is still to be seen, and was whitewashed every year by local people.

From Creggan parish, Patterson recorded the following convictions:

Do you know her house on the mountain and the lake beside it? Well, if he [Finn] was fleet of foot and strong limbed, well sure she was stronger still in spells, as if she did not entice poor Finn into it. And he went in fresh and youthful, and came out a done old man, and they had a high time making him right again. Often I started up the mountain to see the lake, but I could never tread the whole road, I was so afraid; for you know, a wedding party went into Cally Berry House once and they were turned into stone. Her house goes down and down, and in the very bottom chamber sits the Cally herself, to this very day, and will, maybe till the end of time.[69]

In Irish tradition, the Cailleach is infinitely old, and has many lovers. Her veil (*caille*) barely hides the fact that she is the great goddess of pre-Celtic and Celtic times. As recently as 1927 the folklorist Eleanor Hull wrote that 'In Ireland, the goddesses are held to be both more

Neolithic chambered tomb on Slieve Gullion, Co. Armagh (left), known as The Old Lady's, or Cailleach Birrn's House. The chambers are shaped to evoke the goddess-as-hag. Folklore says that Finn entered the Slieve Gullion chambers in full vigour and emerged as an old man

numerous and more powerful than the gods...and still regarded as the builders of mountains, the impersonators of winter, and the harbingers of spring.'

Ulster, as the Northern nadir of light, was *the* natural home of the Cailleach, although of course she was acknowledged in each of the provinces including Munster, where her chief stronghold was on the Bheare peninsula.

In Ulster, the *cailleach*, or *caillighe*, was the eternal mother. Figured in prehistoric monuments and whitewashed stones, she also appeared as the hag at the end of harvest, when she was severed from the earth out of which she had sprung in a sickle-throwing rite.

An old man from Ballymoyer recalled in 1944: 'I saw the Cailleach cut by the scythe only. It was afterwards taken into the house and put around the woman of the house. It was always put about the neck of the woman of the house. That was the right thing to do'.[70]

Neolithic-chamber-standing-stone-oat-sheaf-housewife: the mythic chain joining the first harvest wife to the most recent was completed every year. The cailleach sitting on the woman's neck was an awesome sight for all. Then the goddess was hung above the table during the harvest feast.

The Tomb of Bith

From the archaic strata of Irish myth concerning the original settlement of Ireland, as recorded in *Lebor Gabála*, the first man and woman to land were Adra – 'The Ancient' (alias Ladra) – and his sister Cesair,

(Top) Knockmany chambered tomb, c. 3000 BC, Co. Tyrone. Stone A (top left) is engraved with an image of the goddess Áine-as-hag, spouting serpentine forms from her open mouth. A 'four quarters' pattern is generated beside her right eye. (Above left) Corn harvest at Toome, Co. Antrim, before 1914. The grandmother of the family eats her field lunch. She embodies the Hag-deity, since of all the human family she comes closest to first-hand experience of the complete cycle of birth, death and rebirth. (Above right) Cutting the 'Churn' or Hag, when the last handful of oats is plaited, and ritually severed, in a sickle-throwing ceremony with their father, Bith, together with a number of subordinate women.[71]

Bith travelled north through Ireland from the Munster landing place and died at Slieve Beagh, on the Ulster mountain named after him. There, the 'seventeen magnificent maidens' who accompanied him on the journey to the Northern province buried him under the mountaintop cairn which they constructed, the Carn Móre or Great Cairn.

The Irish word *bith* means 'cosmos, world, eternity, everlasting, being and existence'. Thus his name, his body and his cairn carry the load of the entire universe. He brings a truly cosmogonic myth to the southern fringe of Ulster.

An alternative name for Ulster is Uladh. *Uladh*, as a language word, reveals 'a monument, a hoard of hidden treasure, a stone tomb, a charnel house, and a pile of bones'. In these senses, Uladh (Ulster) is synonymous with Bith's tomb. Uladh is where the personified Cosmos drops into the dream of Northern night, prior to its recreation by the next wave of conscious envisagers, the next generation, as they voyage into awareness by cutting themselves free from the coils of oblivion. Like Cesair, Adra and Bith, they too are survivors of The Flood – that amniotic ocean which fills the entire horizon of every unborn child.

In 1894, Canon O'Connor reported that the cairn was being undermined by quarrying,[72] a fate which seemed to symbolize the collapse of an entire cosmology. For Bith was Cosmos, and regarder of Cosmos, the universal idea, beholding, and so creating, the Universe. Thus Carn Móre embodied the merging of subject and object, of interior and exterior worlds, of thing with action. It stood for integration of body with spirit. From its lost summit the agonizing mind-body split of Christian Lough Derg would seem unnecessary.

Although the Great Cairn on Slieve Beagh Mountain has gone, Bith has been given a new lease of life by modern physics. Scientists like J.R. Wheeler believe that the universe can best be understood in terms of participation.

As we have seen, participation was fundamental to the archaic position, which Bith exemplified. Anthropologists have identified it as fundamental to the world view of 'primitive' tribes of every continent. Lévi-Bruhl even formulated a law of participation, as the key to understanding *How Natives Think*, as his book, translated in 1926, was resoundingly entitled. He wrote: 'In varying forms and degrees, the mystic relations which primitive mentality so frequently senses in beings and objects...involve a participation by contact, transference, sympathy or telekinesis...[so forming] a collective representation.'[73]

Wheeler suggests that the entire Universe is brought into existence by observations made by all conscious beings. This is his Participatory Universe. So it may be with pilgrims on Station Isle: creation and re-creation is seen to depend on staying awake and alert during 'Creation Eve'.

Wheeler goes on to suggest that lesser degrees of noticing require the co-ordination by a supreme intelligence[74] (such as Bith), capable of embodying them in an organic whole – a commonwealth involving all species throughout Time. This new cosmology revives a pre-Platonic 'Bith', and heals the mind-body split.

Thanks to the women who accompanied Bith and Cesair to Ireland, we may also see the net of consciousness extended horizontally, for, as Macalister realized, many of their names are the thinly disguised countries of Europe and Asia,[75] nutritious yolk to the foetus of Ulster, in preparation for its birth into fuller awareness, on behalf of Ireland as a whole.

However dim and overgrown, in an era of fragmentation, the northern track over Bith's grave has become, he nevertheless stands for the underlying unity of Christian, pagan, and scientific myth. To him, they are different avenues in the same cosmic park. Encouraged by his synthesis, we turn south, to walk to the opposite province of Munster.

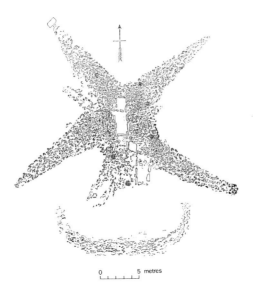

0   5 metres

Ox-tomb at Doohat, Co. Fermanagh. Bith, the primordial being, often reappeared as a bull, giving his life for communal good. Thus the mythic bull of Cualgne 'belched out his heart, like a dark stone of black blood'

Part Two MUNSTER

The Sun Goddesses

Inherited Words

South: Áine and Dess

People first landed in Ireland nine thousand years ago, and watched the sun climb to the top of its daily arc over what is now Munster, Ireland's southern province. This repeated event helped to establish the sun goddess Áine and her sister Grian as Munster's chief pre-Christian deities, while they were worshipped in some form throughout the country. Áine was also known as An, Ana, Anu, Dana and Danu. Cormac called her *mater deorum hibernensium* – 'the mother of the Irish gods', adding 'it was well she nursed *deos*, i.e. the gods'.[1] It was in Munster, the southern quarter, that her power stood highest, both in the sky and in terms of human response.

Since myth is primarily a verbal affair, Áine's proper name was also an Irish-language word, *aine*. Áine the goddess lives on as *aine* the word, which means: 'Delight, joy, pleasure, agility, expedition, swiftness, play, sport, amusement, music, harmony, melody, experience, truth, veracity, brightness, glow, radiance, splendour, glory, brilliance, wit, and drinking up.'

The name of a deity is a godhead's first expression and last resort, and often tells what the deity does and *is*. In the Irish language, *aine* and related words are, like sunbeams, now largely separated from their divine solar source. Yet they still shower down through a space rapidly turning neutral, to animate Munster life.

The switch from Irish to the English language which has occurred in most parts of Munster during the last two hundred years has all but killed off the use of *aine* words, and for the same reason there has been a change in the perception of 'south'. Whereas in English, 'south' is a largely transparent word, used to establish an abstract geometry, its equivalent in Irish – *dess*, or *deas* – reinforces and overlaps with Áine's southern persona. *Dess* meanings include 'south', 'right hand', and 'being to the right of a person facing east'.

(Previous page) Da Chích Ánainne (Paps of Anu), Co. Kerry. The sun goddesses, Áine and Gráinne, touch the twin summits with the milk of sunlight

Áine's gold. Gold solar disc, engraved with the equal-armed cross of the rotating seasons, and a sheet-gold 'lunula', c. 2000 BC

As Stokes noted, the Irish, 'like the rest of the Indo-Europeans determined their orientation by looking at the rising sun'. Therefore south was *lam des*, the 'right hand', which was considered more propitious than *lam cle*, the 'left hand', cognate with Welsh *cledd*, 'north'.[2] With *dess* firmly attached to the ascending side of a sunrise greeting, its 'south' was never a neutral zone, but a subjective condition, from which many positive qualities flowed, as further meanings of the word *dess* reveal: 'right, just, meet, agreeable, well-arranged, fine, neat, precise, correct, pretty, elegant, decent and dexterous'. This is the legacy of the Munster quarter.

A specific solar connection comes in *dessel* – 'direction of sun, sunwise', and therefore 'lucky, favourable and propitious'. This leads via *deisceart*, 'southern quarter', towards Áine's regional characteristics in *desse* – 'seemliness, comeliness, beauty, pleasant aspect' – echoed in the golden *deasac*, 'ears of corn'.

'Ah yes, Áine Cli, that's Áine of the light, the Beautiful', explained Tom Harnon to an officer of the Irish Folklore Commission in 1972,[3] for in the neighbourhood of her principal Munster síd, Cnoc Áine, she is still recalled with affectionate respect. The territory around this 161-metre-high, sickle-shaped hill in Co. Limerick, was known as Deise Beag, literally, 'Little South', and stood for Munster in miniature, where the vast and varied province overseen by An was represented on a more intimate scale and inhabited by Áine. In this way, *dess* and sun goddess came together at their provincial headquarters – a coalition emphasized by an alternative name for this part of Co. Limerick, in use till 1690, 'The Seignory of Any'.[4]

Cnoc Áine

Áine's sanctuary hill, Cnoc Áine, and the nearby sacred lake of Lough Gur have a central place in Munster's mythology. Ceremonies held annually at Cnoc Áine on St John's Eve (23rd June) marked the summer solstice and were vividly remembered in 1879. 'Every St

John's Night, men used to gather on the hill from all quarters. They were formed in ranks by an old man called Quinlan, whose family still lived on the hill in 1876,' wrote Fitzgerald.[5]

Reports spoke of bunches of hay and straw, tied upon poles. These 'cliars' were lit and carried in procession round the hill, and around the little moat on the summit. Afterwards people ran through the cultivated fields, and among the cattle, waving the cliars, which brought luck to crops and beasts for the following year. The torches showed that Áine had visibly climbed to the top of her annual axis and highest solar achievement of the year, which was also the start of her annual decline. The 23rd June gathering therefore combined triumph with sadness, and some accounts even speak of the ritual as her 'funeral', at which 'the good people' or fairies emerged 'from every lios [enclosure] and rath [hill-top earthwork] throughout Ireland', and they all trooped to Cnoc Áine bearing lighted torches in her honour.[6] These otherworld multitudes may have been matched in former days by human pilgrims, drawn island-wide, and enjoying the opportunity to mingle with the supernatural legions.

When, one year, out of respect for the death of a local man on 23 June, the torches in the human procession remained unlit, those in the supernatural phalanx were seen, as if to compensate, to burn with exceptional brightness. 'Áine herself was observed in the front, directing and ordering everything.'[7]

In the nineteenth century, many families living around the hill, including the O'Brien's, Dillanes, Creeds, Laffins, O'Deas and Fitzgeralds, claimed direct descent from Áine. They spoke of her in near-human terms as 'the best-hearted woman that ever lived', yet on occasions she reminded them of the difference in kind between her supernatural pantheon and common humanity.

For example, on one St John's night a number of girls had stayed late on the hill, watching the cliars, and joining in the games, when suddenly Áine appeared among them. She thanked them for the honour they had done her, but said she now wished them to go home, since her Otherworld friends wanted the hill to themselves. Some of the mortals then looked through her ring, whereupon the hill appeared crowded with fairies previously invisible to them.[8]

Áine was sometimes seen on Cnoc Áine as a *cailleach*, or old woman, comparable to the Ulster hag of Knockmany (p. 57). Those who accepted her modest demands enjoyed good fortune. If, on the other hand, they slighted or exploited her, difficulties soon overwhelmed them. The need to observe the divine balance by means of an exchange of gifts is the theme of these anecdotes.

Mr Harnon of Bruff recalled his grandfather saying of the Dunworths who lived on the hill during the famine of the 1840s:

One night a knock came on the door of their houseen, and a little old woman was there. And they asked her in, to come to warm herself. She could not delay long, she said, as she sat by the fire. . . .

Map labels:
- quarry
- Site of Áine Cliar's Cave
- ring fort
- Three rings of Áine Eogabal, and Fer Í
- Áine's Well
- Síd Áine
- North Cairn (Cairn of Uainide)
- 500'
- Castle of Áine's leap
- Knockainey village
- 400'
- River Camoge
- Cloghaunainey (Bridge with Áine's footprints)
- 0   250 metres

ELEVATION

PLAN

North cairn "of Uainide"

Dún Áine (conjoined Rings perhaps those of Eogabal Áine and Fer Fí.

Síd Áine

SCALE of FEET

Síd Áine, Áine's cairn on the summit, is now destroyed. The other barrows are associated with her father (Eogabal), her brother (Fer Í), and Uainide, 'The Green' (Westropp, 1917)

(Top) Cnoc Áine, Co. Limerick. A twelfth-century text says that this hill was given to the goddess Áine, 'till the end of the world', and was 'the abode of kings and queens . . . the best hill . . . both ordinary and extraordinary that stood on Ireland's wondrous land'. The stone bridge on the river Camoge, Cloghaunainey (above), demolished in 1930, was believed to have been built by Áine, and to carry the impress of her feet on its slabs

(Right) The sculptured stone at Áth An Charbaid, Co. Kerry, is perhaps a full-length portrait of the Sun-Moon deity

65

Then she left, and thanked 'em, and she said they would not regret it. She wasn't gone too long when they heard, as they thought, another knock on the door. So they went out. 'My goodness,' they says, 'What now?' She couldn't carry on, the old woman said, so she came back and she stayed, and into the kitchen *walked a nice sheep.* The family were in an awful state over the sheep, for in that time people used to be hanged for stealin' a sheep, if it could be proved, or even if the skin of a sheep was found in a peasant's cottage you were hanged immediately and especially on the O'Grady estate! In the mornin' old Dunworth went...to Kilballyowen House, to the oul' O'Grady, and told him about the sheep. Oul' O'Grady sent his herdsman out, and all the sheep were intact in their pastures and paddicks. 'No' he says, 'the sheep don't belong to us.'

Dunworth then went to Oul' O'Grady again and asked him what would he do with the sheep. 'What'll you do with him?' he says, 'he's yours. Keep it!' And he did keep the sheep.

Right, the sheep grew up, and she had two lambs. Those two lambs grew up, and had two lambs, and they had two more lambs.

And then the next was, they got the idea that the sheep was getting old, and that they'd take her to the fair of Hospital to sell her. The night before the fair, a knock came to their door, and the little woman came, and she came in, and she always asked for something. First she asked for the heat of the fire. That time when she came she asked them to give her a pinch of salt and they asked her to stay. 'No' she said, 'I have a journey to go on, and I must go!' 'But, she asked, 'are you goin' to the fair with your sheep tomorrow?' 'I am.' 'Let me give you advice, and keep that sheep, and don't go to the fair!'

Well, they went to the fair the next day and they sold the sheep, and from that day on their luck changed. In fact, within a week all the sheep were dead. That was the Dunworths'. They came down in the world again, and they became just as badly off or even worse than they ever were. The remains of the houseen might still be there, for all I know now. On up above David O'Grady's...up beyond the quarry there, at the sunset end of the hill.[9]

Just east of the village and hill of Knockainey runs the little river Camoge, over which Áine was said to have built a primitive stone bridge, Cloghaunainey. It survived until 1930, when it was demolished, along with the locally revered impressions of her footprints, said to be visible on its broad flagstones.

According to a local belief, it was on the Camoge river bank that Áine conceived the mysterious Geároid Iarla, the male phantom who haunts nearby Lough Gur. The story tells of the rape of eternity by history – the violent meeting in the early thirteenth century of the first Norman lord in the area (the Earl of Desmond) with the regional deity. In Irish myth, Overlordship or Kingship depended upon the male claimant making love to the territorial goddess. By that means he won his legitimacy, as described in Fitzgerald's transcription of a folk tale current in the district:

The first Earl of Desmond led very much the life of a libertine, and walking one morning along the river's edge, he saw a beautiful woman seated by the water, combing out her long hair after bathing.

Her cloak lay behind her on the grass. The Earl, whose name was Muiris (meaning Great), advanced noiselessly on her from behind, knowing that if he had but possession of the cloak, he would have her in his power; and he seized it before she was aware of his approach.

The beautiful woman was Áine-n'-Chliar herself, and she told the Earl that he could never have had his will with her, had he not seized her cloak. She told him further that she would bear him a son, Geároid, whom he was to bring up with all possible care, like any other gentleman. One caution however she gave her love: he was not to show surprise at anything, however strange, his son should do. When the usual time of nature was accomplished, Áine brought the infant to the Earl, and the father's pride was great in him.

The boy grew up from year to year to manhood, and excelled in the accomplishments of his age and rank. But one memorable evening it happened that there was a gathering of great ladies and gentlemen at the castle of the Earl of Desmond, which still stands in Knockainy village. There was dancing, and of all the ladies none could vie with a certain one among the guests. The grace and the endurance of this young woman were however beaten, everyone said, by those of the young Earl Gerald himself. When the dance was ended, this lady engaged him in another contest, for while all were seated at the supper-table she suddenly arose, and at one leap cleared guests, table, dishes and all, and then leaped back again. The old Earl of Desmond turned to his son and said 'Can you do anything like that?' 'No,' said Geároid. 'Well, stand up and try. Don't let yourself be beaten by a woman.' Thus commanded, Iarla rose to his feet, and making a spring from where he stood, leaped right into a bottle, and then leaped out again. There was great admiration at this feat; and with the rest the Earl of Desmond looked in the greatest astonishment at his son, saying he never thought he had such power. 'Were you not warned', said the young Earl, 'never to show wonder at anything I might do?'

By his public show of amazement, the old Earl unintentionally cast his son out of the normal world, for once people had identified Iarla's feats as Otherworldly, patterned on those of the goddess his mother, he became classified as a demi-god and could no longer sit wholly comfortably in the mundane, but was now bound to follow her into the supernatural. 'Now you have forced me to leave you,' were his last words to his father.[10]

Iarla's jump takes us into the supernatural realm.

The Tuatha Dé Danann

A collective term for many of the nature gods, coined in the Middle Ages, was the *Tuatha Dé Danann*, the people of the goddess An, Áine or Danu. They were the Neolithic and Bronze Age pantheons of gods which Áine was credited with founding. As we have seen, belief in her has not yet died out, while in the manuscripts of Christian clerics, her 'people', the pagan gods, 'are fully recognized as such till the late tenth or mid-eleventh century', and called 'unfading . . . whose duration is perennial'.[11]

It was recorded that the boy sun god, Cúchulainn of Ulster, had led a drunken raid of the Ultonians to Cnoc Áine. They reached the hill in winter and set up pillars to shelter their horses from the snow.[12]

In a peace treaty recorded in the twelfth century, each province is allowed, through their gods, a share of Cnoc Áine – an arrangement confirmed by the monuments on its summit. Previously, two gods from Mide, called Uainide (Green) and Eogabal (*Eo*, 'tree' and *gabal*, 'a fork, a gable') laid claim to the hill. In these attacks the characters of a seasonal drama emerge, for Irish mythological names generally mean what they say. The Mide raid was not warfare in the secular sense, but the desire of verdure and forest deities to establish themselves in and from the goddess's earth-body, saturated as it was at Cnoc Áine by the solar ore of her name.

Through the warmth of the southern sun goddess, the bringing to leaf of an island-wide tree, inherited from the central province, was intended.

This interplay between provincial and national centres is implicit in every act of centering, since myth normally has cosmic ambitions, whereby each sub-centre instinctively reaches towards infinity, and therefore joins up with all other centres. A faint echo of this expansiveness was remembered in 1972 by Tommy Hannon. He spoke of

a little small man [who] lived somewhere at the side of Knockainey Hill . . . Spellman was his name. He was a tailor, and he used to go up to the highest pinnacle of the hill every morning very early. He used some words, or recited somethin', or said somethin', anyway . . . he'd point his needle to the four cardinal points of the compass, and around in a circle, and [then] come down. And there was no journeyman tailor would enter Knockainey that day.[13]

This constraint on free trade may derive from an earlier ceremony in honour of Áine – a marking of the 'sky cloth', prior to the swift cut of her scissors, the blades of sun and moon. (Tailors are connected with the Neolithic goddess through a shared interest in textiles, which she introduced to Ireland.)

Perhaps Spellman was reciting a version of the traditional greeting to the rising sun, chanted by John Macneill of Barra, in the Irish-influenced Hebrides:

> Hail to thee, thou sun of the seasons . . .
> Thou art the glorious mother of the stars.
> Thou liest down in the destructive ocean
> Without impairment and without fear.
> Thou risest up on the peaceful wave-crest
> Like a queenly maiden in bloom . . .[14]

Throughout Ireland, Áine was known as the wife of Manannán the sea god, from whose bed she climbed every morning. She was also said to be the wife of Echdae the sky horse. By leaping regularly from one spouse to the other she joined sea and sky together and landed at Cnoc Áine within the summit monument, Síd Áine (p. 65). This much-disturbed mound is placed on the eastern end of the hill, and is balanced by the traditional site of her 'cave' (destroyed *c.* 1900 by quarrymen), which lay at the western or sunset foot of the same sacred hill.

The Irish word for fairy is *síóg*, or *ben síd*, literally 'woman of the síd'. Fairies were the army of the hidden goddess, or versions of the gods in her pantheon, seen much reduced in size and power, yet persistently working for the neglected values of a goddess submerged by Iron Age warrior patriarchy, Christianity, and modern materialism. They symbolized an endangered vital relationship – the cohesion of Culture-in-Nature, and the sense of a sacred whole.

In rural Ireland, fairies, or 'the Good People', were taken seriously, at least until the arrival of television. Appearing at dusk, they displayed something of their former divine powers, and resisted the process of genteel emasculation which was their fate in nineteenth-century England.

The deities and fairies of the Tuatha Dé Danann found allies in the poets, or *filí*, who were collectively known as *aes dana*, 'men of arts, servants of the goddess Dana' (Ana-Áine). They moved freely through tribal areas and across politico-social boundaries, and were especially well represented in Munster, the province of poetry.

Poets were specialists in liminality; they operated at the thresholds, between categories of space, time, or identity, in dangerous, 'frontier' conditions, among uncomfortable truths. These they shaped into harmonious knowledge on behalf of the community.

The poets were expert in native learning – legal tradition, history, genealogy, and the science of natural phenomena – all viewed as aspects of the divine myth, and realized in verse. Because myth is repeatable, they claimed to predict the future pattern of events, and were the bridge between mundane and supernatural spheres.

But as the folklore of the Cnoc Áine district makes clear, access to the divine was not restricted to poets. Rather, almost the entire human population of Munster could claim direct descent from pre-Iron Age stock,[15] and so held to an unbroken thread of identification with Áine, reaching back to the Neolithic. In this sense they were collectively 'the folk of the goddess Dana or Áine'.

Myth and the Folk Voice

Irish folklore resounds on a mythic frequency. Traces of the primary sacred narratives permeate its apparently inconsequential scraps. This is because they represent a collective wisdom and speak with an open voice, unconstricted by the claims of excessive individualism, and so are relatively immune to disruption by personal mortality. Instead, by word of mouth, folklore opens a free passage between the generations, a route confirmed at intervals by parallel written records.

In Ireland, the literate and oral traditions have remained unusually close together, for, as MacCana explains, 'while the native men of learning, the *filí*, did not eschew the use of writing, particularly in the post-Norman period, the fact is that they inherited something of the druidic preference for the oral mode, both in their teaching and in their composition.

'Consequently, the Irish oral tradition embraced the literature of greatest social prestige as well as the common lore of the mass of the people.

'Thus Irish literary tradition is ideally the manifold *oral* tradition which in a sense had no beginning – and has hardly yet ended in the Gaelic-speaking areas of Ireland and Scotland.'[16]

Irish folklore is pluralistic (it works by inclusion), and polytheistic (gods are often disparaged in the stories, but rarely turned away). Its world is made from the merging, conservation, and recycling of *all* available sacred insights. 'Move up!' the storyteller cries to his assembled divine characters, 'I hear another god at the door. It may have come to destroy us all, but I will talk it into some kind of accommodation.' This is both a habitual gesture towards mythic comprehensiveness, and, on a political level, the art of compromise of a much-invaded people, living in an ancient land. Thanks to such tactics, the spirit of the old gods managed to survive, and continued to join people and place together.

Irish folklore is open-ended partly because it has no holy book. Consequently its earliest deities have interbred with later gods, historical characters, and monotheistic saints, in the interests of overall synthesis and continuity.

Post-modernism now advocates a comparable 'double coding', but is operating in different and difficult circumstances, for so deep is the rut dug by centuries of linear progress, affecting most aspects of modern culture, that the Great Plain (Magh Mhór) known to folklore is now all but invisible to the dominant forces of narrowness. Yet for that very reason, Áine's barely audible Co. Limerick tales have taken on a peculiar relevance to the world at large. They have something to say about a timeless (yet increasingly betrayed) sense of belonging on earth.

Ironically, her stories are fading out just as serious alarms are sounding in environmental research institutes. Having dismissed Áine as superstition, experts are now taking over one of her roles – that of mourning banshee (*bean síd*), and have begun to lament the imminent demise of all our worlds, real and imagined, resulting from a neglect of the balance which she had successfully advocated for so long.

Given this situation, Áine's last reported lingerings around Cnoc Áine become a matter of more than Irish interest. In Munster folklore she stands for a sacramental marriage of the elements, and sweeps people into nature's holy wheelings, which are presumed to animate sun and *síd*, river, hill, and ocean, flame and breeze, art and science, means and ends.

With her dying breath, the archaic Áine affirms the fundamental need for a pattern of continuity, and declares that an earth which is loved (even after an estrangement), may not, after all, be doomed.

Folk Tales

Conversations with people in mid-Limerick in 1989 and 1990 suggest that traditional attitudes to Áine are fast declining, but have yet to disappear. Stories told in 1971 undoubtedly drew on local topography and historical events, and put them at the disposal of mythic themes, known in some form throughout the Indo-European hegemony, and stemming ultimately from the beginnings of human speech.

In the summer of 1990 Pat MacNamara of Lough Gur, near Cnoc Áine, favoured me with a monologue on neighbourhood traditions, delivered in a rapid, matter-of-fact tone, as though it was his duty to repeat *everything necessary*, like a St Patrick's Purgatory pilgrim doing the stations. His repertoire has eluded death by Bronze and Iron Ages, incineration in one and a half millennia of Christian Hell, incessant tribal warfare, Norman invasion, English settlement, Protestantism, rationalism, famine, emigration, mechanization, television, and at least one change of language.

Around Cnoc Áine, anecdotes passed thus between the generations have stretched the communal horizon towards the primeval. What was heard prepared the mind of the local listener for the re-emergence of the archaic as a contemporary event. In other words, the doings of the gods were known initially through listening to older people in house or inn, and then *experienced* as walking apparitions, if and when conditions were favourable. Such 'preparation by anecdote' no more disqualifies the outcome-as-event from a claim to authenticity than tutorials in mathematics rob numbers of their abstract standing. Each type of education operates and produces results within the structure of its own cognition. Moreover, even in decline, oral education gains something of the systematic quality it would appear to lack by means of a lifelong network of social obligation, including a shared involvement with farming. Further support comes from the recurring events of the natural cycle, which envelop and test every word.

But because they were so valued, accounts of supernatural events were often withheld from strangers, as T.J. Westropp discovered in 1917:

Knockainey's ancient observances were in full force within the last forty years, [but] a suspicious feeling in the present inhabitants prevented my learning whether the rites are not, still, performed, but certainly the ancient goddess and her brother Fer Í [Fí] are still remembered.[17]

Fortunately other collectors have been more successful than Westropp, including David Fitzgerald in the mid-nineteenth century, and Canon

Lynch *c.* 1900. In the 1930s, the newly established Irish Folklore Commission gathered more material through a local schools survey, and in 1971 Daithi o'Hógain of the Commission, a native of the town of Bruff, conducted many tape-recorded interviews with older members of the community.

The typical Folklore Commission interview is an exchange of mutual trust and a shared passion for a Past erupting as Present.

In collecting these stories, the rhythms of the speech are usually transferred directly from tape recorder to manuscript, in the same way as a musical score contains a symphony.

However some contributors, like Tommy Hannon, fell silent when the tape was switched on. *He* had not received the relay of ancestral confidences through a machine, and would not agree to pass them on by that means!

In Ireland, the Divine is nourished by conversation. At its best, Irish talk retains a sacramental quality and so needs no other justification. Like any creative act, or rather like *The* Creation of the gods, 'the crack' is understood to be a primary event. In its stream, idea, emotion and thing combine in whirlpools (whose equivalent in traditional Irish music are jigs and reels), alternating with placid stretches and furious falls. At times, submerged cargoes, long supposed lost, rear up, waterlogged yet intact, to bump and nuzzle in the ceaseless flow. Such supernatural talk is no mere description or illustration of a parallel reality. It *is* the Other, returned to life – a life made between speaker and listener (who exchange roles, turn by turn), and where eye and gesture contribute like the glitter of sunlight on a wind-stirred lough, to the business of serious delight.

Equally, if the trust on either side is compromised, utter dismay results. (On one occasion, O'hÓgáin found that his appreciative laugh at a man's story of the Black Bull of Lough Gur was mistaken for ridicule, and the speaker was too upset to continue.) But when empathy is sustained, the goal of the exchange – almost every phrase declares it – is the construction by *re*construction of a complementary world. This was and remains an ingrained Irish ambition, mythic in scope and archaic in pedigree.

Lough Gur

The Enchanted Lake

Four kilometres north-west of Cnoc Áine a group of rocky limestone hills spring from the plain. Among them lies a sacred lake – Lough Gur.

Before its eastern side was drained in the nineteenth century AD, its broad reaches formed an approximate square around a large triangular island, called Knockadoon. Throughout the prehistoric era, Lough Gur appeared as an unbroken ring of water, nine kilometres in circumference, to which An the traveller was drawn, in the person of the goddess, Áine.

'As all Munster knows,' wrote Fitzgerald in 1879, 'Lough Gur is enchanted...in the past, no minstrel, piper, or poet would willingly spend a night within a mile of its shore, such was its fearful reputation and potency. Even to fall asleep in daytime on its banks was considered among them to be reckless folly.'[18] The sense of danger arose from the belief that the original poets of Lough Gur were either descended from, or *were* demi-gods, like Geároid Iarla, able to draw human poets out of their depths.

Oral tradition places Lough Gur under the aegis of the goddess Áine who made it. 'The old people used to say that the sky was widest over Lough Gur,' reported Tommy Hannon in 1972. As sun goddess, Áine looked at its grey waters, caused them to sparkle, and so made her entry into another element.

Sometimes she or her agents appeared over the lough as a *sí gaoith*, or fairy whirlwind.

'Is it dangerous?' Mr Hynes was asked.

'Oh, 'tis. You shouldn't look at it at all. 'Tis fairy, you see. It'd be moving around as if there was some machine overhead. And 'twould twist, twist, twist, until it would bring up a certain amount.'

Tom Carroll added:

'I watched it one night. I saw it carrying a wind of hay anything up to a hundred yards into the sky. I bent down; I kept looking at it, I said: "Let the fairies do what they like!" The old people used to say 'twasn't right to look at it.'

...but a growing prosaicism gave Mr Carroll new-found daring.

Pat Coffey spoke:

'We saw it one day, and Ned Hynes said to go down on our knees and bless ourselves and not to look. [I said "Don't look, lads," agreed Ned Hynes.] Away over BallyKilleen and far away over the bog. Where it went I couldn't tell you!'[19]

Flickering traces of Áine Cliar, The Bright, may explain why the night air around the lough is sometimes seen to be filled with unearthly fire, as Ned Hynes recalls:

'It came from Grange one night down by Lough Gur, near th'oul land down by the *carcas* [causeway]. And when I came along by the bend of Knockfennel, I had plenty of light. And 'twas a wonderful dry year. So I was standing listening, and I could hear the fire tearing. I had plenty of light. Says I, "will I go up and tell Mrs Connolly? 'twill burn the whole place!" I said to myself, I'd mind my own business... it must be *them* lit up. And I was talking to myself like that comin' away. And comin' round by the Carraigin now, I came out. And when I came to that bend! God, young man! There was no more a fire there than there was [one] up on that counter now! That's God's truth. It must have been some other class of fire. It wasn't from this world, anyway.'[20]

Lough Gur enjoys or suffers multiple realities, and is more than one place.

'My own father and mother... always told me 'twasn't right to be out late at night. Especially in the hills at night, You know... Especially in the hills around here. He said we'd get some kind of feirin' [fairying] out of it,' commented Tom Carroll.

Around the lough, Áine can appear as an old woman, a young princess, a mother, and a mermaid. Nineteenth-century reports claim that 'Áine is frequently to be seen, half her body above the waters, on the bosom of Loch Guirr, combing her hair.'[21] Áine, Danu, or Anu, the principal pre-Celtic, Celtic, and modern deity of Munster, is the constant traveller who yet sits still, the feminine in the man, and the embodiment of world-as-woman.

An account of how the lough was formed from Áine's urine was given by Ned Hynes in 1971:

'Do you know how the Lake came there? St Patrick came around Ireland, didn't he? He came to Patrick's Well. But he passed Lough Gur. But there's a well in the Avenue. And he came along, and there was a poor oul' woman makin' her water, in pardon to you. And he said: "God increase you!" And she kept on makin' it away until she made the Lake. And the Lake was comin' all around her.'[22]

Cause and effect work in both directions in the unusual sensitivity of the lough to atmosphere, as indicated by *The Dublin Magazine* of 1764, which reported that 'the waters became disturbed and fetid at the approach of bad weather'.

Lough Gur, looking south over Garret Island from Knockfennel. The tip of Knockadoon island can be seen on the east, or left

Another Lough Gur story relates how Geároid encounters a young woman on the shore of the lough. He points to a ring on a stone, and when she picks it up, the waters of the lake rise up red, like blood. When she screams and puts the ring down again, the lake subsides. This emphasizes the immediate effect on the environment of Áine's slightest action. The lough is her divine blood, the world is her extended body.

The belief that the lake sprang from a young woman's failure to replace the lid of a well which overflowed (a common explanation of British and Irish lakes) is also still held in the area, and is another means whereby the bodily fluid of the land, as a living entity, is connected to the actions of a representative female, who is both human and divine.

'There was a princess, and she went for a bucket of water to the well. And 'twas a boilin' well. She took off the cover of the well. And she took up her cup of water. And she came away without covering the well, because the water came up over her. And that's how Lough

Gur Lake came. She got flooded out,' according to Tom Carroll, speaking in 1971.

To a pair of human lovers, Áine of the Lough appeared as a mermaid, said Ned Hynes.

'There's a stone in there [at Knockfennel], and they call it The Mossy Stone. 'Tis on this side, and...there could be briars thrown over it now. And I know two that was courtin' there one night, you see, and 'twas shovin' dusk. And the girl got a fright. Says she: "Who's that fellay? Who's that fellay sittin' above on the stone? With the long head of hair?" And 'twas the Mermaid.'[23]

Eel, Tree, and Horseman

Every human state has corresponding apparitions, which are its supernatural equivalent. This also applies to the human corpses, rotting in the lakeside graveyard at Grange on the western shore. Fitzgerald was told by Mr M. Whelan in 1877, who had the story from an earlier generation, that the graves of this ancient burial ground used to be found every morning:

...all bored with holes, and as it was thought that this was the work of dogs, a neighbouring gentleman directed two of his men to go to the place provided with guns, and watch during the night. To their amazement they saw a great eel rise from the lake, and coming ashore, roll on and on over the ground, till she had worked herself into a church-yard. Then she began to bury her snout in the soil over a grave, and was fast making her way into it to feed on the people, when the men fired and hit her. When they came up they found her lying motionless, seemingly dead. In this state they carried her to their master's place and threw her down in a corner of the kitchen where she lay all next day. The following night, the mournful cries of another eel were heard about the lake.

'Tadhg a bhí im lorgsa!' said the eel in the corner, raising herself up. 'Tadhg that was looking for me.'

'Go to Tadhg, in the name of the Devil,' cried one of the astonished onlookers, and the creature glided through the door, rolled herself towards the lake, and there disappeared.[24]

Tadhg is an Irish word meaning poet. At every stage in her life-cycle, Áine required him to sing her praises and to offer physical companionship. At Lough Gur Tadhg was given a poet's dirty work to do – sucking words through collapsing coffin walls in lakeside graveyards, where the flesh of ancestors is arranged in death sentences which must be joined to the mute hopes of the yet unborn. Supernatural skill is needed for the task; that is why the best poets were often demigods, like Tadhg, and Oisín son of Finn.

In the nineteenth century, Lough Gur was believed to disappear by magic once every seven years. At these times, as an old woman from Askeaton asserted in 1879, a supernatural tree was revealed, growing

Lough Gur and its monuments. The 59° Lughnasa sunrise-Samain sunset alignment can be seen to link several important sites and monuments

from the bottom of the lough. This tree might be regarded as another appearance of Áine's tree-trunk father, Eogabal, united with his green foliage brother, Uainide. Both 'men' had travelled from Uisnech, Ireland's central sacred hill, to confirm Cnoc Áine and Lough Gur as Munster's provincial equivalent of a national *axis mundi*. In Lough Gur, a version of their Tree of Trees was rooted into the lake bed, and so drew several layers of reality together. Eogabal + Uainide = *axis mundi* = World Tree, the mythic synthesizing vegetable, which brings the worlds of the gods and humanity together. It stands, like the Christian Cross, at the centre of many European cosmologies.

At Lough Gur the magic tree 'is covered with a green cloth'. (This evokes both Uainide, and Áine's river-bank cloak.)

A certain bold fellow was at the spot one day at the very instant when the spell broke, and he rode his horse towards the tree and snatched away the *Brat Uaine* or Green Cloth that covered it. As he turned his horse and fled for his life, the Woman who sat on the watch, knitting, under the cloth at the foot of the tree cried out:

> *Chughat, chughat, a bhuaine bhalbh!*
> *Marcach ó Thir na mBan Marbh*
> *A'fuadach an bhruit uaine dhom bhathas.*
>
> Awake, awake, thou silent tide!
> From the Mortal Women's Land a horseman rides,
> From my head the green cloth snatching.

At these words, the waters rose; and so fiercely did they pursue him, that as he gained the edge of the lake one half of his steed was swept away, and with it the *Brat Uaine* which he was drawing after him. Had that been taken, the enchantment would be ended for ever.[25]

Here the Otherworld goddess, perhaps Áine, calls on the waters to return to protect her tree from a greedy human horseman. She allows him to touch but not to remove Ireland's green mantle – a message that each generation in turn needs to hear and to understand.

Supernatural trees played a central role in the Irish imagination until late medieval times. Mythologically speaking, the country revolved around them. The tree of Eo Rossa was praised as 'a king's wheel, a prince's right, a wave's noise, best of creatures...a firm-strong god,...a measure's house, a mother's good...a fruitful sea, Banba's [Ireland's] renown, judgement of origin, judicial doom, faggot of sages,...dearest of bushes, vigour of life, spell of knowledge,...shout of the world.'[26]

The Lough Gur tree stands for a divinely renewable prosperity. It is envisaged in poetic form because poetry is the language of the gods. Especially when sung, poetry takes us beyond categorization, and allows us back into the primordial forest where the tree of life is synonymous with the tree of knowledge. In this pre-dualistic commonwealth, the aesthetic of sound is inseparable from the logic of sense.

As the Lough Gur stanza shows, verse, with its accumulating rhythm, can also convey the spatial expansion of the image, by which the deity radiates from the local to the universal. So 'the green cloth from my head' could mean literally a headscarf no bigger than a handkerchief, the leafy canopy of the tree under which she sits, the green mantle of Ireland, and the world in its entirety. This ambiguous scale is a feature of the task that all deities take on, in proposing microcosm and macrocosm as interchangeable terms.

This sense of sharing permeates the Lough Gur vision, and takes many forms. So, for example, the horse surrenders its rear half to the

Cloch a bhile, 'The Stone of the Tree'. It stands two metres high, grey, runnelled and lichened, a reminder of the phantom tree formerly revealed beneath the lough at seven-year intervals. The stone is a permanent reminder of the ideal World Tree, for lack of which all the forests of the world fall into danger. In myth, the divine tree has the power to en-green the entire earth. (Modern Ireland has few forests)

returning water, and the lough tree joins the underwater milieu (of which it takes measure) to the normally hidden realm beneath that, where it is rooted – the Supernatural, revealed to mortals during rare times of insight. With an economy of means typical of a classic symbol, the tree unites thing, idea, process, and aesthetics, in a physical display of divine energy. The poets and musicians whose job it was to help bring it into focus were given a place of honour in its branches by the prehistoric societies which modelled themselves on its structure.

The exchange between the under-lough tree and the surface world is reiterated by the standing stone called *Cloch a bhile* (Stone of the Tree). This megalith, described by Ó'Ríordáin as 'a large upright stone, measuring seven feet by four feet at ground level and six feet high',[27] is sited close to the west shore of the lough, and south-east of the great henge monument, erected *c.* 2500 BC, at Grange. The stone, now dappled with green moss and gold lichen, may have served as a solid reminder to those in the real world that the phantom tree beneath the lough, the ideal tree, was also substantial, and would be seen again. Equally, the Cloch a bhile was itself an outpost of the sacred, where tree-trunk and Áine's female trunk merged into one effigy, cosmological axis, and living force in the land.

Another (very faint) echo of the magic tree might lie at the root of this tattered memory from Tom Carroll: 'A Mrs Riordan had a platform here under a beech tree somewhere and someone said somethin' about it – cursed it or somethin'. I don't know what they said about it anawa'. But the beech tree withered.... whatever happened, they don't seem to know, like.'[28]

Did Mrs Riordan ever knit as she sat there? It is too late to find out. Mr Carroll is dead, and no-one else remembers. This particular image of a primordial inherited synthesis fell apart in the memory of an old man, and vanished forever, because his children and grand-children did not choose to restore it in their talk or song.

The Giants' Grave

Around Lough Gur, Otherworld voices are heard crying out in alarm, when their hopes of eternity are plundered. For example, Tom Harnon recalls the 1938 archaeological excavation of the Giants' Grave, a Neolithic tomb, standing close to the south shore:

'Giants' Grave: they excavated that. They took the bones, put 'em in a bag and brought them here to the castle. I worked with them. But I believe, – I've been told it by several people, that if every *bean sí* in Ireland were ever clanned together that night, that the greatest keening and crying was heard all around the lake, and through the hills, and even farther on, away even into the bog, the Red Bog, and across even to Knockderc.'[29]

The *bansíde*, as the name implies, are the queens of the *síde* or underworlds, and led by Áine. She was upset by the desecration of the monument, till then the house of living spirits, including her own, so the banshees of Ireland united to mourn the death of a five-thousand-year-old tradition.

Until the nineteenth century, a family banshee was often heard wailing outside a house, to escort the dying individual to the *síd*. After death had occurred, human keeners echoed the sound in their mourning. Keening as a social custom survived in the Lough Gur area till the early twentieth century. Tom Carroll knew the last of these women, Dinny Fitzgerald's mother in Balincoloo – 'They'd keep it up all night around the bed.' Another local custom, still remembered in the 1930s by older inhabitants living around the lough was that:

On the night of full moon, the people brought their sick close to the lake so that the moonlight shone brightly on them. The old people called this night 'All Heal', and if a sick person was not better by the 8th or 9th day of the moon, he would then hear the *Ceol Síde* which Áine would sing to comfort the dying. The sick person would then fall asleep at the music called The Banshee Wail, the whispering song of sleep, which Áine's brother Fer Fí played. He was a red-haired dwarf, and it was considered good luck to hear him laugh. He played only three tunes: Wail, Sleep, and Laughter, on his three-stringed harp.[30]

Fer Fí's Wail was played at Lough Gur by a Mr J. Butler as recently as 1898.

The locally-used Gaelic name of Giants' Grave was *Leabthacha Dhiarmada is Ghráinne* – 'the bed of Dermot and Graney', where the youthful Dermot had lain with the sun goddess Gráinne (Áine's alter ego), below the level of the horizon, in a night of love-making, as described in the Finn Cycle of poems.[31] (By the twelfth century the

Giants' Grave, or Bed of Dermot and Graney, c. 2600 BC. This ruined gallery grave, excavated in 1938, yielded remains of at least eight people, and many bones of ox and hare. The 'giants' were the god and goddess, whose combined bodies the tomb describes in effigy – probably Donn, the underworld god, and Gráinne, the sun goddess. They became Dermot and Graney in medieval romance

'hanging hair' wall

Plan of Giants' Grave. Three hundred and sixty-six Neolithic tombs named after Dermot and Graney are said to exist in Ireland – enough for every night of their year of lovemaking. Until the late nineteenth century, young human couples traditionally mimed the divine union by mating in such tombs.

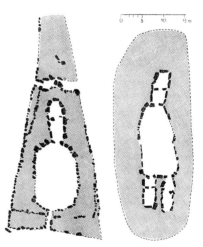

Neolithic tombs of Creevykeel and Deerpark, Co. Sligo (above), designed with heads, eyes, bodies, and (right) even legs

The 'hanging hair' of the outer wall (far left) is echoed in the sleep song of Gráinne, sung to her lover, in which she evokes the long-haired Áine.

Sleep a little, a little bit,
for you no fear, none at all...

Sleep as in the west away
daughter of Gailian, Áine
who went, hair hanging, soft smile,
with Dubthach, come from Oak-isle.

(Finn Cycle)

scribe had reduced the goddess to a woman, and Dermot to a hero in Finn's war band.)

O'Rahilly writes of 'Grian, the sun goddess and her double Áine',[32] and around Lough Gur both modes of the goddess are represented by hill sanctuaries, with Grian, or Gráinne's being at Cnoc Grene, a hill near Pallas Grean, eleven kilometres north-east from Lough Gur (see p. 100). Knockgrean, as it is sometimes called, was named after 'The Lady Grian of the bright cheeks'.[33] (The Irish word for 'sun' is *grian*.)

There are grounds for regarding the Giants' Grave in its entirety as an effigy of the goddess Áine/Grian, with the west chamber (one stone now fallen) as her head, and the outer walls of smaller megaliths her hair. When Dermot entered her main chamber he was entering her body. Though outwardly a mere mortal from Finn's war band, once inside, he grew in her proximity to reach a matching gigantic length, and set an example which young men in every locality were happy to follow.

Neolithic tombs throughout Ireland continued to be used by human lovers, identifying with the divine coition as Wood-Martin reported in 1902:

Even in the present day 'Dermot and Grainia's beds' are associated with runaway couples and with aphrodisiac customs. Cotton went in search of the Ballycasheen bed, in Co. Clare. He asked some country girls the way to it, and was heartily laughed at.

At length, the oldest girl of the group agreed to go, if *certain* he was a stranger, and if he told her his name. But the girl's conversation was in Irish (which he spoke not) and dragged on, and as the evening was growing late, he became impatient and very ungallantly rode away. A mile further, he made the same enquiry from a herdsman's wife. She said . . . it was the custom that if she went with a stranger to Darby and Grane's bed she was certainly to grant him everything he asked![34]

Borlase also noticed much libidinous hilarity passing between young people who had accompanied him to similarly named monuments, which were still believed to cure barrenness. He found no fewer than twenty-two megalithic tombs in Co. Clare alone, named after the divine prototypes.

Upon entering Gráinne's bed at the Lough Gur monument, Diarmait discovered that he had a golden sword. The existence of this precious weapon within the tomb was affirmed in the neighbourhood as recently as 1938. For this magic weapon the chamber provided the stone sheath.

In the Highlands of Scotland a comparable sword is known in oral tradition as The White Glave (sword) of Light. As told by John the Tinker of Inverary in 1860, it belongs in 'the Realm of Big Women', or 'behind the face of the sun'.

The conjunction of Gráinne, hero, and golden sword at the Lough Gur tomb may be compared to the Excalibur-Arthur-megalithic tomb ensemble so often found in Britain, where Arthur's claim to earthly rule derives from his association with the goddess Morgan le Fey.

Sword and sun. Rock-engraving at Östergötland, Sweden, c. 1500 BC. At Lough Gur, folk tradition connects a golden sword with Dermot and Graney's Bed – a phallic tool, tempered in the body of the sun goddess. Irish colg, *'sword', also means 'penis'*

MacCana maintains that the 'human' Diarmaid of the oral tale found in the tenth-century *Aithaid* manuscript was originally the god Diarmaid Donn.[35] In mid-Limerick, Donn's síd is at Cnoc Fírinne, twenty kilometres west of Lough Gur. The name Donn is derived from 'brown' or 'dark', while Irish *firinne* is 'truth'. He ruled the world below ground. For love of him, the original Gráinne drew herself down from the sky to follow him into the abyss, reluctantly leaving her sun-lit plains and warm soil behind. She asserts:

> For him I'd sell earth, – yellow,
> Mellow, all, – though bad bargain.[36]

This explains why Grain, a girl's name meaning 'Brightness and Beauty', merges with MacCana's derivation of the *same* name from the word 'ugliness'. The embrace of her brightness led to her 'loathsomeness, an object of horror', as surely as the splendour of a spear-point (*grain*) was designed for death. She had a foot in both worlds, and reintroduced the hero Diarmaid to the negative power of Donn's personality from which he was in part derived.

Cnoc Fírinne, Cnoc Áine and Cnoc Grene are listed as the last Munster strongholds of the fairies in the eighteenth-century poem.[37] From their respective *síde* the three deities rode out to mingle at the sacred lough which lay between them.

Dead Hunt and Silent Coach

Up and down, from zenith to nadir, the gods ran rings over and under Lough Gur. Their transit sometimes took the form of a hunt in the sky where the hounds of death pursued the individual.

People who live around the lough knew of the Dead Hunt. In 1972 Tom Carroll recalled: 'Willy heard it first, and then I heard it. We heards the dogs' tongues and all, and they beside us. We heard the horses and all, same as it was the middle of the day. That was about 2 o'clock in the morning. I'm only just telling you things we saw ourselves... They say it's some kind of a hunt spirits.'

Ned Hynes also heard it more than once: 'By God, I did... the hounds 'ud go in under your legs. You'd hear their tongues. You wouldn't see them, and they'd knock you down.'

A hunt might be expected to go anywhere following its quarry, but some witnesses believed that its normal course ran from Lough Gur to Cnoc Áine.

Tom MacNamara told me in 1990 that it passed right over him one night, on the east side of the Lough. He had lain down in a cold sweat till it had gone. In Tom Harnon's opinion, 'You never heard the hunt in your youth. That 'twas in your matured years that you actually heard it. When you were young, the older people in the household heard it, but you did not . . . But after that hunt there's always someone supposed to die on the following day in that locality.'

The hunt explicitly links the Lough to the síd of Cnoc Áine, and associates human mortality with the sport of the gods. The person about to die, or to be buried, is the hunted quarry selected by the spirits of the underworld and pursued from one world to another.

Another supernatural event experienced by Lough Gur people is the passage of the *Coitse Bodhar*, or Silent Coach. Speaking in 1972, Ned Hynes described its effect: 'It is like you'd run a tractor down the road now, drawing all buckets after it.' Is it dangerous? he was asked. 'No. But you wouldn't hear it passin' you out' (as it drew close). Hence its 'silent' name.

'I know its path – from here to Johnny Londrigon's old house; right beyond that; and it goes in there, out by the butt of Fox's Hill.'

John Brien of Bruff, aged eighty-two in 1972, believed that the Coitse Bodhar ran along routes laid down in antiquity around the Lough, and still visible, as archeaologists confirm. Brien remarked: 'There are an awful lot of old roads around there y'know – all the double ditches. The Coitse Bodhar travels along the old roads. You should throw yourself down on the ground when you hear it.'[38]

Tom Carroll also thought that it was highly dangerous to get in its way: 'The Coitse Bodhar follyed my Uncle Willy. He was never any good after it.'

The remains of ancient wooden causeways across the Red Bog, immediately south of the Lough, were once part of the ancient road network, and known to local men in the nineteenth century. 'We've been diggin' and burnin' the ould piles for years,' commented Paddy Regan, a labourer, to Mary Fogarty of Lough Gur. Ó'Ríordáin accepts the Cladh na Leac, running round the west side of the Lough, as 'portions of an ancient road clearly visible, a sunken track bordered by boulders.'[39]

The owner and occupant of the coach was Áine, judging by a story related by Mr James Butler in 1897. He told of a herdsman, Sean O'Shea of Knockfennel, whom she summoned to play his bagpipes at a ball that night, and he was 'carried off in her carriage, sitting beside her'. In this manner they passed down winding avenues of choicest fruit trees, evergreens, and sweet smelling roses to a grand mansion. Inside, a great ball was in progress, with good food, drink and company.[40]

The Coitse Bodhar may perhaps be seen as one of the waggons in which the North European mother goddess travelled. Tacitus knew of her in Denmark as Nerthus, or 'Mother Earth'. When not visiting her people in her sacred waggon, she kept it in a grove on an island.

Finn McCool at Lough Gur

The trail left by Áine around the lough attracted mythic heroes in pursuit. Among these was Finn. 'Finn McCool used to pass that way – he was after her,' Tom Carroll affirmed in 1972. Finn was the demigod son of the warrior Cumhall, and of Muirenn his goddess mother from the síd of Almu in Leinster.

Finn's name means 'bright', and he was bound to chase the sun goddesses Áine and Grian (Gráinne), in their southward career, especially since Diarmait, one of his men, had eloped with Gráinne. Indeed, Finn camped on the summit of Cnoc Grene, as the name *Seefin* (seat of Finn) there makes clear. From Cnoc Grene he travelled the few miles to Lough Gur, and arrived for the Oenach, at the start of harvest.

The twelfth-century *Duanaire Finn* states: 'At the Hill of Doon, the rock above Loch Goir, the horses of the Fiana came to race at an Oenach [great festival] with the Munstermen.'[41] Cormac derived the word *oenach*, 'religious festival', from *aine-ech* – 'delightfulness of horses', and in 1911, Canon Lynch was told by an old man that the Lough Gur racecourse was on Knockfennel, the hill bordering the north side of the lough. Others recalled how people came from all quarters to games and amusements there, for what Lynch deduced was a First Fruits Ceremony at the start of harvest, or Brón Trogain, the month when the earth labours for her fruits. Compatible with this annual effort, the word *gur* means 'keen and painful', as in *Mná re gúrlámnad* – 'women in painful parturition', and *gure*, 'pangs'.

As with the Ulster horseracing at Emain Macha (p. 218), the event is inseparable from the divine birth. Lough Gur is probably Áine's birth-lake, hence it was known locally as 'the hatching lake'.[42] What she gave birth *to*, at least from Finn's perspective, was a horse. A certain black mare, which belonged to a druid, Dil, son of Two Raids, won the three chief prizes of the Lough Gur oenach, or assembly, 'unto the rock over Loch Gair', and it was presented to Finn by Fiáchu, the local potentate, who had obtained it from Dil, his druid grandfather.

> There for thee is the swift black horse,
> Said Fiachu to the prince of champions [Finn],
> There is my famous chariot,
> And there is a horse for thy charioteer.

This mare, a horse-goddess born from the lough, was the perfect gift for Finn. She acquired extra value through being presented via Fiáchu and Dil. At Lough Gur the Black horse passes from Dil the priest to Fiáchu the farmer, and thence to Finn the warrior. This represents a transaction which, according to Dumézil, might be expected of any Indo-European community from the Bay of Bengal to County Clare.[43] It ritually united the three chief sub-divisions of Indo-European society. The divine horse accordingly carried the secret of social cohesion, and Lough Gur folklore is seen to gallop with the orthodoxies of two continents.

A lakeside farmer, Edward Fitzgerald, knew of the Lough Gur horse in 1911, when 'people had various tales of the wonderful black mare'. Was *this* the horse involved in the attempt to snatch the cloth from the under-lough tree? If so, the fragments of one myth touch the remains of another, and the mare who produced political stability on the surface plane also engaged the vertical unifier, the tree, shared by gods and men.

Archaeological evidence steers the ritual horse racing in the direction of charioteering, for in addition to the Cladh na Leac trackway around the lough, a pair of bronze chariot-tip hand-holds survive, and are dated by Fox to *c.* AD 100. These have lain in the British Museum since 1850, and are labelled 'From an island in Lough Gur'.

Fox writes: 'Structurally and decoratively, the Lough Gur bronzes are phallic, with circular shaft, roll, dome, and central ring.'[44] They may have functioned both as magical protection (Roman soldiers in Britain often wore a phallic charm around their neck), *and* as practical hand-holds. Intentionally placed on an island in one of Ireland's most sacred lakes, they might be seen as carrying forward the daily and annual affair between East (Leinster) and South (Munster), where 'Finn' dipped the chariot into Áine of the lake, to join the stable of her Coitse Bodhar.

These bronzes belonged naturally in the depths of the feminine, to be received again, like the sword Excalibur, by the Lady of the Lake.

As the returning sun goddess, Áine was probably driven around the Lough in a ceremonial showing at the summer festivals. Parts of bronze and gold votive models encapsulating such an event have been found in Ireland, and are based on Bronze Age Scandinavian designs, notably that of the Trundholm sun chariot. A gold leaf sun disc, 12 cm diameter, made *c.* 1000 BC, and probably carried by a model chariot, was found at Lattoon, Co. Cavan.[45] Two bronze Irish backing discs, similarly incised, and with loops for attachment to a model chariot and horse, suggest a nation-wide tradition, while a bronze horse, 15 cm tall, with holes for axles and disc attachment, extends the practice into the late Celtic period.

Knockadoon and Tír Na n'Óg

After the charioteering and the Harvest gathering on Knockfennel, the demi-god Finn cast his eyes across the water of Lough Gur to Knockadoon, the large rocky island, rising in the middle of the lake. According to one medieval text, he then crossed the water with his men to visit 'Dun over Lake', which O'Grady and MacNeill take to be the fort, Dun Gair, on the summit of Knockadoon.

Once there, he and his Fianna or military troop, 'three score hundred' strong, enjoyed three days and nights of feasting, says the poem 'The Headless Phantoms'.

The meaning of this short journey may lie partly in a mythic rebirth

*Coitse Bodhar, the 'Silent Coach'
as Sun Chariot. A gold disc from
Lattoon, c. 1000 BC, is perhaps an
image of the sun goddess,
displaying her solar journeys, and
incorporating a perpendicular
vagina-sheath motif to receive the
phallus-sword. Old Irish* faighin,
'sheath', *also means 'vagina'*

*Bronze horse (below), c. AD 300,
15 cm tall, apparently pregnant,
with pierced fetlocks for chariot
attachment*

*Restored Irish solar chariot (above), based on Irish
material and the Danish Trundholm sun chariot. A
chariot-wheel was* droch óir, *'hoop of gold', in Old
Irish*

*Chariot bronzes (left), hand-holds for a chariot, 16 cm
tall, found on an island in Lough Gur. Here, the
Lough Gur 'Silent Coach' merges with the solar
chariot, and its circuits of the lake suggest an island
waggon-deity comparable to Nerthus, as described by
Tacitus. At Lough Gur, Áine unites sun and water*

87

of Finn by the Munster sun goddess, Áine, from the midst of her principal birth lake.

Knockadoon is a picturesque intermingling of grey limestone cliffs and outcrops, with deciduous woodland and pasture. The remains of prehistoric habitation sites, and of stone circles, dot its hilly surface. These combine with folklore survivals to offer nearly five thousand unbroken years of a sacred economy, while the name *Gur*, being derived from 'pangs', suggests that mythically speaking, Knockadoon stands at the centre of a birth process involving the lough-as-womb of the presiding goddess.

As late as AD 1685, Knockadoon was still a true island. By 1833 it had been joined to the mainland by two wide causeways. After that, the east end of the lough was drained. Despite these alterations, it is legitimate to read the prehistoric island in its entirety both as a child of the lake, *and* as an image of Áine the mother of the gods, squatting in labour.

Throughout the world, Stone Age art is centred on the birth act, and serves to link human and divine parturition with sympathetic topographical events, such as the emergence of streams from caves, and of islands from lakes. The sight of Knockadoon, apparently rising from a ring of water, was probably the underlying inspiration for the extraordinary concentration of monuments around the lough.

For all prehistoric peoples (and for Munster's rural community in more recent times), the features of the landscape are considered to be alive. At certain locations, favoured because of their particularly evocative appearance, this background vitality takes on a supernatural intensity, and reveals the chief deity of the province. Thus Knockadoon *is* Áine, arising from her waters of parturition, just as the Paps of Anu, *Da Chíche Ánainne*, in South Munster, were recognized as those of the same goddess, and emphasized by the nipple-shaped cairns constructed on their summits in antiquity. At both places, natural endowment and human response were mutually supportive. The synthesis also permeates the 'art' of Áine, like the low relief of the goddess (p. 99), found 2 kilometres north of Knockadoon, at Caherelly Castle, where the limestone torso becomes a landscape of paradise.

In Croker's day, the south-west lobe of Knockadoon was known as Back Hill, perhaps because it makes the rump of a giant rock woman, facing north, whose vulva coincides with a cave regarded locally as the entrance to Tír Na n'Óg, the Land of Eternal Youth.

In 1910 a local man showed Lynch an entrance to the Tír Na n'Óg cave on the north cliff, and said that it was believed to have been occupied by 'a mysterious old man and his wife'. This may have been the cavern visited by Fitzgerald in 1826, and found to be twenty-two feet (6.7 metres) deep. Croker was told 'that at various periods of danger, even so late as the year 1798, it had been used as a place of retreat.'[46]

So Knockadoon, an eminence thrusting up through water from the depths, reciprocally gave access to a hidden realm, and the dream of

The Island of Knockadoon, seen from the shore of Lough Gur. Croker's map of 1833 (below left) shows two relatively new causeways, yet Knockadoon still suggests the plump form of the international Stone Age deity, squatting in the birth act

The squatting goddess has been drawn, sculptured, and perceived in landforms since Palaeolithic times. Silbury Hill and lake in Wiltshire, England (above right), were constructed c. 2600 BC, when the stone circles of Knockadoon were being erected. The same image appears in the seated figurine from the Vinča mound (Yugoslavia), sixth millennium BC (opposite)

uterine return. In these terms, Knockadoon and all its many caves comprise 'one of those unexpected landscapes which sometimes inspire a strange familiarity derived from pre-natal emotions, which the unconscious mind clothes in pictures of a fairy land. Strange yearnings of the heart, and fantasies of floating are associated with these pre-natal "memories".'[47] In Irish culture, they are translated as the possibility of entering the mistress of eternity.

In Irish tradition, Tír Na n'Óg is sometimes accessible to the living. Instead of the gloom and pain of the Classical Inferno, those who travelled there found that living itself achieved perfection. Tír Na n'Óg is variously described in early Irish literature as the Land of Youth, of Honey, of Promise, the Wonderland, the Silver Cloud Land, the Land of Women, and the Land of Bliss.[48] These were different names for a single, flexible, poetic realization, over which the figure of a 'queen' ruled, and called mortals to her side. Entry was by invitation and enticement, or by courteous exploration of adult voyagers. In either case, human access was dependent on the poets, whose words were needed to carry the adventure over the threshold. To equip them for this task the Irish poet's traditional apprenticeship was spent in the dark, in underground chambers, where the rules of composition were taught, and poems committed to memory. As Edmund Spenser observed in the sixteenth century, even when poets emerged to hear their works sung by bards at social events, out of respect for the divine source of inspiration, they lay in darkness (facing Tír Na n'Óg) as they had been taught to do while students of the art.

Entrances to Tír Na n'Óg occur throughout Ireland. They are found in lake-isle caverns (as at Knockadoon), down wells, under lakes, or where the sun sets, or on islands in the Western ocean. These doors all led towards music (often played on a harp), a magic tree (frequently of gold or silver, from which a sacred branch was plucked), divine horses and birds, of dazzling colours, a banquet where a cauldron of ale was always full, and where an unearthly kind of Time was enjoyed. Central to the vision, its source and overseer, stood the figure of a beautiful woman. Combining generosity with authority, she was the goddess revealed.

In a more dispersed fashion we have already encountered many of these elements around Lough Gur. At Tír Na n'Óg, they combine to make a primary world, from which earth is a derivative.

All the Tír Na n'Óg splendours may be anticipated down the wet limestone cavities of Knockadoon, where:

> A woman abides in this noble house
> Above all the women of Erin,
> With hair of gold she welcomes us
> In her accomplished beauty.[49]

A silver branch, mentioned in other Tír Na n'Óg descriptions, establishes a further link with the craft of poetry, since in inauguration ritual it was customarily held over the new poet's head. In keeping with European tradition as a whole, the Irish poet's muse was feminine, and typically envisaged as goddess of the Otherworld. He went there to meet her, and to confirm her existence.

Money Hole and Bull

All traditions are liable to decay, and on Knockadoon that of Tír Na n'Óg has produced an offshoot, where endless joy may be sold off for cash. Local opinion now insists that there *is* something of value hidden under Knockadoon – money. The Land of Women is prostituted in keeping with the rising commercial ethic.

The precise location of the Money Hole is disputed. Earlier this century Mr John Hynes used to point out a large flagstone, a little under a metre high, in the fence of the old road between Knockadoon and Knockaroe Hill, which lies to its north. He maintained that a woman from Co. Clare had dreamed on three consecutive nights that a mass of golden treasure lay beneath the stone, and led a body of Clare men to dig there. However, before they could find it they were attacked and driven off by local people, who later regretted that they had not delayed their response till after the gold had been located.[50]

Yet Lynch was told that it was 'located a short distance above the Black Castle on the *southern* slope of Knockadoon Hill [though] somewhat concealed now, as...it is situated in the centre of a so-called 'grove'...which consists of bushes and briars.'

This Money Hole has been the rendezvous of many exciting efforts to discover the much coveted but hitherto unobtainable crock of gold which is believed to have been buried there long ago, by a Geraldine chieftain before going to battle. He compelled one of his soldiers to swear he would guard the treasure dead or alive. The chief then shot him and placed his body over the Hidden Treasure, and the soldier's spirit, in the form of an enchanted bull, still guards it.[51] His informants said that anyone who dreamt of the treasure three nights running qualified for a search, which began by tracing out concentric circles of holy water which the bull could not cross. His frustrated bellowings were heard for miles around. Tongues of flame shot from eyes and mouth. The search started at midnight, and lasted till dawn, but the unexpected death of one of the party often caused the attempt to be abandoned. The Eastern Circle on the brow of the Hill is directly over the Money Hole, Lynch concluded. In 1972 the Money Hole was still spoken of, though in Johnny Brien's belief the gold was in a cave on the Knockfennel shore of the Lough 'Where a big bull or a dog is supposed to be guardin' it.'

But Tom Carroll saw the bull at Knockadoon:

'...A big black bull, about seventeen feet high at the shoulder, jumped up out of Knockadoon and followed the three of us one night...and his backbone as thin as a glass...he was comin' out of Knockadoon, and he walked along to the runnin' water, and he seems not to come...he wasn't able to come across the runnin' water. They say he was mindin' the money. There's money buried there.' [Tom had himself dug for it, but forgot to keep up the circle of holy water round about.]

Irish myth says that prosperity partly depended on a bull. He was the epitome of strength and virility and through his annual sacrifice he regenerated the exhausted world.

In 1837 the eastern part of the Lough running up to Knockadoon was drained, and huge quantities of ox bones were revealed in the mud of the former lake bed, suggesting ritual slaughter, possibly at Samain, over a long period. (At Samain ritual slaughter and the practical need to cull the stock before the winter fodder shortage, worked together.) 'More than one hundred cartloads of bones were removed, and sold to dealers in such articles. And later, during the potato famine [of 1845], the poor of the town of Bruff obtained a scanty living, by collecting and selling bones from this locality ... the remains of *Bos Longifrons* [the most ancient type of domestic cattle], the heads of which almost all exhibited a fractured front, produced by the blow which had killed them.'[52]

In 1977, on a wet Sunday morning in September, the writer was challenged on the slopes of Knockadoon by an angry inhabitant who believed an attack on the Money Hole by metal detector was about to take place. Once satisfied that it was only a camera being carried, he explained that during the Famine the English landowner, de Salis, had dug from Knockadoon a great mass of old weapons and vessels, to furnish his London mansion. In fact, prehistoric bronze chariot fittings, shields and axes *were* taken from the Lough. 'There is scarcely a museum or a private collection in Great Britain and Ireland which does not include some object from the lake and its vicinity,' is Professor O'Kelly's assessment.[53]

In their starvation and despair, local people rightly felt that the embodiment of community values (their chief treasure) was being stolen, and with its disappearance, a framework of beliefs which had supported them for millennia was being dismantled. Hunger's bitterness was then complete, and those who had the strength to crawl to the emigration boats departed, truly bereft.

Yet in 1977 enough trace of the Money Hole remained for a young man to fly to its defence as a working proposition. If not indelible, the last version of Tír Na n'Óg is proving hard to eradicate.

Finn in the Bruiden

One way to approach the hidden Otherworld of Knockadoon is to follow behind the gods – to let *them* locate the entrance, and so slip across the threshold unnoticed at the rear of their party. We can tag on to Finn and his Fianna; but if the ride is free, it is far from easy.

As Finn frequently discovered, the burden of heroism is a heavy one, and unenviable. Abnormal and anomalous, the hero must mediate between the paired men-god opposites and be the first to face the terrors of divine caprice, which in this case involves destruction.

Finn, the most volatile of demi-gods, is hard to pin down, but he *was* seen feasting on the summit of Knockadoon, as Samain, the Hallowe'en quarterday, approached. Samain, Summer's End, was a zone of instability, being the void between one year and the next, in which feasting and sexual adventure merged with monstrous wintry images of disintegration.

Nothing better illustrates these perils than the Bruiden type of story, connected with Hallowe'en, where the god-hero is enticed into a magic house which *could* be in Tír Na n'Óg, but where he is unexpectedly abused, ill-treated, and often killed. He has been tricked. Too late does he realize that the banquet hall belongs to another type of supernatural realm, which is bound into the bleakest segment of an annual cycle. That is where the poem 'The Headless Phantoms' takes us. These words, attributed to Guaire (alias Oisín), Finn's blind son (who was believed to have spent three hundred years in Tír Na n'Óg), slam shut behind his father, giving him no choice *but* to go downwards.

The Headless Phantoms

Both Guaire's descent into Tír Na n'Óg and Finn's entry into the Bruiden are widely known in Irish oral tradition. From that enduring source, the twelfth-century writer drew his material. 'There are many points to indicate that the folktale served as a model for the literary version,' writes Murphy.[54]

He concludes that beneath the Heroic, aristocratic, 'realistic' crust of the Finn Cycle, as written down in the twelfth century, lies an elemental magic as old as humanity's settlement of Ireland.

This nature religion came to make equal use of text, memory, and oral recitation, with the written cross-references giving extra authority to the pronouncements of Tom Carroll and his friends.

The growth rings of successive seasons contribute to the trunk of the pagan world tree, but as every forester knows, its life entirely depends on the current flow of sap *immediately* below the bark being renewed every year. Finn had to be lured into the house of treachery at the start of each November. This also explains why Bruiden poems (whether memorized or read) were recited at Hallowe'en, for on the words spoken and heard the demi-god rode to his annual destiny on behalf of a fearfully grateful humanity. The words projected the deeds that *ought* to happen as between men and gods, with the demi-god in the vanguard of the exchange. (If, as has often been noted, there is something cynical in Finn's character, so there is in many another veteran who is repeatedly pushed into the front line.) True to the incantatory mythic method, it is on lines of verse that he and his Fianna lower themselves into the chamber of the supernatural.

Near the entrance, the blind poet Guaire stands. (Has he ruined his eyesight, for a glimpse of the dark behind the Bruiden door? If so, that is a poet's fate.) Finn, meanwhile, confronting the Celtic New Year, speaks in terms of physical appetites. He wants shelter from the growing cold. He needs more food and drink for his men. In search of these commodities, The Headless Phantom verses send him on a rapid circuit of Munster. By telling the tale, under his *Guaire* pseudonym, Oisín drew the action towards Lough Gur, and to Dun Guaire on Knockadoon, the sum of its province, and therefore a good site for the nebulous and enchanted lodging that Finn eventually finds, with darkness descending.

Entrance to the magic hostel might be under the large flat stone close to the north-western shore of Knockadoon, traditionally called Leac Rudhraighe Rueidh, connected in local belief with 'Red Rury', a mythic, Charon-like ferryman.[55] As named on the 1927 Ordnance map, the slab may mean literally, 'The Flat Stone' (*Leac*), 'of long occupation' (*rudrad*), or 'a searching groping sojourner, a darkening, and a dark gloomy countenance' (*rudhrach*), and going on 'a great journey' (*ruidh*), with a 'rush, a vault, a bound, and running jump, a throw or cast' (*ruid*), into the Bruiden.

At the door stood 'a grey-haired churl', a Giant. 'My welcome, O famous Find [Finn], saith the Giant cruelly.' The Giant quickly seizes Finn's horse, and fastens the door with iron hooks. Finn and his men 'sit down on the hard couch that has to rest us all at once; the log of elder that is on the hearth has all but quenched the fire.'[56]

The elder-log is a well-known emblem of the goddess-as-hag – Áine in her winter underworld, for example. The privation of the scene is reminiscent of the flea-ridden, smoke-blackened barn in the Welsh *Mabinogion*. The Book of Leinster version reads:

The Giant flings firewood of elder on his fire: it almost smothered us with smoke. . . . A hag abode in the great house, with three heads on her thin neck: a headless man on the other side, with one eye protruding from his breast.

The churl urges the people of the house to rise up, and sing a song for Finn. . . . Nine bodies rise out of the corner from the side next to us. Nine heads from the other side on the iron couch. They set up nine horrid screeches; matched in loudness, but not in harmony.

This is the birth cry of Chaos and winter dismemberment, complementary to the harvest birth, due to occur nine months later at Lughnasa, which has to be earned in the pit.

They are a screeching, wailing, shouting, and clamorous rabbly household.

That strain which was sung to us would waken the dead out of the mould. It almost broke the bones of our heads.

The Giant then lifts the firewood axe, and deftly smites, flays, and destroys the Fianna's horses, but Finn tells his men not to complain, saying 'Well for us if he grants life to us.' [Finn knows, if his men do not, that they are no longer in control, but in the power of a different kind of sense.]

The giant then sets out 50 spits of rowan, but each came from the fire with the meat still quite raw. Finn rejects these: 'Take away thy food, O

Giant! For I have never devoured raw food; I will never eat it from today till Doom.'[57]

Rowan, in Irish belief, keeps the dead from rising, and for that reason was planted in graveyards. In rejecting the offer of raw flesh on rowan spits Finn was therefore declining the role of a supernatural corpse eel, which *is* allowed to eat the uncooked flesh of the Grange graveyard. Had he accepted the meat, he would have shifted the balance of his demi-god status firmly towards the divine, and so spent the rest of his existence identified *totally* with the Knockadoon síd and with the Tuatha deities.

In refusing, Finn retains a grip on the human aspect of his double personality. He opts instead for a borderline role, and the ability to move freely back and forth between worlds.

'If thou has come into our house', saith the Giant, 'to refuse our food, it is certain that we shall go against yourselves.'

Then fighting ensues, the fire is quenched, and Finn and his men are driven 'into a dark, black nook, where they lay head-to-head till morning, till the sun lighted up the house.' (At the same instant, in the Otherworld of the famous New Grange tumulus, Co. Meath, the sun pokes its golden wand at midwinter dawn through a stone roof-box to the central chamber, with a touch of hope.) Here, the smile of Áine may alight on the Fianna's distress and confusion. But instead, having declined her raw meat, with implacable logic her sunbeam strikes them with the spear of mortality. Consequently, 'When the sun rose, each man falls hither and thither,' and 'A mist falls on every one's head so that he was dead on the spot.' Such is their welcome back into the world of mortals.

They are born dead; it is midwinter.

But this is not the end, for though the Fianna have opted for humanity, they are granted a special kind of *eternal* humanity. Thus: 'For a short time we lay in our rest. We rise up, We are whole.' Now conspicuously 'human', the Fianna pay the price (in this relentless education), for the fairy Otherworld immediately vanishes from view: 'There the house is hidden from us. Everyone of the household is hidden.' But mortal life goes on: 'Thus arose Find of Inisfail, with his own horse in his hand. Whole were we all, both head and foot, every blemish was absent.' Yet this is no robust return. Instead, like animals re-emerging from long hibernation, 'We fared thence wearily, feebly. Those we met in the real world, they asked of us tidings. We had no wish to deny it. "We found", saith Find, "on our way Tribulation for our billeting." '[58]

Inside Knockadoon, his imprisonment may be connected with the cave known as Carrignagol, named on the 1927 Ordnance map. It means 'Rock of Weeping, Wailing and Lamentation' (*gol*), and stands close to the Leac Rudhraighe Rueidh (p. 77). There he might reflect on *gola* – the pit, prison or pre-Christian 'Purgatory' from which he has escaped.

Through the mean days on the far side of winter, traumatized by his otherworld treatment, Finn seeks a motive for the attack, and concludes: 'Those that came against us, the three shapes out of Yew Glen, [came] to take vengeance on us for their sister, whose name was Cullen wide-maw.'[59]

Cuillen means 'holly tree'. Perhaps it was *her* burning, as an annual yule-log sacrifice, that stirred her evergreen sisters to avenge the incineration, by attacking Finn the fire-god. ('Yew Valley' also evokes Áine's brother, Fer Í or Fer Fí, whose name means Man of Yew.)

The Red Cellar

At Lough Gur, the cycle of violence still reverberates in a brief story, related by Ned Hynes, concerning Knockfennel on the north shore.

'An oul' woman was going up there...sewing. And the White Boys saw the line of the red thread, and they followed her up the cave, and they murdered her there. And that's why it's called the Red Cellar.'[60]

Finn means fair skinned, and 'The White Boys' is another name for the Fianna. 'The oul' woman' may be the one who sat knitting under the magic lough tree, the mother of crafts – textiles were a Neolithic innovation. Here she comes into alignment with the three-headed hag (the triple winter goddess) who so tormented Finn's men. His 'white boys' tracked her down and dispatched her from this world, back to her underground retreat on the north shore of the lough, behind which the sun is never seen. The murder of solar Áine as an old woman is performed daily after sunset, when the last red threads lining the clouds are extinguished in deepening twilight. The see-saw of violence in and between worlds is attributed to the Fianna, the mythic war-band who, as warrior-mercenaries, were also involved in endemic warfare across the political surface of Celtic Ireland.

However, since Finn and his men were solar derivatives, they often regarded Áine favourably, and called her Buanann, meaning 'Nurse of the Heroes', for 'as Anu was mother of the gods, so Buanann was mother of the Fiann'.[61] Further, the Colloquy of the Sages states that Áine was Finn's mistress. 'She was with Finn for seven years during which time she abundantly gratified all Ireland and Scotland, and bore him two sons.'[62]

These benefits are implicit in the siting of the Red Cellar Cave; for although it lies on the north shore, it *faces* east, to the goddess of sunrise, while on the ridge above, the *oenach* races of full summer were run.

Excavation of the Red Cellar floor brought to light bones of bear, elk and arctic lemming – creatures that had sheltered there between the end of the last Ice Age and the arrival of humanity. The seasonal movements of these beasts, responding to solar and lunar cycles, amounted to a performance of moves subsequently scripted by human mythology. In essence, we have followed where the lemming led.

Bronze trumpets of bull-horn shape were used in Munster, c. 1000 BC, to imitate the bellowings of the mythic bulls. At the Red Cellar Cave, folklore tells of a bull, a trumpet, 'an oul' woman', and the divine hero, Geároid Iarla

Pre-Christian Irish religion habitually perceived all life to hang from a single thread.

Two decades ago, Tommy Hannon told of 'a farmer coming home late from the fair of Bruff [who] stumbled into the Red Cellar Cave, where Geároid Iarla sleeps with all his warriors, waiting to be risen. There was a beautiful trumpet there . . . the farmer picked it up, and put it to his lips, and blew a small little bit. All the warriors sprung up, and the farmer ran away terrified. If he had blown a proper blast the spell would be broken, and they would all be freed.'[63]

There may be more than a hint of Finn and his Boys in Iarla and *his* men, with the local demi-god echoing the work of the national Finn, in his Bruidhean adventure. Irish myth often works by multiplication of echoes. For that reason the Red Cellar 'trumpet' may be related to the bronze horns, made *c.* AD 1000, and found at Dowris, Co. Offaly. Coles derives these from the Nordic lurer, always found in pairs, and says that the Dowris instruments give a note 'which resembles the bellowing of the bull',[64] and can be assumed to have had a ritual function in a bull myth ceremony. In 1972, Johnny Brien insisted that there *was* a magic bull in the Red Cellar, echoing the ox known to Carroll at the Knockadoon Money Hole.

From shore to shore, folk belief effectively brings to life the archaeological evidence of lurer, and oxbones in the lough, while animating the landscape of the south with a version of the *Táin Bó Cualgne* bull epic of the north. Voiced anecdote is the link. When sounded, it can raise the riches of antiquity and early literature to the lip of contemporary experience.

Suideachan, the Birth Chair

To witness the birth of Áine's child, we have to return to Knockadoon, where her birth chair is situated. There, 'at the old edge of the lake, beyond the Western Circle of Knockadoon,' writes Lynch, 'is Suideachan, the little seat of the Housekeeper (*Bean tighe*).'[65] Here Áine comes up from Tír Na n'Óg and sits to give birth, in the manner shown by numerous Palaeolithic and Neolithic figurines.

The chair consisted of a small grassy mound, with the rock seat on the west side overlooking the lake. Other descriptions of the mound say that it was eight feet (2.4 metres) high, with a hollow in the middle. It is sited 'just this [the north] side of Ash Point' according to Tom Carroll. Pat MacNamara (who lives close by) calls it a rocky outcrop on the shore near the gravel pit, and before Garret Island is reached, walking from the north. It was here that Sean O'Shea, a herdsman from Knockfennel, met Áine on a fine evening in August.

Next morning his wife told him that she had had a bad dream, in which the starch for her Sunday cap had turned yellow as gold, and she then saw a fine lady in a carriage who was throwing up gold balls with one hand and catching them with the other. Worse still, this lady never ceased grinning at her, and mocking her, till she was wakened by the fright. (The 'lady' was probably Áine, juggling with her solar self in miniature, the theme of so much of the golden 'art' of Irish prehistory.) Sean, ignoring his wife's misgivings, then drove off with Áine to her mansion.[66]

'Inside, a great ball was in progress, with good food, drink, and company. He then saw shoals of freshwater fish gazing in admiration through the windows of her enchanted banquet hall, for he was in one of the submerged palaces of Geároid Iarla. At the end of the night, the lady gave him a purse of gold, which on awakening he discovered contained only yellow furze flowers.' This story was related by Mr James Butler in 1897.[67]

At some time in the 1870s Áine appeared at the Housekeeper's Chair to another local man, Mr James Cleary. 'She was every inch a queen', he told his friends. A few evenings later he was out on the lough in his curragh when it capsized and he was drowned. Her call, they concluded, could not be resisted. Anyone who saw her, it was believed, was driven insane by the spell of her beauty, or died shortly after. (Madness is a voyage to another reality, where 'normal' behaviour dies.)

Both O'Shea and Cleary may be said to have enjoyed or suffered a *reverse* birth into Lough Gur, and a return to the divine as sacrificial victims.

In the mid-nineteenth century it was told how on one occasion Áine came up from the depths of the lake and sat on the housekeeper's seat to comb her hair with a golden comb, while in 1971, Tom Carroll affirmed that she *still* sits on the Suideachan, 'combing her hair with a golden comb, and she'll continue to do so till her comb is worn out and her white hair...'.[68] At that point, words failed him.

In Hiberno-Scottish tradition, solar-lunar suggestions play about 'a fine golden comb and a coarse comb of silver; they are worth a deadly fight with a giant in many a story',[69] while the pre-Christian Greek

The Knockadoon Suideachan, or Housekeeper's Chair, is seen at the left, above. On this flat-topped limestone slab, Áine, the supreme Housekeeper of Lough Gur, was reputed to sit. On her birth-chair, during the month of Brón Trogain, when 'the earth is in travail', she turned green corn to gold and bore it to triumphant harvest. Punnann, 'sheaf of corn', was Áine's child

The 'Housekeeper' (far left), carving from Caherelly Castle, Lough Gur

The Lady of Pazardzik, Bulgaria (left), c. 4000 BC, the Indo-European goddess-in-labour rites of Ge-Themis, the earth goddess, were centred on a comb (*kteis*), which was regarded as synonymous with the female pudenda, from which the earth goddess gave birth to sun and moon.

At Lough Gur, a man called Cuacaill, or Herdsman of the Island, coveted Áine's comb and stole it. Afterwards, misfortune befell him, and on the verge of death, he ordered that it should be flung into the lake, where Áine is sometimes to be seen, half her body above the waters, 'combing her hair', as reported by Fitzgerald in 1879.

The Harvest Birth-line

Áine as mother-to-be appears in the word *ain*, meaning 'in my womb', and 'the period of fasting prior to a feast day vigil', while *guaire* (gur) can mean 'on the point of parturition'. With these words, the mother goddess sits on her *suidechan*, or maternity chair, at the eve of the harvest quarter-day, Lughnasa (1st August), and waits for the dawn birth of her son Lugh. Sunrise occurs at 59° and joins the Cnoc Grene síd of her solar 'sister', Grian, to the Knockadoon birth chair. On the way, it passes over the Money Hole site nominated by John Hynes, and over the north end of the Lough. There, a Bronze Age spear with two gold rings and 'sunbeam' gold inlay on the socket was dredged up in 1857, and presumed by O'Kelly to have been a votive offering.[70] The same alignment passes from the Chair across a circular stone platform of Neolithic age on Garret Island (named after Áine's Norman son, Geároid Iarla), and thence to the western shore of the Lough, where it enters Ireland's greatest embanked stone circle.

The one and only entrance to this monument is narrow, well-defined, and aligned precisely to receive the Lammas sunrise at 59° East of North. The enclosure is named Rannach Crom Dubh, after Crom Dubh, the porter-god of harvest, who in Irish folk belief carried the first sheaf, or *punnann*, from the goddess (its mother) to the people.

The Lughnasa dawn at Lough Gur threw a spear of light between Grian's síd and the birthday island of Knockadoon, where her sister Áine laboured to produce the harvest child. Archaeology, place-name evidence, topography, solar behaviour, and folklore combine to help recreate what was the most joyful day in the old Irish year, and to return the mythic narrative to the physical symbols through which it may become visible again.

Crom Dubh

In her majestic survey of harvest folk-belief, MacNeill (1962) found a harvest god, Crom Dubh, spoken of in most parts of Ireland, especially in the provinces of Connacht and Munster, from Donegal Bay to the Dingle Peninsula. Crom Dubh, she writes 'is a pagan deity' whose name means 'the dark bent one'. He is popularly regarded as the dominant God in the land till the coming of St Patrick, and mid-nineteenth-century sources in Munster continue to refer to Crom

Dubh as 'the god of harvest'. He was believed to emerge in most parts of Ireland at the start of harvest, on 1st August, midway between summer solstice and autumn equinox.[71] In Co. Limerick the day was called Black Stoop Sunday. Crom stooped because he carried on his back the first great sheaf of wheat, the inaugural and sacred gift from the Otherworld. He was dark or black because in order to find the wheat, he had been into the winter underworld of Grainne-Áine's subsoil and síde.[72]

That Crom Dubh and Áine were anciently linked together as harvest deities is clear from a mid-nineteenth-century report from Co. Louth, which calls the festival *Domhnach Áine agus Chroim Duibh* (the Sunday of Áine and Crom Dubh).[73]

Crom-the-giver complements Finn-the-taker, acting as farmer to Finn's warrior, and as a darkness set against Finn's 'bright'. Where Finn goes, Crom follows, and vice-versa, in a double act discernible at Lough Gur. So, Rannach Crom Dubh, the low-lying ring, complements Seefin, Finn's seat, on top of Cnoc Grene.

Subsequent to the Neolithic era, Crom was expected to carry extra loads imposed by cultural change, including the impact of bronze workers, Iron Age warriors, and attacks by Christian saints. Emerging as he did from the very foundation of Irish culture, all these challenges were loaded on to his shoulder for assimilation, on the assumption that, like an ox, he would continue working, whatever happened, and however low his reputation sunk in the eyes of clever newcomers, who needed him more than their abuse implied.

Both Crom and Finn can be seen as degraded versions of the high gods, Donn the dark one, and his dazzling opposite number, Lugh.

After reviewing a mass of folklore and early literature, MacNeill concluded that Crom is indeed a version of Donn, 'and that he can be regarded as identical with the pre-Celtic food-providing gods – Cormac, the Dagda, Elcmar, Midir and Balor',[74] all of whom were engaged in conflict with a Finn-Lugh opponent. Yet the outcome of these struggles was a joint affirmation; Lugh's spears came to hit their mark on Crom-Donn's shoulder as bundles of golden corn-stalks, each tipped with a precious wheat or barley head. The spear was the staff, or *rannach*, of life, carried to the people by the dark god.

Crom brings the entire legacy of Neolithic goods from under the hills, including knowledge of ploughing (his nickname, 'Suicin', is probably a diminutive of *soc*, 'a ploughshare'). Corn, a granary, a feast, influence on weather and, (as we shall see), a bull, are also in his gift.

The sheaf that Crom brought to the feast on his shoulder was probably the golden corn child, Eithne. In folklore this girl is sometimes presented as Crom's fairy mistress, while the attempts of the god Lugh to wrest the sheaf from Crom is portrayed as a struggle to abduct the corn maiden, Eithne. The word *eithne* means 'kernel' or 'grain'. Eithne has been Anglicized as Annie in Ulster; she can be regarded as daughter of Áine, and seen in 'Maiden' corn dollies, and the astrological Virgo.

Corn Maiden and Crom Dubh. The harvest god, Crom Dubh, carried the corn child, Eithne ('grain'), from Suideachan across the lough to the henge monument that bears his name. He is personified (above) in its biggest megalith, 2.3 metres tall. Eithne, as daughter and mother-to-be, was annually plaited from barley, oats and wheat

Rannach Crom Dubh, alias The Lios, or Stone Circle B. Crom Dubh entered by the 59° entrance passage, coinciding with the Lughnasa (Lammas) harvest quarter-day sunrise. The embanked arena of Ireland's biggest henge, erected c. 2500 BC, is ringed by 113 megaliths

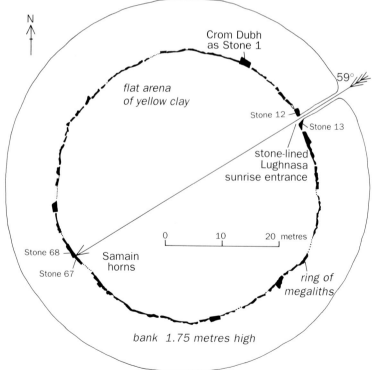

N

Crom Dubh
as Stone 1

59°

flat arena
of yellow clay

Stone 12

Stone 13

stone-lined
Lughnasa
sunrise entrance

0   10   20 metres

Stone 68

Stone 67

Samain
horns

ring of
megaliths

bank 1.75 metres high

Entrance passage (left) and arena, Rannach Crom Dubh. A gold-feruled 'spear of Lugh' was dropped into Lough Gur as a Bronze Age votive offering on the 59° sunrise line which strikes through this stone-lined passage (see p. 77). As 'Lios', 'cattle pound', the walled arena (right) could secure Crom's bull. The entrance alignment, as Windle observed, also fixes firmly on Samain sunset, between horn-shaped stones 67 and 68

Her womanliness and long sojourn in Crom's underworld shows in *eitre*, 'furrow'. Eithne's November self is the new furrow waiting for the seed.

The Samain Bull Ring

The opening of Rannach Crom Dubh at 59° for Lammas sunrise also admits its replica, the May Day sunrise, which falls along the same line. Moreover, if the 59° axis is projected *across* the ring to 239° East of North, an alignment with the complementary twin events of Samain and Imbolc sunsets is registered. Windle writes: 'One thing is quite clear, when all [modern] obstacles were removed (such as Holy Cross cottages) a person standing with back to the entrance passage would get the sharpest possible sight of the sun going down [at Samain] through the notch between stones 67 and 68'.[75] The 'notch' is the 'V'-shaped space which the two stones (touching at their bases) offer as they rise to make a pair of tall stone horns, even though the tip of 67 has since been knocked off. They are now 1.9 and 2.3 metres high. Apart from Stone 1, they are two of the tallest in the ring. The horns and the notch stand at, and make, the gate between the years.

Both the pre-Celtic and Celtic annual circuits ended at Samain, Summer's end. The red sunset is therefore the blood-light of the old year, shed on the 'gate-post-horns' of the new. Layer upon layer of organic debris, found immediately behind the horn stones, suggests that the annual bull was devoured as a roasted carcass on the spot, in repeated Samain feasts.

In Munster and Connacht folklore Crom's bull was believed to be immortal. By trickery St Patrick once killed and ate it, and then ordered the bones to be thrown into the hide, whereupon the animal returned to life. Around Galway Bay at Samain every household skinned and roasted a bull in honour of Crom Dubh, and one may assume that Crom Dubh and the Bull were originally synonymous.[76]

Evidence for sacred communal cooking places at, or attached to, Neolithic monuments in Ireland, is now abundant. Often, as at the Drombeg stone circle, West Cork, the tradition can be shown to have extended into the early Christian period. Now called *fulacht fiadh*, these 'ox-cooking' sites are frequently associated with Finn and his Fianna, and probably derive from a Neolithic prototype exemplified here at the *Lios*, or 'Enclosure' of Crom Dubh.

The *dubh* of Crom's name accordingly means burnt as well as dark. In Crom-the-Bull we witness the old year sinking to his knees, his huge weight falling, in fire and smoke, to the winter underworld. At Samain the monument became a bull ring. One meaning of 'Lios' is cattle pound, which may explain its sheer and remarkably continuous inner wall of touching megaliths erected to prevent the bull's escape. At the Lios the third bull of a trinity bellows across the lake, to his mythic brothers, in the Red Cellar, and on Knockadoon.

The Samain human congregation desired to share in the bull's descent into the underworld, just as they craved for a crumb of Eithne, in the new Lammas loaf. For the same reason, they ate a morsel of the beef (*rann* means crumb *and* morsel). They re-enacted the bull's downward journey in their own digestive tract. Samain, as the start of a *new* year, was also the season of maximum virility, epitomized by the bull and emphasized in human liaisons. *Gam* (November) was the month of weddings, with birth nine months later, at Lammas.

In terms of Áine's physical needs, the sacrificed bull can be said to enter her lake, and the body of her síd. The early twelfth-century account of Cnoc Áine specifically states that it opened at Samain to King Oilioll Olum, and Áine herself came forth, playing on a copper timpan or lyre, whereupon he violated her.

Another legend, current in the 1870s, says that when Áine emerged, she was accompanied by a red bull, and was then raped by the Earl of Desmond, and so gave birth to Garad (Geároid)![76] Bull, síd-opening, Áine, and fruitful coition are clearly associated, in a mythic union at Samain, whose progeny was born the following Lammas, nine months later.

Bulls and Faction Fights

If Rannach Crom Dubh served to pen sacred bulls, it may have been the scene of ritual contests, ending in the death of a beast. In the early literature, a Brown Bull kills the Great White Horn of Connacht, and in Co. Limerick up until the mid-nineteenth century, contending human factions played out a battle of rival bulls (such as can be envisaged at the Lios), at the November Fair Field, beneath Cnoc Grene, situated on a Samain sunset alignment with the Lios.

Although in recent times the Bryanes and the Conways were the chief clans involved there, the rival teams were known as the 'Three Year Olds' and 'The Four Year Olds', implying a contest between beasts, perhaps bulls, with whom the people identified. The beastly origin of these team fights, with ash staves, is confirmed by many Co. Limerick people. Some say that two farmers disputed at the fair over their respective animals, while a more archaic tradition insists that it was the animals *themselves* that originally fought. Human injuries, and even fatalities were expected every year, imitating the annual instatement of a bull god and the deposition, in a trial of strength, of his rival. A hierarchy of contests is suggested by the Co. Limerick faction cry: 'Parish against parish, county against county', leading to inter-provincial bouts.[77]

Rannach, the Buried Staff

The faction fighter's ash stave may have originally been regarded as allied to the magic staff of the Dagda, another form of Crom Dubh. Sealed under the yellow clay which was laid across the surface of the Lios at the time of its construction in 2500 BC, Ó'Ríordáin found (but did not recognize) the Samain symbols of a Neolithic god and goddess.[78] Made of stone on a gigantic and matching scale, these were the staff or walking stick of the god and the crescent new moon of the maiden-goddess. Both measured 36.4 metres from tip to tip, and came together close to the Samain horn stones. MacNeill's conclusion that Crom Dubh may be regarded as identical with the food-providing god called the Dagda, helps to solve the mystery of the buried 'Staff' created from carefully arranged limestone rocks, since it was the Dagda's primary symbol of office, described in the ancient literature.

For example, with his double pronged staff 'he cut the double trench of Lorg an Dagdae'. He was known to have been active at Samain, as the Second Battle of Mag Tuired (the Plain of the Pillar) describes:

He trailed behind him a wheeled fork which was the work of eight men to move, and its track was enough for the boundary ditch of a province. It is called 'The Track of the Dagda's Club' for that reason. His penis was uncovered. He had on two shoes of horse-hide with the hair outside. . . .

As he went along he saw a girl in front of him, a good looking young woman with an excellent figure, her hair in beautiful tresses. The Dagda desired her, but he was impotent on account of his belly. The girl began to mock him, then she began wrestling with him. She hurled him so that he sank to the hollow of his rump in the ground. . . .

He looked at her angrily and asked, 'What business did you have, girl, heaving me out of my right way?'

'This business: to get you to carry me on your back to my father's house.'

Then he moved out of the hole, after letting go the contents of his belly, and the girl had waited for that for a long time. He got up then and took the girl on his back; and he put three stones in his belt. Each stone fell from it in turn – and it has been said that they were his testicles which fell from it. The girl jumped on him and struck him across the rump, and her curly pubic hair was revealed. Then the Dagda gained a mistress and they made love.[79]

This passage combines important Samain themes, including the New Year's redefinition of land boundaries. Here the god initiates the process on an inter-provincial scale with his club or staff, which has a forked end.

At the Lios, 'the wheel' is represented by the circle of megaliths, incorporating the sunwheel of the four annual festivals, spun by Áine in her critical risings and settings, and encouraged by the God's staff. This is not to claim that the *mechanical* wheel incorporated into the Mag Tuired story, as written down in the Middle Ages, was known in 2,500 BC, but that the divine digging stick helped the year go round from the earliest phase of Neolithic mythmaking in Ireland. Gray considers that the Dagda's staff is synonymous with his penis, a combination confirmed in the word '*lorg*', since its Old Irish usages include: 'club, trace, mark, impression, track, trail, path, course, example, pattern, model, progeny, descendants, troop, company, wand of office, and male penis'.[80]

One might argue that the Lios, like the entire universe, was generated by the *lorg* of the Dagda, in union with the lunar crescent of the goddess, across whose arc it runs. Concealed in the crypt of the temple, which together they produced, their hiddenness under the clay is a testimony to the strength of belief in the Other, the unrevealed, beyond the reach of sight, while harmonizing with the commonsense faith of farmers who now, as then, bury things in the ground, and hope.

The length of the God's lorg-as-penis gave rise to heroic boasting among demi-gods and human heroes on the same matter. Fergus mac Riog was said to be 'seven fists long in the penis, and a bushel bag wide in his scrotum'. At Hallowe'en seven women were needed to reduce him.[81]

Hallowe'en was also the season when hurling was played with staves resembling hockey sticks. An Old Irish name for the game was *Lorg ane*. Its purpose and origin was to mime in the play the union between god and goddess, which determined the prosperity of the year to come.

This is confirmed by local folklore. In 1937 a priest was told by a farmer that every year a battle for the potatoes was supposed to take place in the autumn between the fairies of Cnoc Áine, led by Áine, and those of Cnoc Fírinne, led by Donn Fírinne. The fight took the form of a cross-country hurling match and the victors carried the best of the potato crop to their side of the country.[82] Donn is an alternative

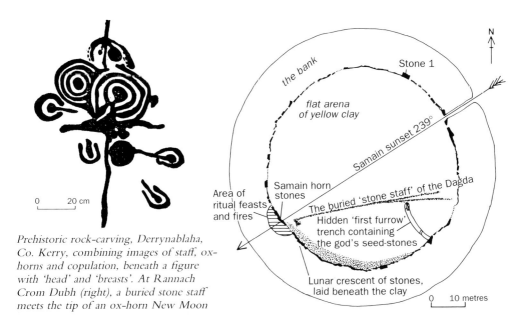

Prehistoric rock-carving, Derrynablaha,
Co. Kerry, combining images of staff, ox-
horns and copulation, beneath a figure
with 'head' and 'breasts'. At Rannach
Crom Dubh (right), a buried stone staff
meets the tip of an ox-horn New Moon

name for the Dagda, being a god of the underworld and of fertility
whose hill, one of the most famous fairy hills in Munster, lies twenty-
one kilometres south-west of the Lios on its Samain sunset side. The
story certifies that the gods and goddesses of the hills around the lough
enjoyed sporting relations, and that, in addition to its other functions,
the versatile Lios staff may also be regarded as a gigantic hurling stick.

The New Moon

The other buried symbol at the Lios, the crescent moon, is a thick
deposit of grey limestone rubble that runs from the Samain sunset gap
(stones 67–8), through an arc of $85°$ towards the south-east. This deep
deposit was immediately covered with yellow clay. Like the staff (the
head of which comes to within 50 cms of the 'moon'), it was intended
to operate from underneath the clay.

Worldwide, the New Moon crescent is understood to combine ox-
horn, New Year, and young women references, and is equated with
many a goddess held responsible for these matters. At the Lios, the
head of the God's staff addresses the lunar crescent, as if bowing its
head in worship, an attitude reflected in songs addressed to the new
moon by young women in South Uist:

> May thy light be fair to me,
> May thy course be smooth to me,
> If good to me is thy beginning
> Seven times better be thine end,
> Thou fair moon of the seasons,
> Thou great lamp of grace.[83]

From first-hand accounts, it seems that in Scotland as in Ireland the response to the new moon was one of a communal tenderness, which, like moonlight, drew things together, and allowed the individual to walk into the domain of the gods. The new moon is more dark than light, and sailed the black sky in a curragh no thicker than a fingernail paring, while returning in a fortnight, with the same boat more laden with silver than a homewarding galleon. This recurring transformation was believed to affect many aspects of daily life, in addition to the behaviour of the tides. The growing moon was written into the world's constitution, and at the Lios was set to rise to fulfilment from the clay.

Adoration of the new moon in Ireland was linked specifically to the well-being of cattle, as the seventeenth-century traveller William Lithgo confirmed:

They also at the sight of each new moon (I speak it credibly) bequeath their cattle to her protection, obnoxiously imploring the pale Lady of the Night that she will leave their bestials in as good a plight as she found them, and if sick, scabbed or sore, they solicit her maiden-faced majesty to restore them to their health.[84]

One function of the Lios crescent may have been to bless the herds at Samain, and Samain was a festival tied to a joint solar-*lunar* calendar. In other words, it fluctuated fourteen days either side of a solar Hallowe'en, in order to follow the new moon's wanderings.

On leaving Rannach Crom Dubh, and pausing for a view of the monument in its entirety, one sees how the criss-cross of quarter days and sun and moon risings and settings make up the circle of the year. All around the enclosure, pots were found ritually broken, and buried against the roots of the megaliths, probably in recognition of the enchantress 'Áine of the Light', who shaped the world from shade to shade.

Geároid and the Lough

Patterns made by stories and monuments around Lough Gur are given physical and intellectual coherence by the water itself, and to the lake we should finally turn. It has claimed the attention and the lives of many. Among human remains found there were lower jaws of large size and heavy outline.[85] If these were the remains of ritual drownings, they bring to mind similar acts in Britain. From Lindow, Cheshire, an Iron Age man preserved by the sphagnum moss in the pool where he was drowned, now lies in the British Museum. He, like James Cleary, took the ultimate mythological walk into the sacred.

The tradition of a regular human sacrifice to Lough Gur survives in folk belief to the present day.

'The lake claims somebody every seven years. Somebody is drowned in it,' stated Tommy Hannon of Bruff in 1972. Was it the seven-year sighting of the tree which drew these people from the shore? Perhaps the lake was dry for them, as they ran across the mud towards the knitter, committing themselves body and soul to an unfamiliar domain.

Geároid Iarla, Áine's Norman son, is believed to have drowned in the lough. 'He was in a boat, boating...and he got drowned or something. And he was seen [as a spirit] after that,' says Mr Carroll. Here folk belief parts company with the historical record, for O'Clery's pedigree states that he died in his house of Caislean Nua (Newcastlewest) in 1399, while other authorities give Castleisland, Co. Kerry. This island, far from Lough Gur, seems his likeliest deathbed. But the earl did not rest there, for 'There was one earl, as they say, by name of Garrett, that was *by enchantment* carried away from Newcastle in Connellagh.'[86] By magic, he was conveyed to Lough Gur.

The magnetism of a sacred centre pulls at what is historically dispersed and gathers further weight thereby. In this case, the historical fact that both the brother and nephew of Geároid were drowned (brother Maurice while crossing the Irish Sea in 1358, and his son Sean, in the River Suir) was pressed into service. These drownings were transferred to Geároid because as a poet, he was required to submerge into the muse of the birth lake, for the benefit of society in general. (In Ireland, poetic truth tends to take precedence over historical fact because the benefits of poetry can be more widely distributed in time and space.)

Historically, Geároid was Geároid Mac Geárailt, second earl of Desmond, son of the first earl, Muiris, and born in 1338, who died (or disappeared) in 1398.[87] His thirty poems in Irish are much concerned with Finn, Diarmaid and Grainne – appropriate subjects for a man who came to emulate Lugh's and Finn's roles at Lough Gur in joining the world of men to that of the gods.[88]

Geároid, son of an invader, a foreigner, was taken to the heart of the Lough Gur myth cycle, and installed there by local people as 'an enchanted magician, a periodic rider, a lost leader whose return is awaited, and a feared King of the fairy host'.[89] 'I am the son of the King of the Norman fairies and my name is Geároid Iarla' was a verse still sung in Co. Limerick in 1879.

Geároid's disappearance into the Lough had also to satisfy the demands of Christian myth. Accordingly, Tom Carroll was told that Geároid was banished under the lake 'because he was working witchcraft. He was some kind of evil man.'[90] In this way the reunion of demi-god with goddess is simultaneously represented as Christian punishment-by-separation.

The nineteenth-century population of Lough Gur attributed Geároid's 'drowning' to Áine – the same old woman-knitter who sat under the mid-lough tree. She was out there, watching him.

'She could have saved him when he called on her to do so, but she replied: "I'll not come at any rate till I put the needle in the back of the stocking," as knitters do, when coming to the end of a row they lay aside their work. That much delay ruined him, and the enchantment came on him.'[91]

Here the knitting needle is the equivalent of Excalibur, safely stowed.

Geároid's life-blade was a shared thing – a sword flung from generation to generation, via periods of immersion within the Lady of the Lake. Old Irish *colg* – 'sword', also means 'penis' *and* awn, or 'grain-sheath of wheat'. Thus the language itself urges Geároid to perform the role of a Neolithic vegetation god who must go under, for the sake of the next harvest. Local belief affirms that he lives on Garret Island, *and* beneath the lough in a bright city.

As if to complement his downward plunge, numerous votive offerings of carefully crafted objects were dropped into the lough in prehistoric times. O'Kelly lists 20 bronze axes, 12 bronze spearheads, 2 leaf-shaped swords, a rapier, several daggers, and 120 stone axes. To these Harkness adds 'a great quantity of stone discs, about three inches diameter, and beautifully rounded in outline'.

These sacrifices are still being rewarded by visions of Geároid, reappearing to local people. Tom Carroll recalled that:

'There was a night's frost about nine years ago [1963]. There was a man skating on the lake. I saw him. He looked like an ordinary man – going up and down, and making all kinds of figures on the lake. There was only about an inch of ice there, it wouldn't hold a bird!

He was a black figure of a man with a cloak on him. A lot of people heard the swishing of him sliding over the lake. They say "'tis him …" When the ice is thin, and on a bright night, you'd see him.'

Tommy Hannon recounts how Geároid is

'… supposed to go on hunts with the cavalcade. He leads them around the lake every Midsummer night. It is dangerous to meet them. The oul' Geároid Iarla must be spoken to, to break the spell on him, but he himself can't talk till then. He gets very cross when not spoken to.'[92]

Midsummer night matches Áine's appearance at Cnoc Áine, and the belief recorded in 1839 by the folklorist Lady Chatterton that at the end of every *seven years* Geároid may be seen riding on the lake, mounted on an enchanted charger, fits the Lough Gur 'World Tree' cycle.

The Goose and the Housekeeper

In 1985 Lough Gur was declared a wild-fowl sanctuary and geese are now nesting in numbers on Garret Island. Among them is Geároid Iarla, the male spirit of the lake, one of whose folk titles is *Gé an Oileáin* – the Goose of the Island.

He had been transformed into a goose following the leaping match with Áine, held in the castle at Knockainey. Fitzgerald records the local belief:

'He walked from the hall, his father and others followed him. He walked out onto the brink of the [river] Camo'g, which almost washed the base of

Garret Island, Lough Gur. In folklore it is the Otherworld home of Geároid Iarla, Áine's Norman son. As a goose, his spirit still haunts the lough. 'Goose of the Island' is his title. The barnacle goose was named gigrand *because of its circular flight, following the arcs of the sun goddess, Gráinne. Its wing-bones were found beneath a Neolithic Knockadoon house*

the castle, and they saw him step from the bank on the water. When he touched the water he was transformed into a goose, and in that form away he swam before their eyes.'[93]

Geároid's goosiness was applied to the Fitzgerald family as a whole; they were said to have webbed feet, and a song from Co. Waterford refers to 'Gentle Áine Fitzgerald, close relative of a swan'.[94]

The right and left wing bones of a black and white barnacle goose were found beneath the floor of a Neolithic house on Knockadoon, and may have been a foundation burial in honour of a bird whose annual migrations mysteriously seemed to join known to unknown worlds.[95] The goose was a demi-god on the wing.

The otherworldly quality of all the geese on Lough Gur was appreciated by Tom Carroll as a continuing reality, in 1963:

'Myself and Willy, we went in there to Charlie Hayes', one night, in there at Carraigin. Dinny Hayes was with us. He got in dread, you see. About 12 o'clock at night the geese came on down the lake, and they came right into us. Into the shade, you see, in the middle of the night. And we thought, you see, we were goin' to kill what was there of 'em. We fired 4 or 5 shots...I don't know...6 shots at 'em. And we had a good dog, and he went out to 'em. There wasn't a stir at all after we firin'. I thought we had all the geese, the 20 geese killed. And the dog turned back in, and he started shakin' and cryin', and screechin', and he turned back in under my legs. We thought the hill was movin' away, and the next thing was the geese rose up out of the lake, like a flock of children...and they started laughin' at us like. But we got a woeful fright, didn't we?

'The next night away we went again, and we went that night after them. And the geese came again at us and we fired again at them. And we saw a child, as we thought, or a young fellow, lifting his hand up and hitting the dog down on the head. And he turned then and left us.

'The third night we went, and we went the third night, and the wind was gone this way. Comin' down from the east, you see. And they'd more of a shade, just inside here. And the gate opened inside there. Well, a man walked in the passage, with a pair of nail boots on him, and he was up against me. And I couldn't see him nor neither could Willy. Nor the geese took no notice of him. 'Twas as bright as 'tis now, with the moon.'[96]

Before dawn, a goose wakes on Garret Island, opening an eye on the future. As the lough begins to polish its greyness, the bird slips into the water. With a rhythmic clatter, he pounds down the western reaches to rise and to swim in air. Secure in his new element he begins a slow circuit of the lough. The Knockfennel race course, the Red Cellar Cave, and the Money Hole pass in turn beneath him. On he flies, over the Tír Na n'Óg cave, and the Housekeeper's Chair. Beyond Ash point he goes, over Giants' Grave, and St Patrick's Well, to the place on the river bank where the old earl raped Áine. From there, in a great arc over Cnoc Áine, he banks steeply, and heads north again, to see the Red Bog and Black Sow's Bed gradually define their details. Down he glides over Cleadh na Leac, and with legs jutting, fizzles into the shallows near Cloch a bhile and the Lios shore.

Then, the Goose of the Island witnesses Knockadoon float free from an eiderdown of mist, to become the embodiment of *ain*, and *aine* – words that in Irish and Scottish Gaelic still mean: 'beauty, splendour, gladness, delight, reeds and rushes, oil, butter, music, harmony, heat, light, wisdom, knowledge, peace, and praise-worthiness'.

Enthroned as the Housekeeper of these things and qualities, Áine was open to worship. She appeared when the ego subsided, allowing the freed spirit to enter the open house of two worlds. Then she was seen, sitting at her loughside, supervising the comings and goings of the generations, in a myriad of life-forms. As protectress of the foetus and receiver of the corpse, she was the *bean tighe* and *bean síd* (banshee) in accordance with a natural order, supernaturally created out of chaos.

Today a solitary goose skims across the water and perches on Suideachan, an empty lump of rock. He regards the spreading radiance of morning, stretches his neck towards the sun as it rises over Knockadoon, and barks to an elusive mate.

A barnacle goose
Far up in the stretches of night; night splits and the dawn breaks loose;
I, through the terrible novelty of light, stalk on, stalk on.[97]

From Lough to Province

The effect of a sacred centre is not complete until it has driven the pilgrim away. Just as Otherworld voyagers eventually yearned to leave the magic island they had tried hard to find, so every satiated pilgrim is eventually happy to disperse the intensity of the peak experience along the ordinary roads that lead from it.

Yet it must be admitted, that wherever one travels in the province the sacred is usually close at hand, for the entire Munster landscape retains something of its archaic sanctity. A stream of sacramental invention keeps the land numinous in the present tense. By means of current activity the great resources of a divine past are tapped afresh, for though religious perspectives may differ, the sense of the sacred remains indivisible. Thus a prayer said for Mary breathes fresh life into the entire panoply of Irish deities, and the sign of the cross simultaneously hands tomorrow's dawn to the old sunwheel.

In Munster one is reminded that in Old and Middle Irish, there was no word 'superstition'. Whether embraced or not, *all* matters of belief were treated seriously. This attitude has often been characterized by foreigners as an abdication of judgment. Equally, it may be read as a declaration that every religious impulse keeps the entire issue of the Sacred alive as an idea – an idea which evades containment by sectarianism; for like water, once raised from the rock, the Sacred will run down the valleys of earlier long-lost habits, to confound the bigot, and reunite the community with the ancestral spirits. For this reason, Munster's world-renouncing Christianity goes to the land to affirm its truths, seeking out those very locations most beloved by other gods. Consequently an often unspoken reconciliation is achieved, below the level of dogmatic particulars, where the body of the land opens to all.

Paps of Anu, Co. Kerry

Áine-Anu held sway throughout Munster. Finn went into the mountain paps to sleep with her younger self, Créide. The poem says: 'The couple slept in bed-espousal prepared by willing hands; and they spent seven days there, drinking and making merry.'

But Finn's attitude to the visit is ambiguous: 'It has been fated for me to go there . . . to spend four days in trouble,' adding ominously,

'Wounded men, spouting heavy blood would sleep to the musical fairy birds singing above the eaves of her bright bower.'

On balance, Finn believes, he will have a good time: 'It will be pleasant for me in her mansion, both in regard to bedding and bed-down...She has a vessel into which the juice of berries drips; in that juice her black shawl was washed.'[98]

This black shawl is possibly the underworld and wintry equivalent of the green cloak of the Lough Gur tree.

On the East Pap summit stands a six-metre-high mound, with a large cairn on top. The mound is believed to be prehistoric, and a likely síd entrance. The West Pap also has a mound and cairn, with a visible chamber entrance. Between the two stand the threatening rocks known as Fiacla – The Teeth.

Finn sat down between the Paps on Hallowe'en night:

and they opened, and he saw a great fire in each, and he heard a voice from one of them which said, 'Is your sweet food good?' 'Good indeed' said a voice in the other fairy-knoll. 'A question. Shall anything be taken from us to you?' 'If that be given to us, something shall be given to you in return.' Finn saw a man coming out of the knoll. A kneading trough was in his hand, with a slainsi pig upon it, and a cooked calf, and a bunch of wild garlic upon it; and as the men came past Finn to reach the other knoll, Finn made a cast with his spear, but did not know the outcome, till he heard a wailing and a chanting from the knoll.

The man carrying the pig was the Lord of the Otherworld Feast, in his typical guise as swineherd.

The Harps of Clíu, Co. Tipperary

Fifteen near-parallel watercourses are gouged into the massive north face of the Galtee Mountains. 'Here a man of the fairies made music, Cliach of the harp sweet sounding,' according to the *Metrical Dindshenchas*.[99] He played to King Black Marrow (Smir-Dubh), till 'a loathly dragon that dwells in this place seized the harper'.

This is a late variant on a myth where the Dagda comes from the síd to harp the seasons into being. His 'finger breezes' play across the gulley 'strings', where falling waters contribute to the melody.

The five gulleys of the eastern instrument meet in a coomb called 'Lyre' – meaning Fork (as one might expect of the Dagda) – and separated by Glenageehy (Windy Glen) from a western harp of ten channels. The Harps epitomize the spirit of Munster as the province of poetry, music and song – her natural and supernatural endowment.

Latiaran's heart, Cullen, Co. Cork

At the start of harvest it was customary for women in Cullen to curtsey to a waist-high, heart-shaped boulder on the village green. It marks the spot where Latiaran, the youngest of three sister-goddesses,

The Harps of Clíu, Co. Tipperary (above and below). In legend, the supernatural harper, Clíu, emerged from this mountain síd to make music on the stringed watercourses. He hoped thereby to attract a goddess of neighbouring Slievenaman, daughter of the pre-Celtic god Bodb Dearg

The harp (right), is said to have belonged to the Munster King, Brian Boru. Harpstrings and rivulets carry words to and from the invisible

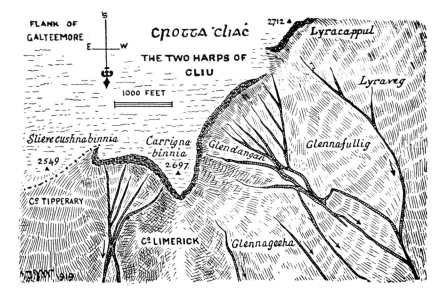

FLANK OF GALTEEMORE

CρoττA Clιac

THE TWO HARPS OF CLIU

1000 FEET

2712

Lyracappul

Lyraveg

Slieve cushnabinnia
2549

Carrigna-binnia
2697

Glendangan

Glennafullig

Co TIPPERARY

Co LIMERICK

Glennageeha

The stone 'Heart of Latiaran',
Cullen, Co. Cork, marks the
spot where this fire goddess
entered the ground at
Lughnasa

Roadside shrine, erected 1982,
at Rath Luirc, Co. Cork

disappeared. A smith praised her feet as she was carrying hot embers, the seed of the fire, in her apron. His remark broke her concentration, and so the embers burned through her apron. Crying out that no smith should ever again work in Cullen, she sank into the ground, to re-emerge at the round well, a hundred paces away, below the modern graveyard.

In its present form, the myth shows Christian influence overlaying the conflict between the Stone Age population and Iron Age invaders, and the celebration by all of the start of harvest. Latiaran's Day is a Sunday in late July, when the Feis or festival of Latiaran, of traditional Irish song and dance, is still held. Up until twenty years ago this was accompanied by a great gathering of travelling people's stalls and sideshows, filling the village street. Today, the boulder remains as an abiding (if somewhat lonely) symbol of harvests to come, a gift from the heart of earth. The village lies between Lough Gur and the Paps of Anu, sixteen kilometres from the latter.

Roadside Shrine, Rath Luirc, Co. Cork

Set beside the main road from Limerick to Cork is a small shrine made of chickenwire-reinforced concrete, honouring one Michael Fitzgerald, who died on 10 December, 1982, in an accident there. A fresh spray of wild flowers, placed round the cross, speaks of a memory tended daily.

Travellers in Ireland share the roads with deities, who themselves go about the repeatable events of their colossal lives sustained by the journeys of every mortal whose life-route happens to pass through the same myth. In the medieval Tales of Places, or *Dindshenchas*, a place-name is derived from the adventures of a deity that come to a climax at a particular spot, often involving the death of the prototypical being. By this means places come to be regarded as *place-events*. Without the Happening, the place would cease to exist. Therefore the god and the man do not die in vain. Together they help to make reality for later generations.

Part Three LEINSTER
City Myths

LEINSTER 1
Leinster Approaches

East

The eastern province Leinster, or Laigin, as it used to be called, faces the sunrise. Bursting with sunrise confidence, the courts of Leinster's kings have sometimes aspired to national control – a pattern successfully followed by Leinster's and Ireland's greatest city, Dublin.

The Irish word for east, *oithear*, is filled with sunrise meanings, such as 'beginning, forepart, future, and day to come' and 'a day in the east', as well as 'the façade or front of a house'; and the leading edge of the land is *oithir* – 'the coast'. Another form, Old Irish *air* – 'east', leads to *airech* – 'first', and *airechus* – 'supremacy'.[1] The east, then, was called the chief or principal place, and the quarter from which the others were reckoned; hence *airtherach* is the perceiving intelligence, 'the front part of the head'. Head, home, sun, shore, time and space, came together in Irish 'east' words, which were lit from within by the divine eye.

The *Laigin* is the old name for Leinster's inhabitants, and in popular etymology derives from *láigen*, 'a spear', and so puts dawning sunbeams into the hands of warriors. The myth tells how they, like the rising sun, came across the sea from darkness, to conquer night's black territory, and were transformed as they advanced, with the broad blades of their spears taking on the deep-blue, green, gold and silver hues of daytime experience.[2] Laigin myths dramatize eastern-ness, and incorporate dim memories of migrations to Ireland from that quarter. O'Rahilly cites movement of Celtic people from Brittany to Leinster in 300 BC as feeding extra material into a body of migration myth which also refers to settlement of Leinster from Britain.[3] These intermingled memories and oral traditions, accumulated throughout Irish prehistory, are centred upon the desire to identify an ancestor-deity from the east. Early Laigin literature is 'obsessed' with that issue, says O'hUiginn.[4]

'When we *mean* and don't just *say* words,' wrote Wittgenstein, 'it seems to us as if there were something coupled to them.'[5] In Laigin that 'something' is an ancestral god of sunrise, and his army of demi-

---

(Previous page) Gold boat, found at Broighter, Co. Derry, and now in Dublin, after a voyage from the hidden sun of the North

Labraid Loingsech (left), the 'Speaker-Mariner', mythic founding father of Leinster. Horse-eared, he has sun-horse connections, reflected in the Bronze Age Swedish sunboat, engraved at Östfold (above). Leinster's inhabitants – Laigin – were the 'People of the broad spear' – láigen (Irish Bronze Age spears, right)

gods, pointing their spears at the province of eastern opportunity. (The spear, transferred to civic hands, was thrown annually into the sea by the Lord Mayor of Dublin, to mark the limit of his jurisdiction.) Arriving out of night, sometimes they called themselves the Black Foreigners, or *Dubh Gael*; 2,200 strong, they carried their lances over the sea from the Continent. They were led by Labraid Loingsech, meaning literally the Speaker-Mariner, or Sea Rover.

Leinster myth may be said to begin with the first word that this Speaker-Mariner uttered. His founding proclamation created a province later renowned for its agricultural prosperity, for he spoke his grandfather's name, Ugaine. To the virgin forests of Leinster, he probably brought Ugaine's knowledge of farming, which undoubtedly *did* come to Ireland from the Eurasian continents lying to the east. Ugaine may well be a corruption of *ugaim*, 'plough traces', and of 'horse harness', or 'harnessing' – *ugmaim*.

Descriptions of the Speaker-Mariner emphasize his solar, super-human quality. He is 'Gold, brighter than the sun . . . he slew kings . . . he overcame men and gods' (says a sixth-century panegyric),[6] and was himself a god – son of Áine, the goddess whom we have met in Munster. He was also known as Moen, from the word *moen*, 'mountain', miniaturized as *moin*, 'a heap of sods, or turf'. 'The one god is Moen', cried the poet,[7] as Labraid came to earth, and was identified with a symbolic heap of Leinster soil, so founding the province.

But rather than simply exchanging a solar for an earthly habit, archaeological evidence implies that the king-god of the province brought the two aspects together in a fire-mountain ritual, dating back to the third millennium BC, nearly two thousand years *before* the Celts arrived, and confirmed in later literary accounts, which suggest that each new king of Leinster burned his predecessor to death.[8] Moen himself (despite being the *first* king!) is said to have avenged his father's 'murder' by burning King Cobthach ('Whirlwind') at Dind Rig, on the southern border of Leinster.[9]

The Night Ferry

Labraid's journey is repeated by everyone who takes a ferry boat from the east, and crosses the Irish Sea to land in Leinster.

The apparently self-enclosed world of contemporary reality, seen in a ferry at a certain moment in the summer of 1990, in fact floats on an ocean of myth, whose tides have rolled on to Leinster's shores for the previous six thousand years, before returning to hidden depths within the general circulation of ideas.

A one-way ferry ticket from Holyhead in Anglesey to Dublin cost £20 sterling in 1990. On her summer service the *SS Columba* leaves just before midnight and heads west for Leinster. The ship is named after the Irish mariner-saint, who established the first Christian community in Scotland, at Iona, and is equipped with the usual facilities – a cinema, a duty free shop, restaurants and bars, cafeterias, bureau de change, fruit machines, life jackets, assembly points, rafts and lifeboats.

Once under way, some passengers try to sleep, while others eat, smoke, drink, talk, play cards, or compulsively re-read newspaper headlines, grown crumpled beyond their twenty-four-hour span, and facing either redundancy or a different kind of time. Fatigue and alcohol combine with the pitch and roll of the saintly craft to pull at common sense, and make room for a more comprehensive dream.

The few who walk the open decks, spray-soaked, gasp at the white wake, as it wanders beyond the range of cabin lights into a salty blackness.

Down below, a rhythmic creaking sets in, as partition walls bend under the pressure of legends, swelling beneath the hull.

They threaten the integrity of the vessel, and recall the *SS Victoria*, a car ferry on the Stranraer-Larne run, that went down *circa* AD 1950 with the loss of many lives, after waves smashed open the doors on the car deck, near Coire Breccáin. Breccán's Cauldron is a whirlpool off Rathlin Island.

'It is the meeting of seas, from east and west, from north and south; and each of them hurls [itself] round another place, so that they fall down into the deep, and it resembles an open cauldron which casts the draught down [and] up, and its roaring is heard like far-off thunder.'[10]

There the seas 'whirl around like moulding compasses, each of them taking the place of the other like the paddles of a mill-wheel until they are sucked into the depths, so that the cauldron remains with its

The devouring whirlpool regarded as the hag's cauldron, into which the seas ran together from every quarter. Olaus Magnus, Historia. (The Vikings founded Dublin)

Below: the international Sun boat, Bronze Age engravings from Östergötland, Sweden

mouth wide open; and it would suck even the whole of Ireland into its yawning gullet. It vomits ITERUM, once more, . . . so that its thunderous eructations and its bursting and roaring are heard among the clouds like the steam-boiling of a cauldron on the fire.'[11] St Columcille, Columba of the Churches, the saint of today's Sealink ferry boat, had been there, 'when the sea rose up against him, and upheaved the bones of Breccáin, who had drowned in the cauldron with a fleet of fifty boats, years before. And the saint said "That is friendly, thou old Breccán," and 'he prayed for Breccán, and got for him the reward of heaven'.[12]

'It would take more than the entire host of old Adam's seed to fill [that cauldron]. There lives not the man that would cover at speed, – long the space! – its circuit, from edge to edge, within a month . . . its white paven floor, . . . the mighty whirlpool's home . . . the loud roaring gravel . . . '[13]

On a rough night crossing, it seems as if Ireland will never come. One suspects that she has quietly slipped moorings, and headed off into mid-Ocean, determined to retain her status as an elusive Other-world when approached from Britain or the European continent.

She is 'the high ship Ériu, Ériu lofty, very green' referred to in poems attributed to Amergin of the Sons of Míl, *c.* 500 BC, in which Ireland is also called 'the mighty lady Ériu'.

> I seek the land of Ireland,
> Coursed be the fruitful sea,
> Fruitful the ranked highland,
> Ranked the showery wood,
> Showery the river of cataracts,
> Of cataracts the lake of pools,
> Of pools the hill of a well,
> Of a well of a people of assemblies . . .[14]

The most important sacred ship, coming to Ireland from the east, was the sun boat. It carried the sun, led the sun, and was synonymous with the sun. It was carved on the wall of the west recess of the New Grange monument, facing the northern border of Leinster, *c.* 3100 BC. The idea remained popular in Bronze Age Scandinavia, from where so many cultural influences continued to flow westwards into Ireland.[15]

The famous gold ship, made around the first century AD, and buried one mile from the eastern shore of Loch Foyle, Ulster, shows the continuation of the cult.

A gold boat hook, mast-yard, steering oar, a miniature grappling iron, and two oars were found with the boat in 1892. Other parts of its riggings were sold to a jeweller and lost. Did he also purchase a crew of gods?

The sacred boat moved easily from sea to land; Borlase believed that most prehistoric Irish burial chambers were intended to represent ships, with the dead being conveyed across the otherworld ocean.[16] The physical ocean flooded people's imagination.

The religion in which Ireland now sails – that of St Columba – has perpetuated the ship symbolism. Christ is viewed by the congregation from the nave (Latin *navis*), so called because it represented the ark, or ship of the Church. Incense was held in a navicula, later called an incense *boat*, whose function is to erect a sail of perfume from the world ocean to the deity above the crow's nest.

Landing

Dawn, and on deck a mirage can be seen hanging in the sky. Designed in the manner of a Chinese watercolour, on the port side are the fanciful silhouettes of the Wicklow Mountains, range behind range, and to starboard, the thrusting peninsula of Howth Head, with Lambay Island beyond.

A cheer goes up, and smiles are exchanged between total strangers. Returning migrants pass the names of their counties and small towns around, like cigarettes, to be briefly inhaled by others – so many destinations, lying beyond Dublin Bay, with tables set for home-comings, balanced on the far tips of railway lances and road spears.

Then, from somewhere astern, a fat new sun pulls itself above the horizon, and rolls a red carpet across the waves, inviting us shorewards, as we pass between the now *pink* lobster claws of Howth Head and Bray Head, towards a Dun Laoghaire anchorage.

Beneath wheeling sea birds, and tiers of blue mountains, poke church-spires. Villas display their pilasters and cornices amidst voluptuous gardens, which run down to eau-de-Nil and apricot terraces, lining the palm-fringed esplanades. Everything is agleam in the scintillating air.

At the Bay's centre two red and white spears, or *láigen*, rear skywards, the chimneys of the power station beyond Ringsend.

As if suspended by invisible ribbons from these poles, the entire panorama combines in one of the great urban dances of the world. Whatever disappointments may lie waiting in ambush, the thing as a whole is obviously divine. With that conviction, a multi-national babble of sound goes down the gang plank, passes through a perfunctory customs check, and along the Leinster shore.[17]

Dublin, The Real Dream

Dublin re-Joyce

The incoming tide of tourist voices merges with the world language devised by James Joyce. He reclaimed Dublin on behalf of myth. After piratical raids on many languages, he brought to his native shore the intermingled treasures of a verbal ocean, thereby returning the province to the state of Total Life which it had enjoyed in antiquity. Together with Yeats and other Leinster poets of our century, he worked towards a new day in timelessness, called modernism.

Unlike the nineteenth-century Romantic taste for ruins (remote in time and space), modernism and the archaic concur in their shared fondness for an eternal now, an ever-new light of 'East'.

During the last hundred years writers from Leinster have led the country and perhaps the world in 'attempting to raise the archaic sacredness of language itself from below the horizon of consciousness to an *Autem generatio* of all the gods and their works.'[18] Their hope was to turn the explicitly Christian words: 'In the beginning was the word, and the word was with God and the word *was* God', into an affirmation applying to every divinity ever known, with new forms of the divine being continually reborn on the human tongue. Leinster was the setting for a project of total re-creation.

As argued in the Introduction, this enormous task suited Irish and Anglo-Irish writers, since of all Europeans they had inherited from antiquity a peculiarly primitive concreteness of expression and imagery, largely undisturbed by theoretical Greek thinking, which had never taken root in Ireland. Recently orphaned by the death of the Irish language, Leinster writers brought their collective habits of mind to bear on the emergent International Modern Movement which sought to 'give back to language its pre-logical functions', and 'set the imagination in search of a fabulous word'.[19] The writer Patrick Kavanagh maintained that there were never less than 10,000 poets living in Ireland. Many of them converged on Dublin.

Joyce carried with him the belief that 'all language originated from the human effort to arrive at the meaning of the divine thunderclap'.[20] In his *Finnegans Wake*, the rumble reverberates above and below Dublin, like all the deities in the world speaking together. They talk of 'multiple stratifications reaching back millions of years . . . related to the entire history of mankind, past and present, and brought to the surface with the hallucinatory eruption of images in the dream, the day dream, the mystic-gnostic trance, and even the psychiatric condition'.[21]

But Joyce's endowment to Leinster only yields its full dividend if it stimulates readers to recreate the 'province-as-cosmos' in their own terms. (The labour of digesting *Finnegans Wake* is nothing, compared to the tasks which it invites us to undertake.) Alas, there are no free rides to mythic Ireland, the passive paradise isle vanishes as soon as it is touched. To find it again, one has to walk, and in a mood of informed innocence, towards *Magh Mhór*, the primary plane of being. But at least Joyce shows that such a Great Plain still exists, and exists in contact with the mundane world. He habitually used the pun as a bridge between the two states, old and new, so that in a word or phrase, 'a street full of traffic is also a panorama of prehistoric places and animals',[22] Joyce's jokes told the truth, that oldest and newest are interdependent terms in a continuing dialectic.

To a peculiar degree, Joyce the novelist invites each new reader to collaborate in re-making his novel, *and* the city – a process unimpaired by the physical demolition of many of the buildings he describes. Rather than imposing a set of architectural preservation orders, his legacy to Dublin was a self-renewing mythic methodology.

He advocated mythmaking using whatever materials and circumstances came to hand. *Any* Dublin could have served his pattern-making from cross-references, as the life-work for every generation.

Should the tunnel vision of road engineers, or some other self-isolating system-builder dissect the city, the task would be the same; namely to draw this new material, however intractable, into a wider network of relationships.

But even for a man of Joyce's energy, the perfecting of the method within a literary framework took a lifetime. From the picaresque descriptions of *Dubliners* (1904), through the transposed heroic saga of *Ulysses*, it was not until *Finnegan* woke in 1939 that a new myth arose. With that work he touched the heart of an a-historic 'All-life', lying beyond the clutch of chronology.

River Liffey

The most permanent thing in Dublin changes all the time – the river Liffey. Its self-purifying motion became for the author of *Finnegans Wake* a symbol for the regeneration of the spirit as a cyclic female process. The river begins and ends his last novel, written between 1921 and 1939.

He envisages the river as she – Anna Livia Plurabelle, incorporating the Irish Magna Mater, Ana, or Anu, coupled with Life and Liffey (Livia), but as a goddess of a thousand names (Plurabelle). This composite being runs through Dublin into Dublin Bay to meet the sun-god hero, Finn, whose head he identifies with the Howth

View of the river Liffey, Dublin. The name 'Liffey' is
derived from Livia, the deified wife of the Roman emperor
Augustus. The Gaelic name was Ruirthech, 'The Impetuous
One', because of her flash floods

Carved head of the river Liffey in
the Dublin Custom House, *1791*.
'It was me that lent my dutiful
face to his Customs,' says Anna
Livia Plurabelle in James Joyce's
Finnegans Wake

Map of Dublin Bay and Dublin

promontory. The novel begins in mid-sentence stream: 'river run, past Eve and Adam's from swerve of shore to bend of bay, brings us by a commodius vicus of recirculation back to Howth Castle and Environs'.[23] It ends, six hundred and twenty-five pages later, with Anna Livia slipping Finn, her lover, in again, as she enters the bay at Ringsend.

So soft this morning ours. Yes. Carry me along, taddy, like you done through the toy fair! If I seen him bearing down on me now under whitespread wings like he'd come from Arkangels, I sink I'd die down over his feet, humbly dumbly, only to washup. Yes, tid. There's where. First. We pass through grass behush the bush to. Whish! A gull. Gulls. Far calls. Coming, far! End here. Us, then. Finn, again! Take. Bussoftlhee, mememormee! Till thousendsthee. Lps. The keys to. Given! A way a lone a last a loved a long the[24]

And so back to the first word in the book. Three years after Joyce had begun his great work, the poet Yeats wrote: 'Our 'natural magic' is but the ancient religion of the world, the ancient worship of nature and that troubled ecstasy before her, that certainty of all beautiful places being haunted, which it brought into men's minds.'[25] He referred to: 'Men who lived in a world where anything might flow and change, and become any other thing; and among great gods whose passions were in the flaming sunset, and in the thunder and the thunder show.'

Joyce found urban existence equally dramatic, and demonstrated that we do not have to choose between two worlds, since the imagination can turn them into one. In his work, 'the end product is always fusion, rather than fragmentation'.[26] Everything comes together in the river.

Hill of Howth (Benn Étair)

Of the Hill of Howth, overlooking Dublin Bay, the mariner St Columba wrote:

> Delightful to be on the Hill of Howth,
> After coming over the wide-bosomed sea;
> To be rowing one's little coracle,
> Ochone! on the wild-waved shore.[27]

The Gaelic name of Howth is Benn Étair, named after the mythical hero whose cliff head confronted the ocean, and protected Ireland from attack. With a view over comings and goings, Étair (or Étar) was *alive*, a living supernatural being, as the *Dindshenchas* makes clear: 'Étar forehead to the flood...the grey sea roars against his shoulder.'

The word *etar* means 'great'. As the living headland, Étar of Benn Étair looks east, with the Dublin rivers Dodder and Liffey, or Ruirthech, to his south:

> His right shoulder fronts the Dothra (Dodder)
> the Ruirthech dashes wildly against his side,
> onset of the flood-tide, wave of the ebb,
> furious are the seas against the shore.[28]

This defensive stance is revised in the prose version, which makes Étar the son-in-law of Manannán, the sea-god, by marriage to Áine, said to be Manannán's daughter.[29] Land, water and sun thus are brought into family relationship at a critical point. As a wedding ring, Étar's wife 'puts a golden chain about him, [so that] the sea should not drown him while he wore it, nor should sharp spear points pierce him'.[30] Sunlight on the surf makes this ring around the head, to the narrow land neck on both sides.

The completed union dissolves the sexual divide, and Étar then becomes an androgyne, able to appear as female. 'She' is 'Étar softly-bright, splendid and stately, of the royal harbour.' (George IV built massive harbour walls on the north side of the headland, in the early nineteenth century, hoping to make it the Holyhead terminus, but it rapidly silted up, and is now used only by shallow draft coastal vessels.) The text implies that Étar was a primordial if not prehuman figure, who introduced the act of dying of grief for one's husband.

By way of balance, the male Étar was said to have died for love of Áine, 'and his grave was dug on yonder peak', again, at Howth.[31] At Howth, the front door of Ireland, and its point of morning arousal into consciousness, the myth-makers established that the task was not merely the *reconciliation* of opposites, but their complete integration in androgyny. In many religions the androgyne is an image of wholeness and of an original state of being.[32] Howth shares in that international perception, through the dual sexuality of Étar.

Dublin Airport

Over Howth, Boeings glide down from the stratosphere, to land at Dublin Airport, ten kilometres inland. From Manchester, Amsterdam, Rome and Athens, out of the rising sun, flocks of planes descend on *Mag n' Elta Edar*, 'The Old Plain of the Flocks of Edar'. This was 'the first plain in Ireland', says *Lebor Gabála*. On it, 'birds settled to sun themselves, for never did branch or twig of a wood grow through it'.[33] It was *the* primary glade, in an otherwise forested island, where Partholón, a mythical founder, died. Elta is said to be named from 'a woman, Elta, daughter of Oes Uindset'. Both *ealta* and *uinde* mean 'see, act of seeing, or beholding'. This clearing, tucked in behind Howth, did not have to be made. It was given, as an original fact, divinely granted; a first garden. The collective noun *elta* can in Irish be applied to all manner of birds and beasts, including human tribes. Nine thousand and eight followers of Partholón were said to have settled on its treeless extent, which ran across the area of modern Dublin from Swords to Tallaght, a distance of eighteen kilometres. So every street in the conurbation is crowded with the ghosts of mythical birds, soaking in the dawn warmth, after their migration flight from the east, on what was sometimes called the Plain of Moynalty. Their descendants sit on bird tables, to peck at bacon rinds, offered every morning, while the rush hour traffic goes by.

As Heidegger points out, the ancient Greek word *techne* belonged to mythic thinking, and was then the name 'not only for the activities and skills of the craftsman, but also for the arts, including poiesis'. *Techne* involved a bringing forth in poetry, where *aletheia*, truth, happens, illuminating the presence of the gods and the dialogue of the divine with human destinies.[34]

At Dublin Airport one might complain that modern technology has grown too big, but in fact *techne* is much shrunken in scope, compared with its archaic role. Where once it revealed the glories of eternity, it is now obsessed with the pursuit of mere convenience.

One cannot blame our machines for this decline. Indeed, if given an adventurous flight plan, they could still work the routes of the fabulous imagination, known to the great white-speckled birds of unusual beauty, seen by Conaire as he rode in his chariot across the Plains of Liffey. They retreated on his advance, and 'stayed a spear's cast from him, till they betook themselves to the wave, and he was obliged to plunge into the sea to overcome them. Then the birds quit their birdskins, and turned upon him with spears and swords. One says: "I am Némglan [*nem*, 'sky', *glan*, 'pure, bright'], king of thy father's birds, and thou has been forbidden to cast at birds." '[35]

With their ability to fly between worlds, and different kinds of reality, those birds were a protected species.

Dublin's Mythic Foundations

Stone Corinthian acanthus leaves sprout from Dublin, the capital of the Irish Republic; yet neither Greeks nor Romans settled here, nor anywhere in Ireland. (Some Phoenicians apparently sailed around her coasts, and gave a few names to the map-maker Ptolemy, working in the second century AD, which he duly incorporated into his cartography of Europe.)[36] But Ireland remained a rural society of scattered farmers and wandering pastoralists, whose 'cities' were the seasonal *oenach* encampments, raised for a few days from a background of remembered myth, and then dismantled again, leaving only yellow patches in the grass, which soon returned to green.

Not until the late ninth century AD did invading Vikings establish Ireland's first urban settlements. Of them all, Dublin, facing Britain and Europe, prospered most, and was made the chief city by the Anglo-Normans, who followed them ashore. If, as Rose asserts, Irish 'East' comes from *airech*, 'first', Dublin has obliged by growing to urban pre-eminence.

The founding of a Viking town or city was essentially a mythic affair; at the outset humanity sought the advice and approval of the gods for the new enterprise.

College Green is considered to be the centre of modern Dublin. There, where today's Church Lane and Suffolk Street meet, the Vikings constructed their *thingmote*. It was an artificial conical hill, twelve metres high, made as a place of assembly and justice, with a seat on top for the king, above tiers for his sons, and noblemen, according to rank.[37] (A comparable Tingwall on the Isle of Man survives as its ritual and ceremonial capital.) Standing stones and carved stone balls placed on the summit connected these Viking monuments to the cult of the earth goddess, in whose soil previous kings were interred below the summit, as at Uppsala, in Viking Sweden. Wherever they travelled, the Vikings took with them a belief in the divine ancestry of kings. Dublin's Thingmote, which survived into the seventeenth century, as Speed's map shows, was nothing less than a creation mound, combining the tomb of the traditional order with the womb of a new reality. Around it were constructed other burial mounds, between which the population practised archery and throwing games, in imitation of the wars between the pantheons of Aesir and Vanir – which reproduced the Irish Sons of Míl versus Tuatha Dé Danann encounter, by other names. In both cases the weapons included sunbeams, thunderbolts and flint arrowheads. (Neolithic flint arrowheads, regarded as 'fairy darts', were *the* prototypical missiles, and in nineteenth-century Ireland and Norway they continued to be revered.)[38]

The Dublin Thingmote, or Haugen, was levelled in 1682. Shortly afterwards, a new world mountain arose close by, in the form of the coffered dome of the Irish Parliament House begun in 1728. This was modelled on Hadrian's Pantheon, erected in Rome in AD 126, as a temple for all the gods, dedicated to the planets, and intended as a simulacrum of the universe.

The English architect of the Dublin building, Edward Pearce, had studied in Italy and France, and was in close touch with Lord Burlington's Palladian enthusiasms (expressed at Chiswick House) before arriving in Dublin in 1726. He produced a parliament in a foreign style, in keeping with the wishes of the Anglicans, who took control of Ireland, following William III's victory on the Boyne, in 1690, and who, by law, were the only people allowed to sit in the new organ of the Protestant Ascendency. Both in scale and style, his building expressed domination by a foreign power – a colonial victory, comparable to that of the Sons of Míl.

Yet in deference to Anglo-Irish Protestant suspicion of symbols, the building was designed to ring somewhat hollow. Erected in the heyday of Newtonian reductionism, the Hadrianic devotion was turned into a stylistic exercise, following a foundation ceremony which was only a caricature of ancient Roman practice:

On 3rd February, 1728, the first stone of the new building was laid with great ceremony by the Lords Justices, attended by several Peers, the King-at-Arms, the Sergeant-at-Arms, Captain Edward Lovet Pearce, architect, and Thomas Burgh, the Surveyor-General. The foundation stone, a large hewn white block, with a cavity in the centre, was placed in its bed by Primate Boulter (of the protestant Church of Ireland), by removing the prop with which it was supported, after which it was adjusted by the Lords Justices, assisted by the King at Arms, who at certain intervals, waved his handkerchief for the State musicians to play. A large silver plate was inscribed with the dignitaries names, and dedicated to George II.[39]

Several gold and silver coins of George I, George II and his queen, were deposited with the plate, and the aperture was closed by a small stone, bound down with iron bars, presumably to prevent theft prior to the next stone being laid on top.

An accompanying full-size bronze equestrian statue of the triumphant George II has now been moved to Birmingham, England, but the gold and silver coins of his Irish dominion still lie, like suns and moons, imprisoned in the wall, overlooking College Green.

By 1805, divine power was worshipped for what it was becoming – Money, and the building on College Green turned into the Bank of Ireland, a function it has kept ever since.

The transit of the prehistoric gold disc, from deified solar symbol, to emblem of emperor-king, ruling by divine right, to an abstract token, finally declining on to a bed of paper currency, is a voyage beyond symbol and its flat shadow, Allegory, to the Otherworld of pure number – a place inconceivable to the first Laigin spearmen. In order to retain *some* grip on physical reality, the bankers commissioned Edward Smyth to carve statues of Hibernia (Ireland), flanked by Fidelity and Commerce, and sat all three on the pediment, from where, as abstractions, they have adorned the skyline of the former parliament house, since 1809.

These changes are both recent and important. They transport Ireland from rootedness in mythic values towards intrinsically meaningless signs, and to a land where accountants reign by declaring quarterly, half-yearly, and annual results in a mock echo of the archaic cycle, robbed of supernatural resonance. Nineteenth-century bankers promised to pay little or nothing to Ériu, either as goddess or as colony. Instead, her role was to give and not to receive. (She lay beyond the pale of Dublin's privilege, across barbarous bogs, where natives spoke a foreign tongue, and bathed the Pope in pagan superstition.) Georgian Dublin regarded Ériu as an object to be exploited, and this intention glittered through the windows of the city's neoclassical mask, until, in the twentieth century, it acquired a mythic soul.

The Missing Augur

The future of Irish mythology increasingly depends on Dublin. More than a million people now live in its conurbation, compared with 1.8 million for Leinster as a whole, and 3.5 millions for the entire Republic.[40] Late twentieth-century urbanism, a world-wide phenomenon, has transformed Ireland from a largely rural, to a city-orientated country.

Two fifths of Eire's people now dwell in her capital city, and are searching for new roots beneath pavements, where most of the pipes and cables run horizontally, rather than up and down. Without roots,

'The Templum of the Sky', Corpus Agrimensorum, *sixth century AD. Quartering of the sky and earth together was achieved in the augur's gestures in founding a city*

the city may prove more ephemeral than the gathering of tents at the old *oenachs*, since *they*, like annual flowers, grew from fresh seed every year. By contrast, a city, claiming to be *perennial*, needs to find purchase in the subsoil, as the founders of cities in antiquity knew.

It can be said without exaggeration that the future of Dublin, as of modern urbanism everywhere, depends on some form of mythic re-engagement, if a drift towards psycho-physical triviality is not to end in disaster. This is the issue which, one way or another, will be resolved in the city, on behalf of the province and the country.

The founding of a Roman city required the services of a priest-surveyor, known as an augur. In him, 'practical' and 'sacred' coalesced from the outset. His first task was to ask the gods for guidance in choosing a propitious site. An important aspect of his prayers was careful observation of natural phenomena in the district – the flight of birds, the movement of stray animals, thunder, and the motion of clouds. Then the liver of a sacrificed ox was examined for portents.[41]

Had a Roman augur ever stood on the Old Plain of Etar, in AD 100, among the mythic flocks and herds of creatures sunning themselves, he might well have decided to mark out the site for modern Dublin precisely where it now is – across this primal fruitful plain – on the grounds that humanity should follow the instincts of other species. By chance and good fortune, without the assistance of an augur, the sprawl of modern Dublin represents and recapitulates a zoological creation legend. If farmyard, wilderness, and zoo have mainly negative connotations for today's urban sophisticate, Dublin's location nonetheless suggests a reconnection of jumbo jet with bird, car with horse power, and Phoenix Park (the largest urban park of any European city) with the original field of praise.

According to Varro, a Roman writer born 116 BC, the augur stood at the centre of the proposed city site, holding his curved wand, and scratched around him on the ground a diagram called *The Templum* (from Greek *temenos*, 'sacred enclosure'). The design was always a cross within a circle. The direction of the augur's eyes followed his gestures, and by viewing the proposed town site together with the country beyond, he contemplated it, and 'united the four quadrants or templa into one great templum by sight and gesture', which simultaneously 'marked out the space in the heavens' into quadrants.[42] Livy says that the first stroke was engraved towards the east,[43] while

Varro makes clear that this was a qualitative process, 'con-tueor', involving 'mature pondering, caring, and guardianship'.[44] The eyes, and 'the vision of the heart', cortumio, were engaged together. This primary measuring was an act of devotion, acknowledging every aspect of the genius loci, or spirit of place.

The templum symbolized the integration of sky, earth, and underworld. Prosperity on the land-surface depended on a collaboration which also revealed the sky over the future city to be the temple of Jove. (In Dublin, 'Jove's' domain had in deed, but not in thought, been brought to land, in the dome of the Parliament House.)

Then the four divisions of the templum (divided and reunited) were transferred to the proposed street pattern of the city. The main east-west route, the decumanus, crossed the chief north-south future thoroughfare, called cardo maximus, in an enlarged version of the templum, whose outer circle became the sulcus primigenius, or 'first furrow', cut along the foundation line of the city walls. For this, a white male ox and a white cow were yoked to a bronze plough. Once again, links with non-urban ways are emphasized. City-making is regarded as a special kind of agriculture, an urban field, visualized as an intensification of the natural order, rather than its betrayal, and deliberately placed 'at the intersection of the co-ordinate axes of the universe'.[45]

The templum ritual secured the union of sky, land and underworld. The drawing was accompanied by the correct verbal formulae, which, in Rome, ran: 'Temple and wild lands be mine in this manner, up to where I have named them with my tongue in proper fashion.'[46]

Existing trees were invoked, one on each quarter, around the augur at the centre of the pattern. The trees were a reminder of the primeval wilderness, denoters of chief quarters, and the vertical links between sky, earth, and underworld.

The augur's anxiety concerning the right form of words arose because the templum was bounded by the words of incantation, by verba concepta, which drew a magical net round the landmarks that he named. It was this naming which actually fixed the boundaries. By word and gesture, the priest hoped to 'open up' the normal passage of time to allow the primal time of the deity or mythic ancestor (the time of perpetual Beginning) to slip into the urban foundations, so ensuring that the future city would enjoy divine favour.

Mundus and Byzantium

At or near the spot where the augur stood, a pit was dug, called the mundus. Into it were cast 'first fruits' and 'good things', along with earth from the settlers' home country. Conversely, some of the virgin earth *from* the hole would be taken for incorporation into homes to be built along the new streets. The cavity was consecrated to the infernal deities called the Manes, meaning The Good Ones. Their stone, the lapis manalis, was laid on top. It was regarded as a gate to

Dancing at Glendalough, Co. Wicklow, 1930. This echoes the traditional 'dancing at the crossroads', where, as a magic act, the province and the four quarters were re-inaugurated through dance. Recreation was also an augur's work of re-creation

the Underworld, and was drawn back at seasonal festivals both to allow extra gifts to be deposited and to enable the hidden deities periodically to re-enter the city from below.[47]

Regarded as the navel or umbilicus of the city, the Roman *mundus* can be compared with the national navel stone of pre-urban Ireland set up at Uisnech in Mide.

Essentially the same idea – that urbanism cannot long be sustained without a recognition of the hidden core (or *síd*) values on which it is based – has returned to haunt the late twentieth century. But one of our difficulties concerns how to fit a Joycean language of mythic expression within a largely technical frame of reference. In the last thirty years, the Dublin solution (as with other cities) has been to ignore the problem. The city engineers and the poets have been working in different departments.

For the ancient classical city, *mundus* digging and ritual filling constituted the birth act. Only then did the settlement come alive and receive its name, or names. (Normally there were three given; one public, one used by priests, and one never uttered. The secret name of Rome is believed to have been that of an androgynous god of harmony, Amor,[48] and the secret name of Dublin might be borrowed from the androgyne Étar, of nearby Howth.)

The inspired search undertaken by many Dublin writers during the last hundred years for their 'city-within-the-sacred' may be seen in every sense as a Classic preoccupation.

Collectively, writers in and about Dublin have constructed the divine city of Indo-European tradition on the banks of the Liffey. Sometimes they have used the method employed by William Blake (who built Jerusalem in industrial England), by consciously turning to continental exemplars.

Yeats' poem, 'Sailing to Byzantium' (1926), written in Dublin, offers Constantinople as a model, and infuses Dublin with his dream. He explained that in the eighth century AD, 'Byzantium was the centre of European civilization, and the source of its spiritual philosophy, and I symbolize the search for the spiritual life by a journey to that city.... There religious, aesthetic, and practical life were one. Architect and artificers spoke to the multitude and the few alike.'[49] Artists, he went on, were almost impersonally involved in their subject matter, which was 'the vision of a whole people'.[50] Yeats re-imagined the co-ordinates of city planning as 'the artifice of eternity', towards which the individual soul might gravitate. Although, as an old man in the new Irish Republic, he felt half-inclined to sail off to Constantinople, the effect of his work was to leave his idea on College Green.

Comings and goings across the Irish Sea, real and imagined, have brought Dublin to life. Joyce chose exile in Paris, in order to create his universal urban language from fragments of foreign speech, mixed with the humus and first fruits of the bi-lingual Leinster he had fled. He then offered the whole deposit to the city which had inspired his endeavour. So Dublin achieved a long-delayed mythic birth, despite its inclination to distrust the poet-midwife.

Thus 'Finn again', as another Leinster sunrising Man-God, shines down the unintentional 'decumanus' of Nassau Street, across College Green, and westwards along Dame Street.

Dublin as Machine

Recent pessimism concerning the future of the city tends to represent its problems in technical terms (pollution, congestion), and to advocate 'social engineering' regarding crime and drug abuse, without reference to a mythological base, or its absence. Yet this oversight *is* the problem from which all others flow, for without a mythological structure a city is unlikely to enjoy good health.[51]

In the vacuum, anxiety, alienation and apathy often replace the communal co-ordinates of god-given location, and The City, which once brought Nature's sacredness into focus, now exhibits an intensification of the absurd. This predicament is articulated with uncommon power by the Dubliner Samuel Beckett.

Following a walk along the Dun Laoghaire harbour wall on a dark and stormy night, he embarked in his novels and plays, from 1938 to 1985, on a courageous voyage to the dead heart of a city whose patterns lack spiritual purpose. He re-opens the *mundus* and finds only a void – or the housing for a machine on the verge of disintegration.

In his play *Endgame* (1957), Hamm, the chair-bound master of a dying Iron Age, expresses contempt for ancestral wisdom by setting his parents in dustbins.

The image of City-as-Machine (the rotation of spiritless matter), has its philosophical blueprint in Descartes' dualism, and in Newtonian positivist science.

Early twentieth-century optimism regarding the mechanical city gained further support with Walter Gropius' rational urbanism (a Cathedral of Reason), and Le Corbusier's designs of the 1920s for La Ville Radieuse.[52]

The need to re-design cities around the motor car added further momentum to the mechanistic tendency. Across the Irish Sea came the influential Buchanan Report (1963), which recommended for Leeds (half the size of Dublin), thirteen radial motorways built through the inner suburbs, with six of them eight lanes wide, and a series of motorway cross-links varying from four to six lanes wide, and all 'free of such obstructions as cross-roads and roundabouts'.[53] 'Beyond all question there will have to be a great deal of urban road building in British cities,' wrote Buchanan, and within two decades cities on both sides of the Irish Sea (and Belfast more than Dublin), have been transformed accordingly.

Yet from the outset, Buchanan himself admitted that 'We cannot hold out any hope that this... vigorous programme of urban road-building ... will go very far towards solving the problem [since]... each new motorway built to cope with existing traffic seems to call into existence new traffic sufficient to create a new congestion.'[54]

Nevertheless, in Dublin, as in so many other cities, a ruthless highway-building programme is now decimating the urban fabric.

But why, if the twentieth-century cult of the wheel is so harmful, are the cults of the Bronze Age gold disc with spokes, or Mug Roth's Leinster wheel, to be preferred? Is not a wheel a wheel in any age? The difference is that the first two were designed to roll *between* categories. They were the vehicles in which the cosmos was delivered. They drove out from the sun and back, enabling free transportation through the poetry of Godhead. Consequently they were a civilized enhancement, and *realization* of nature, rather than a means of its destruction, careering out of control, and currently turning medieval Dublin into a wasteland. Most of the former inhabitants have been bureaucratically dispersed to low density new suburbs, 'so that they should not talk to one another', as Toibin has half-jokingly remarked.[55]

Waiting with Beckett

Ten years before the Buchanan Report, Beckett emerged as a prescient spokesman for disillusionment. This Dubliner offered a dark alternative to Joycean optimism. The chant of Beckett-the-Augur has the sound of empty lorries returning to the depot late at night. Whereas for Joyce language was an intimate part of the mystery of creation, 'for Beckett words are the chief ingredient in the art of failure'.[56] No wonder that he aspired to total silence. Beckett saw words as demons of falsity, false because hollow, devoid of the divinity which they once embodied. Embittered, they could now truthfully speak only of its absence (and in this, above all, they were false, as Beckett suspected). His was a Protestant vision, where symbols were discarded.

Beckett struck a chord, evoking the response 'How true' from modern city dwellers around the world, waiting, as he implies, for their Godot. But the story has not ended with Beckett's death. His character Clov, hovering on the threshold at the conclusion of *Endgame*, prepares (perhaps) to go somewhere else. After implosion, after pessimism, 'nothing *naughtens* itself', as Heidegger remarked, and Beckett's nadir can be seen as the trough in the wave-like pattern of divine breathing. Inhalation can be expected to follow, later, if not soon, shallow if not profound, with or without the human contribution.

In practice, there is considerable overlap between Dublin's phases of spiritual emptying and replenishment. Even while its vacuous suburbs are being constructed, they are generating a new literature. Sometimes, as in the plays of Dermot Bolger, this takes the form of a lament for the disorientated – an Irish version of the English 'New Town Blues'.

When the mythic appetite remains keen, opportunities are found everywhere, including, since 1970, in the archaeological recovery of Viking Dublin and in the new energy-efficient railway, known as DART, which runs around Dublin Bay, carrying the population on an elemental journey, at once ordinary and extraordinary.

The Dart is the latest *láigen*, or spear.

Through the train windows the water presents itself, alternately cloud-dulled, sun-gilded, moon-tugged from high tide to low, planished or wind-fluted and engraved by the world's shipping lines.

Nature is *still here*, and is still offering a place at her sacred mud-fringed table. Off the Sandycove rocks, men (and, since 1989, *women*) plunge naked into the sea at dawn. Their personal recreation may also be seen as a daily community service, re-integrating the natural, man-made, and supernatural domains on behalf of a million citizens still in bed.

The bathers dive under the shadow of the Martello Tower from where Stephen Dedalus set off on his Ulysses journey in search of Dublin.

Áth Cliath and Atherne

Dublin is named after the *Linn Dubh*, or Black Pool.[57] This was the tide-flooded mouth of the little river Poddle, which debouched into the Liffey immediately south of the present Dublin Castle. Used by the Vikings as an anchorage from AD 838 onwards, the pool was eventually drained to become the castle gardens.

Prior to that, Dublin did not exist, but there was a Celtic settlement, a 'proto-town' just west of the castle, and straggling along the ridge now occupied by High Street and Thomas Street. It overlooked a ford across the Liffey. In the early Middle Ages the river was broad, shallow, and tidal, and subject to flash floods from its mountainous headwaters. The ford, *áth*, was approximately 300 metres long, and composed of wattle hurdles, or *cliath*. These made a roadway of rafts, staked to the river bed, and weighted down by massive stones. Its precise location has yet to be ascertained.

Áth Cliath Cualann (*Cuailin*, 'bundle', *cual*, 'faggot') was a wholly Irish settlement – an irregular cluster of huts, perhaps bounded by an earthen ditch and bank.[58] The name remained in use till at least 1368, by which time *Baile Áth Cliath* referred to the walled medieval town which had grown on top of the Celtic settlement.

The *Dindshenchas* says that the Leinstermen made the hurdles of wattling for the Áth Cliath ford, at the command of a greatly feared roving poet, Athirne the Importunate, who wanted to drive the sheep which he had rustled in South Leinster across the river to Dun Étair (Howth).[59] Linked in this way to the critical eastern headland, Áth Cliath arrived on the national mythic map, long before it became a city. Athirne's (or Atherne's) walk had been undertaken on behalf of Connor of Ulster, who lived in the first century AD; yet the poet's task was essentially a mythological circuit of Ireland.

At his King's command, this 'hard, merciless man' went at first left-hand-wise about Ireland [from Ulster] till he made the round of Connacht. Then he went to the King of the midst of Ireland between *the two Fords of Hurdles*[60] [that is to say between Áth Cliath, and its counterpart in the far west, called Áth Cliath Medraige]. The King in the middle was Eochaid, who reigned at Lough Dergderc, on the North-South river axis, the Shannon. There Atherne 'robbed Eochaid of his eye'.

Then he travelled south, into Munster, and demanded to sleep with the queen of the province 'or the honour of the men of Munster should be lost forever'.

Continuing his round, he moved northwards into South Leinster, where he deliberately insulted the population, inciting them to kill him, so that Ulster would gain a pretext for attacking Leinster. He therefore took 'thrice fifty queens of the wives of the princes and nobles of Leinster, and drove them across Áth Cliath, along with the sheep and cattle he had stolen, and took them all to the Benn Étair headland'. (At the centre of a national road and rail network, modern Dublin, which stretches to Howth, makes a comparable sweep of the country.)

Áth Cliath, the pre-Viking proto-Dublin, grew around the zeal of Atherne. His ruthlessness is found in the Old Irish word, *aithe*, 'sharpness', and shows a poet's weapon in *aith*, 'tongue', and victory in *aithin*, 'knowledge'. His powers of prognostication, especially regarding the siting of settlements, is also conveyed in *aithin* – 'the liver' (much used for divination throughout Indo-European lands). His theft of the solar eye is possibly reflected in 'firebrand', *aithinne*.

These solar connections were inherited from his father's brother, who, riding a sky horse, landed in Munster and threw up a great sod. Only Atherne noticed a brooch of four-score ounces of red gold lying beneath the hoofprint, and claimed it by ancestral right.[61] It symbolized the golden wheel of the sun's route, emerging from the underworld, and was the counterpart of the jewels at first offered by King Eochaid (*eochaid* – 'horse'), of the Shannon, before his eye was plucked out.

Gold was found again in the profusely flowering *aiteann*, 'furze or gorse'. This common bush was burnt ceremonially at the February quarterday, and used as May Eve torches or firebrands.

In this guise, the poet walked back into Áth Cliath, Linn Dubh, and Dublin. He was still flaring through the streets on May Eve in the eighteenth- and nineteenth-century versions of those festivals. Throughout the country, wherever Atherne went, *aiteann* bushes could be found hanging from house rafters, and were changed annually for luck.

Atherne was a poet who earned his keep, for when his furze thorns were crushed he became winter fodder for the cattle, and as fuel for the hearth he showed his practical side again.[62]

Etymologists derive *aiteann* from *ote*, 'furze', in Basque – the most ancient language in Europe. This suggests that Aiteann's arrival in Ireland, as a mythic character, may have predated the first waves of Indo-European-speaking settlers, *c.* 2500 BC. If so, Dublin could hardly ask for a more archaic, prickly, yet eternally vigorous founding father.

The Siege of Howth

The Ulstermen, led by their young sun god Cúchulainn, came south to Benn Étair to help Atherne defend his booty from the enraged Leinstermen.

The Leinstermen besieged Howth, so that the Ulstermen for nine watches, were 'without drink, without food, unless they drank the brine of the sea, or unless they devoured the clay'.

And of the seven hundred kine that Atherne had brought, there was not a boy or man of Ulster who tasted the milk, but the milking was cast down the cliff, so that of the Ulstermen none might find out Atherne's food to taste it. And the wounded men were brought to him, and he would not let a drop go into their mouths, so that they used to bleed to death alone.[63]

King Connor was prevented from starving by a slave girl who came daily from his Ulster citadel, carrying food. Her feet and knees pointed backwards, but she could travel around Ireland in a day, and knew what was happening throughout the land. She was obviously the denizen of a Northern Otherworld.

The entire description has the ring of an archaic rite, spoken with the accent of a later warrior society. The widdershins, or anti-solar direction taken by Atherne, as a Northern agent, suggests the stirring of subterranean forces, orchestrated from that nadir to promote a nation-wide sacrifice on Howth, the point of eastern promise, as the prelude to a new round of prosperity in the upper world.

As a poet, Atherne was allowed by law to move freely around the provinces, demanding hospitality. On this assignment he is concerned with more than one kind of existence. His snatching of the solar eye from the head of Eochaid of Dergdec is an attack on the material world *per se*, with the aim of restoring it to an original chaos, a programme which reaches its climax in the inversions and madness at Benn Étair. (As Mary Douglas has shown, such seasons of misrule act as a cleansing process in many societies.)[64]

At Howth, drinking sea water (a recipe for insanity) is balanced by pouring milk (a crazy surf) down the cliffs, and while men eat clay, the only 'real' food is delivered by an uncanny creature who walks backwards in another form of inversion. (Her elevation to King's confidante is, moreover, disruptive of the established social order, since she was the child of slaves, yet born in the King's bedroom!)

Finally, with the booty of Ireland assembled at Dún Étair, Cúchulainn set his foster son to guard the east door of the fort. Three hundred Leinster heroes (presumably spear-men) beheaded this guard, Mes-dead, son of Amargen. His war cry, uttered at the point of death, caused general collapse. 'It is the sky that crashes or the sea that flows, or the earth that quakes.' That is how Cúchulainn interpreted the sound, while acknowledging that it betokened the death of the divinely appointed individual, whose solitary cry shattered the macrocosm, as did Christ's on the cross, prior to resurrection.

Howth was an ending and a beginning, a last shriek, *and* a first light. Above all, the siege was a point of exchange between the uncanny and the real.

Bruiden Da Derga

The view south-west from Benn Étair across Dublin leads to a myth, first written down in the eleventh century, called the Bruiden (or Hostel) of Da Derga.[65] At this magic Hostel, built over the river Dodder at Bohernabreena, three kilometres south of Tallaght (see map p. 127), Leinster's natural and supernatural forces were attacked from the sea by the god Midir of the Northwestern Otherworld.

Seen from Howth, the fireball of Samain sunset goes down over Bohernabreena. Its Bruiden story, set at Samain, probably complemented the death of Mes-dead on Howth at Beltaine. The paired events make the mythic threshold between summer and winter halves of the year, just as their respective sunrises and sunets lie at 180° to each other.

At the Beltaine festival Mes-dead, facing north-east, had to die to inaugurate May-day sunrise and the summer half. At Samain the forces of chaos came in from the sea, and sent scouts to the top of Benn Étair

At root, the magic Hostel or 'Bruiden' Da Derga stories may have been inspired by the Hag's Door – the hairy vulva of the winter hag, seen here in prehistoric engravings from (left to right) Östergötland, Sweden, Gavr' Inis, Brittany, and Sliab na Caillighe, Co. Meath

to spy out the land. They identified the magic Da Derga house, selected for destruction, in the blue haze of the middle distance. It was crowded with revellers, including 'a one-eyed man, asquint with a ruinous eye. A swine's head he had on the fire, continually squealing ... blood has been spilt at every feast at which he has been present.'[66] He came from the great síd of the south, Slieve Femin.

Also present was the hag Cichuil, perhaps named after *cicul*, 'cycle, or astronomical cycle'. She was 'bigmouthed, huge, dark, sorry, hideous ... though her snout were flung on a branch, her lower lip would reach her knee.'[67]

Then another ghastly giantess is reluctantly admitted – a lone woman, coming to the door of the Hostel after sunset, with pubic hair reaching to *her* knees, and her lips on one side of her head. (The Irish word *toth*, 'female pudenda', is thought to be derived from pubic hair, and in the Neolithic goddess imagery of Ireland and continental Europe, her open orifice, sometimes fringed by luxuriant hair, is found engraved in tombs.)

As if to match the cosmic disorder attending Mes-dead's end, the noise of the enemy fleet running ashore in Dublin Bay at Fuirbthe Strand (near Merrion Gate) shakes Da Derga's Hostel, 'so that no spear nor shield remained on the rack therein, but the weapons uttered a cry, and fell all on the floor of the house'. An inmate says: 'I know nothing like it, unless it be the earth that has broken, or the Leviathan that surrounds the globe and strikes with its tail to overturn the world.'[68]

The built-up area of Greater Dublin now stretches from Howth to Bohernabreena, and so the paired myths of Howth and the Bruiden may be said to underlie every home in the conurbation. Each stands on mythologically prepared ground, where construction and destruction, being and non-being, are weighed against one another.

The Bruiden alerts us to the contingent nature of the modern city itself, as it now confronts the prospect of self-induced desiccation in a purgatorial greenhouse.

Today, the men in the Greenpeace dinghy who challenge the dumping of radioactive waste into the Irish Sea perform one of the tasks of the ancient poets. They alert a complacent population to the fragility of what is taken for granted. So in Leinster, Mug Roth, personification of the great wheel of harmony, where all spears function as contributory spokes, is aware of another possibility. 'It seemed to him almost as if the sky had fallen on the surface of the earth, or as if the fish-bounding blue-bordered sea had swept across the face of the earth, or as if the earth had split in an earthquake, or as if the trees of the forest had all fallen into each others' forks and bifurcations and branches.'[69]

Both then and now, the ability to imagine Doomsday is essential to the maintenance of reality beyond the myopia of complacent individualism.

In this respect, the site of Greater Dublin invites general alertness, being precisely balanced on the Howth-Tallaght beam, between the Beltaine and Samain junctions, which were the danger points of the traditional year. These were annually tested by mythic 'fire drills', where, at the twin festivals, the poems were recited, and the contingent nature of surface life was made plain.

The purpose was to find communal security on the far side of whatever divine turmoil and human cataclysm had to be endured. So, for example, following the massacre of those within the Bruiden, Mac Cécht travels around Ireland, searching for one golden cupful of water to give to his dying King. But all the lakes and rivers turn out to be dry. At last, Mac Cécht, who acts like Sir Bedivere to King Arthur, is led to water by a wild duck. Then, with a renewed capacity for admiration of Nature, he cries:

> That is splendid, O wild duck
> The lake water that spreads under thy breasts. . .
> O speckled little, red-bellied bird,
> a drop of gold water from thy wings![70]

In this appeal, he is reassimilated into the natural order, via the supernatural order. The red duck is another 'goose of Lough Gur', an intermediary who will lead humanity back to the sacred spring believed lost, yet preserving the water necessary for cultural rebirth.

Then Mac Cécht 'turned throughout all the well, to bathe himself therein', and said: 'Cold fountain . . . surface of strand . . . sea of lake, water of Gara: stream of river: high spring-well: cold fountain.'

Thereafter 'he took the full of his cup out of it . . . and reached the Hostel before morning, and poured the precious water down the decapitated King's throat'.[71]

Anna Livia

Joyce proposed in *Finnegans Wake* that Finn lay beneath the soil with his head at Howth, with his feet at Castle Knock (the Phoenix Park Cemetery), and that Finn's Dublin was inseparable from the living natural water-scape of Anna Livia Plurabelle. She is the river Liffey, whose recurring history he told from source to sea, so inviting Dublin to take full possession of its soul and to become rooted in its province as never before. With Joyce's Esperanto (the talk of all nations, and of none), the augur's words were belatedly spoken along Liffey's quays, and people around the world heard that still-born, centre-less, cities might be revived, that towns which had demolished their Thingmote might find it again, and that at any stage the City can open a new testament with the environment, if only the *civitas* (citizens) are inspired to do so.

Poets and novelists of every generation imply that all reality is an act of imagining, and Jack Yeats' painting of the swimming race, held in the Dublin Liffey, shows how an old dream of a divine river supports the contestants *in fact*. Like the Ganges, the city's river goddess is someone to be borne up by, and reborn from. Despite Liffey's recently acquired toxicity, the swimming race remains an annual event.

The hurdles of Atherne's ford lie in the river, and in *Finnegans Wake* it is the river herself who has the last word. 'She is the secret of the continuation of the jollification. Men, cities, empires and whole systems bubble and burst in her river of time...All the contending parties...are mothered and cherished by her. Them she affirms and celebrates, as she slips between the river banks on her dream journey to the sea of renewal.'[72] Her unfinished sentence, which brings the book into the Bay, loops back to join immediately with the first word on the first page.

'But in that suspended tick of time which intervenes between her dissolution into the vast ocean and her reappearance as 'river-run', a brave renewal has taken place. We know that she will be drawn up in dew and descend in rain upon the Wicklow Hills, and that the sun of a whole new day will run its course before she again leads us back to Howth Castle and Environs. A great deal will happen to everyone and everything during this day. And when the night comes again, bringing its release from sun logic...the timeless story of that slow combustion which ever consumes and sustains itself in the interior of the spinning atom, in the living world, and in the soul of man', will be retold.[73]

Gold cup and ring from Broighter, Co. Derry.
To rediscover Nature within the sacred cycle,
Mac Cécht sought a gold cup of water

Original Landings

Historically speaking, Labraid Loingsech and the Laigin originally represented Iron Age arrivals in the province where Dublin has since developed. At the same time, they echo much earlier landfalls, celebrated along the Leinster coast in myth and monument, as the following examples demonstrate.

The Drimnagh Fire Mountain, Co. Dublin

A Neolithic monument (erected *c.* 2000 BC)[74] possibly demonstrated how natural elements could be brought into controlled interaction over the body of the mythic founder of the province, the equivalent of Moen (Turfstack). Moen was an epithet of Labraid Loingsech, 'The Speaker', here expressing his silence on entering his provincial ground.[75] At Drimnagh, the presumed solar-king was found in a stone cist on the Neolithic ground surface, with a bowl decorated by an incised 'secrets of ploughing' pattern, in a four quarters design. Over his head, a swastika stone setting (a well-known solar emblem) was embedded in a stack of sods, which were then subject to an intense and even firing, so igniting an outer roof of stout alder-wood spears (perhaps representing pre-Gaelic 'láigen') which shot their flames skywards.

This union of sun and earth was reflected in the belief, current till 1939, that the gold regalia of King John, a King from the east (Britain), lay under the mound, and shows how the original mythic event rolled through and beyond the confines of history.

Here at Drimnagh, location, structure and iconography concur with ancient myth and recent folklore, to represent Leinster as the fortunate province of dawn.

The coastal district of Leinster in which Drimnagh stands was known as Cuala, from the word *cualu* – 'heap, mound, faggots', and sometimes used in the sense 'phalanx of spears', and linked (by Keating) to a mythological invader of Ireland called Cuala. Thus the coast is named after the founder, and his initiatory mound, which *brought it into conscious existence*, since reality was founded on ritual behaviour.

145

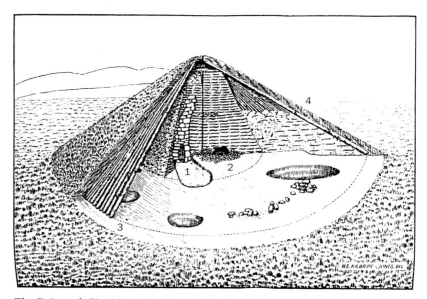

The Drimnagh Fire Mountain, Co. Dublin, later third millenium BC. It consists of: (1) a inner turf-stack with stone flu and draught-pit; (2) primary burial cist; (3) outer covering of alder-wood spears, and (4) turf. With its alder spears associated with flame, it anticipates the Celtic 'bright spears', láigen, by fifteen centuries

Ladra at Ardamine, Co. Wexford

A six-metre-high grass and bramble-covered mound, set on sea cliffs, is said to mark the spot where Ladra, 'the first dead man who went under the soil of Ireland', was buried. He was the pilot and oarsman of the boat of Cesair, the founding goddess of Ireland. On landing, he took sixteen of her women 'and was dissatisfied thereat... He died of excess of women, or it is the shaft of the oar that penetrated his buttock', according to *Lebor Gabála*.[76]

This last droll circumstance is believed to be a medieval clerical insertion, a graffito which fails to conceal the underlying myth.

The name Ladra is related to the word *adna*, 'aged', denoting the ultimate male ancestor of the Irish race, in a cosmogonic or foundation myth, predating Labraid Loingsech, and arising directly out of a primordial Flood. Yet both as mariners and introducers of new knowledge, the two have much in common, and Ladra is close to the word *adma* – 'knowledgeable, skilful, dexterous'.

Ladra and Cesair were brother and sister – son and daughter of Bith (Cosmos). 'We seem here to be on the track of a myth of a divine brother-sister union,' wrote Macalister,[77] comparing it to the Greek Zeus-Hera coupling. In Ireland, he continues, 'the original story knew of only one 'man', Adna (Ladra), with one wife, Cesair, and a number of subordinate women.'

These women were the ancestress-goddesses of Asiatic and European nations, who arrived with the divine couple in Ireland.

So constructed, the story enabled 'the facts' of history and geography and of human settlements and migrations, to be associated with the creative love of two ultimate beings, whose incestuous relationship was a way of expressing the 'one family' nature of the cosmos.

St Maedoc and Ladra

The head of an early Christian cross is set into the north side of Ladra's mound at Ard Ladran (Ardamine), and is said to mark the spot where St Maedoc of Ferns landed, after administering the last sacrament to St David, patron saint of Wales, in AD 598.[78] Here, on the Leinster shore, Maedoc built a church. He then converted the local ruler, Dima, to Christianity, and so represents another beginning.

Irish beginnings are often spun together by myth into a combined cord of hope, and in this case the incorporation of a cross into a pagan mound was matched in Maedoc's life. Like Ladra, he too was a child of Cosmos, conceived when his mother, queen Eithne, saw the moon entering the mouth of her husband, while the king saw a star enter *her* mouth. Thus Maedoc was generated when universal fire entered the lunar bowl, and sailed towards the mind of human wonder. 'My little fire', *mo Aed óc*, was what his nurses affectionately called the baby, hence Maedoc became his name.[79] This 'sunrise' title linked him to pre-Christian Leinster, where eventually he became bishop of Ferns, which lies 19 kilometres inland from Ard Ladran. Ferns was for a while the capital of the entire province.

Maedoc displayed many archaic attributes. After travelling from Wales on the back of a sea monster, he brought a sea-cow out of the ocean to draw a plough for three months. It returned to the sea after each day's work. He could also perform magic of a kind probably derived from the Neolithic, turning barley to gold, and back again, for the benefit of the poor.

Cesair's Landing: Waterford Harbour

Lebor Gabála recounts a creation myth involving the arrival in Waterford Harbour, the southern border of Leinster, of the goddess Cesair. The word *cessair* means 'carries, brings forth, draws out'.

The myth tells how, along with Bith, Fintan and fifty women, Cesair landed at Bun Suainme, in Waterford Harbour.[80] The name *Bun*, 'thick end', and *suainme*, 'cord, string, river confluence', denotes a hill overlooking the Waterford Harbour meeting of the 'Three Sisters', alias the rivers Suir, Nore and Barrow. These rivers have their sources around Árd Éireann, Ireland's central birth-mountain, in Co. Leix. Thus the 'Three Sisters' may jointly be regarded as the freshwater umbilical cord, linking the founding mother on the shore to her 'land-self' and child-Ériu. (The Cesair-Ériu birth process was restaged

Dunmore East, Waterford Harbour (above), the landing place of Cesair (alias Ériu), founding goddess of Ireland, who sailed into Waterford Harbour with her fifty women, reaching shore between the future provinces of Leinster and Munster. The rivers Nore, Suir and Barrow – The Three Sisters – pour their combined flow into this magnificent estuary

The Graves of the Leinstermen, Tountinna (Arra Mountain), Co. Tipperary. The ruins of this Neolithic tomb are said to mark the spot where Fintan, 'husband' of Cesair, survived the Irish Flood. Ireland's 'Mount Ararat' stands on the western border of Leinster, overlooking both Munster and Connacht. The vital founding acts are thus shared between the provinces annually at an Árd Éireann harvest rite, which, in a diminished form, persisted into the present century.[81])

The fifty women who sailed with Cesair are the divine mothers of other nations (Aithne of the Athenians, Inde of the Indians), bringing 'world culture' in the first mythic boat known to have reached Ireland.

As a matter of archaeological fact, Mesolithic hunter-gatherers arrived in Ireland *c.* 7000 BC to fish and forage.[82] Large quantities of Mesolithic and Neolithic tools have been found along the Waterford Harbour shores. Myth and worked flint come together.

The integration of holy word and thing is also seen in the *lam-dia* or portable idol mentioned by *Lebor Gabála* as the divine inspiration of Cesair's voyage. Before setting out, Cesair had advised her followers: 'Take unto yourself an idol... worship it...', and this is the counsel that their idol gave them: 'make a voyage and embark upon the sea'.

Sacred art normally comes ashore with the first wave of settlers; it is their living standard. For the same reason the great Neolithic monuments of Ireland began to be built in the earliest years of the Neolithic influx.[83] They were not afterthoughts, but the architectural images of living gods, the prime-movers of New Stone Age civilization.

Neolithic stone mace-head, Knowth monument,
Co. Meath. God-heads call out of the dark. Divine
speakers deliver Worlds by Words. Irish asbuir,
'say, speak', also means 'to bring forth'. So Labraid
Loingsech 'utters' the Leinster shore

Part Four CONNACHT
War Path and Love Match

Battle of East and West

East and West

The province of Connacht is partly defined by comparison with Leinster. The stereotypes proclaim that Leinster is fertile and Connacht barren. Leinster's sunshine is contrasted with Connacht's cloud and heavy rain, her riches with Connacht's poverty, her urban success with the small and often failing townships of the West. Leinster stands for the triumph of newcomers, whereas Connacht is traditionally the last refuge of the defeated. The wisdom of Connacht, like that of King Lear, comes partly with the loss of power. This most westerly province of all Europe gains and offers insight *in extremis*.

The Irish word for West is *Iar*, which also means 'the end, every extremity, everything last, after, backwards, blank and dusky' – in short, the opposite qualities of East. *Iar* spreads into *iarsma*, 'after-effects, remainder, remnant', *iartharach*, 'furthermost', and *iartestimin*, 'conclusion of a period'. Western time and space combine in *iartaige*, 'unhappy consequence'.

Connacht in its entirety was *Iar*, and is still regarded as the most remote part of Ireland. 'In the eighteenth century, the few travellers who crossed the Shannon had the sensation of entering another world.'[1] Several writers cautioned against taking the risk, and spread rumours of a savage, almost subhuman, native population living on the west coast. Strangers who probed Connemara, like Thomas Molyneux in 1709, found no roads, and no bridges. Not until the nineteenth century did a Scottish engineer, Nimmo, construct a route to Clifden, whilst West Mayo remained isolated even longer. This situation is reflected in the word *conn*, which conveys associations of traditional wisdom, hard of access.

With some misgivings, therefore, the traveller journeys to the west, carrying the burden of myth in the tell-tale haversack of language; the place of the West in the Irish tongue, *and* the act of travelling westwards, were alike loaded with peril.

(Previous page) Achill Island, West Connacht. Atlantic breakers gnaw at the cliffs. Connacht is the storm-lashed, barren, sunset, West end of Eurasia. Connacht's proverbial wisdom arises, like King Lear's, from defeat

The Great Road called Eiscir Riada or Slighe Mhór ran east-west from High Street, Dublin (Áth Cliath), below, to Galway Bay. It followed a path between equinoctial sunrise and sunset, and in the process, bisected the country

St Patrick's Cathedral, Dublin (left) built 1220–5, is orientated from font (west) to altar (east); from birth-lake to reunion with God at the communion rail. It, too, is a Great Road, passing through the forest of Mother Church's rib-vaults

The Lucky Stone, in the porch of St Audeon's Church, Dublin. A metre tall, of grey-black granite flecked with sparkling mica, this Early Christian slab was touched by travellers setting out westwards

The ancient high road to the west, Slighe Mhór, began at Áth Cliath, on the ridge 'whereupon the High Street is sett', say the Annals of Clonmacnoise. Dublin High Street is the start of the road. Before setting off, many travellers visited St Audeon's church (built by the Normans in 1190, over a much earlier chapel dedicated to St Columba). There, in the dark porch, still stands 'The Lucky Stone', which 'was daily kissed and embraced by numbers who believed in its reputed powers of conferring health and prosperity'.[2] This one-metre-high eighth-century Christian gravestone was set up outside the church by the first Mayor of Dublin in 1309 beside a horsetrough. (Stolen in 1826, it was returned to St Audeon's forty years later.) The cross arms, stretching equally north, south, east and west within the engraved banks and ditches of its outer ring, unite the Christian symbol with the four provinces in the body of a greyish-black igneous rock, flecked with mica, like permanent stars, emerging upon the sun's final extinction, from the earth's molten underworld.

The medieval 'Blessing the Road Before a Journey' beseeches: 'May this road be smooth, may it be a journey of profit in my hands. Holy Christ against demons, against weapons, against slaughters. May Jesus and the Father, may the Holy Ghost sanctify us! May mysterious God that is not hidden in darkness, may the bright King save us! May the cross of Christ's body and Mary guard us on the road! May it not be unlucky for us! May it be prosperous, expeditious.'[3]

An't Sligh Mhór ran from the Áth Cliath ford, along Dublin's High Street, through Corn Market and Thomas Street West, and out across the Central Plain. Having negotiated the river Shannon, it finally reached Áth Cliath Medraige on the Connacht coast of Galway Bay.

Throughout this distance of approximately 176 kilometres ran the story of the god Blad or Blod.[4] He had been nurtured under the Atlantic 'by a daring King over Medraige, and over Herot [a territory in South Connacht]. Blod then fared in his ship from the *bottom* of pure-cold Galway from Áth Cliath [Medraige] in wide Herot, to Áth Cliath in Cuala [Dublin].' 'Thence he came by many a turn to Point of Nár' (Howth). Having completed this West to East journey, including the last few miles to Howth, Blod settled on the middle mountain of Ireland, Slieve Bladma, now called Slieve Bloom, halfway between the two fords.[5] From there he balanced his submarine origin in the far west against the sunlit Howth headland in the east. Thus the stage was set for the battle of the sun gods, Finn in the East and Goll from the West, along the line of Slighe Mhór.

The Great Road partly owed its greatness to their struggle. Every traverse of the route was derived from the original event, with 'ordinary' journeys following the divine prototype as far as possible.

Eiscir Riada

An alternative name for Slighe Mhór was the Riding Ridge, or Eiscir Riada. From the Lucky Stone horse trough, the Riding (both as verb and noun) followed a series of natural gravel ridges or *eskers* aligned more or less east-west.

As recently as the 1890s, some geologists believed these eskers to have been left behind by the Biblical Flood. Today they are regarded as the result of the melting of Ireland's last ice sheet, prior to 15,000 BC. Eskers represent the gravel-choked ice caves made by melt-water streams as they wound their way from beneath an ice sheet retreating westwards.[6]

Across Leinster these steep-sided ridges rise and fall in height in what is called a 'beaded' manner, up to 100 metres high, in a 'succession of mounds indicative of the normal recession of an ice-sheet terminating in standing water. Each 'bead' is really a partly formed delta, laid down at or near the mouth of a subglacial stream, and each represents the summer deposit when melt-waters were plentiful, while the less prominent part of the esker between the beads marks the winter phase.' The repeated history of a struggle between sun and ice, and of Summer and Winter forces, is thus written into the pre-human land forms. Riders and walkers rise and fall to the same rhythm.

Because the ridges are so numerous, and documentary evidence so slender, uncertainty exists concerning the exact route of the Riada, west of Lucan. Lochlainn's research of 1938 suggested two possibilities lying up to ten kilometres apart, with the more southerly passing across the Bog of Allen via Celbridge, Taghadoe, Monasteroris, Rhode, Croghan, and Kiltober, towards Durrow Abbey, Ballycumber, Togher and Ballaghurt to reach the Shannon at Clonmacnoise.[7]

The Book of Leinster states that Clonard was on the route, so favouring the more northerly alternative, following the line of the present N4 highway to the Shannon ford at Athlone.[8]

Either way represented a god's route, real as a walker's blisters and aligned between sunrise and sunset. Medieval poets sang the Great Road's praises:

> The line that divides Erin in two
> was Escir Riada (it was no lie)
> whose name held in bright renown
> was the Great Road, greater than any tilled plain.

A road, the poet makes clear, was the sum of its events:

> In this wise were discovered
> the roads, the ancient mearings
> as I found their high origin
> their traditional rights, their local legends.[9]

Some accounts put the western end of The Great Road at White Horse Hill near Clarinbridge, Co. Galway (*Cnoc an ghervain bhain*). Its Gaelic name means hill of the white steed, and can be regarded as another version of a solar deity, repeatedly galloping into the equinoctial sunset hill, having completed the journey from Áth Cliath in the east.

The Hurdle Ford of Medraige lay just west of Clarinbridge, on a

The South Cross, Clonmacnoise, Co. Offaly, tenth century, stands on the mid-point of Eiscir Riada (left), on the Leinster bank of Ireland's great north-south axis, the river Shannon. Consequently, Clonmacnoise is one of Ireland's most celebrated holy places. Whirling solar bosses are a feature of the wheel head cross's decoration

peninsula poking into Galway Bay, in Ballynacourty parish.[10] The ford was built of whitethorn and brambles, against the men of Munster,[11] and seems as much a barrier as a crossing. It was constructed by The Seven Maines – in other words The Seven Days of the Week. They were said to be the sons of Connacht's chief goddess, Medb. Thanks to her and them, space and time were woven together at Medraige, so enabling the western province to enjoy a share of the words *medraige* – 'merriment', and *meadhradh* – 'mirth and song'. From start to finish, the Eiscir Riada appears as a work of the gods.

The discovery of Slighe Mhór, The Great Road, as the East-West axis of Ireland immediately created Northern and Southern halves of the country as variant on the four provinces theme. The halves of Mug (south of the road) and of Conn (to the north) have featured in historical reality, and got their present names from Conn of the Hundred Battles, AD 123–147, and his Munster rival.

Finn's Way

At Cnucha in Phoenix Park, overlooking Áth Cliath, there was a conflict between the solar powers of East and West, with Connacht gaining the victory. The demi-god of the west, Aed (whose name means 'fire'), attacked Luchet (*Luchair*, 'bright') and killed him there, but not before Luchet had blinded Aed in one eye, so giving him the name Goll ('one eyed'). Goll then slew Cumall, the father of Finn, the eastern sun hero, and carried off his spoils and his head, hence there was an hereditary feud between Finn and the sons of Morna, along the line of the Great Road.

By far the strongest directional drive connected with the Eiscir Riada comes from the east-west shadows thrown by Finn the rising sun god, intent on avenging his father by killing Goll. In warrior-Celtic Ireland, the interplay of natural forces was viewed as war. That was the myth which the gods and their human tribes enacted. Similarly, Connacht men invading Leinster had Goll on their side, but as a tenth-century Leinster order of engagement says, 'They must not be suffered to depart alive.'[12]

Sometimes the conflict is conducted with sadistic glee, as when Finn's women tie the aged western hero Garaid to their house-wall by his beard and hair while he is asleep, to prevent him interfering with them. On awaking with a jerk, Garaid tears off his hair, scalp and flesh. In revenge he 'cuts nine stout faggots of ash and kindles fire in the house from floor to ceiling, setting the house in a great blaze; that old man had no mercy.'[13] The women plead to be let out in vain. Finn sees the smoke arising from Drumcree (between Mullingar and Kells, in Co. Westmeath), and gallops to the rescue, but on his arrival there is nothing left 'but the stump of each stake in the earth, and black and charred fragments of the Fianna's 'winsome wives', and his own beautiful dapple-cheeked Aitbe. Seeing this, Finn loses all his strength.

When fierce Garaid saw the women burned, dead and stark, he let fly a peal of laughter over them, to be heard among the Fianna throughout Erin. (His name comes from the word *gaírid* – 'laughs'). 'Pleasant it is to me to find you thus, O women', said Garaid, 'that you may learn for good not to mock at a miserable old man.'

The everlasting war of the east-west road was no joke, yet it was often enjoyable, as for example, when moving west on a bright early morning in late September with the Fianna. Then, for mile after mile along the Eiscir Riada one can sense Finn's encouragingly warm hand on the back of the neck. Pausing at noon, the shadow topiary, trimmed sharp from the base of every tree, is swivelled northwards. On either side of the ridge, stretching to the horizon, lie the sullen colours of the bog, dark brown where exposed by peat cutting and elsewhere an olive green, occasionally hazed over with heather in bloom. Cloud shadows manoeuvre like a phantom navy across this ocean; they are Goll's fleet, steaming from the West, firing their showers, and passing on, through volleys of Leinster sunbeams.

The route to the Shannon is also riddled with the spear and arrow holes of the historical annalists, drawing attention to real armies, advancing and retreating along the route, whose ritual 'hostings' were an important means whereby the contests of the gods were brought to life in mortal combat. In this sense medieval Irish history consists of successive reports on the repeated celebration of a pagan mass, where Finn and Goll, or their fathers, took it in turns to play the sacrificed deity. For the battalions of Leinster and Connacht war was a religious obligation.

The Men of Leinster are urged in the early tenth-century March Roll to

take to their never-failing weapons...ready for every attack, for a battle-rout against united Connacht. Let them march to the battle-rout without grumbling, let them all rise up for the fight to defend the warlike province which their father left them.[14]

The Shannon Frontier

The boundary between Leinster and Connacht was and is defined by Ireland's greatest river, the Shannon. Where it could be forded in summer, many inter-provincial battles took place.

The weapons dredged from the Shannon fords in recent times contribute to the archaeological evidence for religion-as-war. In 1844, at the Keelogue ford, for example, the engineer Griffith found '150 elfstones (stone arrowheads), 10 swords and brass spear-heads, 8 small brass spear-heads, 2 iron swords, 8 small iron spear heads, 10 pieces of teeth, 3 iron battle axes, 10 brass battle axes, 41 sundry broken spearheads, ornaments of scabbards, druids' rings, etc.'[15]

He reported that 'weapons dropped in mortal strife between the men of Leinster and the Connacht men, disputing the passage of the river', belonged to 'distinct and no doubt very distant periods'. At the bottom of a foot of silt overlaying the esker riverbed gravel were 'stone weapons of a very remote age' including 'a great number of stone hatchets' overlaid by Bronze Age and Iron Age material – remnants of battles fought on the same spot, spanning thousands of years. As Griffiths was quick to remark, the struggle reached into his own lifetime, in that the British government had erected two defensive towers on the east bank to repel Napoleon, who was presumed to be leading fresh waves of Connacht raiders. Conversely, the medieval annalists record that in AD 985 'King Moyleseachlin with an army went into Connaught, and from thence brought many captives and rich boottyes.'

Corresponding conflicts in Nature were also much on the annalists' minds. They report hailstones as big as crabs, and how, in AD 688, 'it raigned blood in Leinster, and butter was turned into the colour of blood, and how a wolf was seen and heared to speak with a human voice'.

In 734 'there was a Dragon both huge and ugly to behold this Harvest seen, and a great Thunder heard after him in the firmament'.[16] This snake with wings, escaping St Patrick's attentions, could be regarded as a smaller version of the Eiscir ridge itself.

The dragon of 734 was both an historical singularity *and* an occupant of a cave in the depths of myth. There also, the gravelly ice sheet meltwater trembled, in geomorphological fact, under a groaning ice-roof, as the esker was slowly born.

Finn's opponent in the Shannon wars was Goll. Goll had ranged all over Leinster to the east coast. At Cnucha, he had killed Finn's father in battle, ensured Finn's emnity, and started another cycle in the East-West conflict.

Then having lost his comrade-in-arms, Suca Greatnose, Goll decided to retire into South Connacht, to the west bank of the Shannon. There 'ten hundred handsome shield-bearers of the house of the grandmother of keen Goll gathered around him on the hillock of the rowan tree, to defend their province against the advancing Finn'.[17] (Both the hillock and the rowan tree are emblematic of a divine ancestress.) Goll set his captains Feorann and Modha to guard adjacent fords while he protected a third.

Athlone, Shannonbridge, Banagher and Keelogue were probably the fords concerned. They have been standard crossings throughout the human occupation of Ireland.

'Goll watched against Fionn (Finn) seventeen days without sleep' before sinking into an exhausted slumber. 'Pleasant Goll...handsome of body', lay there, while Fionn led up six battalions, representing not only Leinster, but all the powers of the eastern world, including those of Britain and France – all directed against Europe's most westerly province.

Then 'at close of night upon his couch, when men and woods were in one hue, Fionn of bright aspect awoke'. Like the sun that he was, he climbed into the early morning, reached the ford, heard Goll snoring, crossed the river, and finding his enemy in a heavy sleep 'unsheathed the hard sword above the son of mane-red Morna. Goll awoke and raised his spear'.[18] There the pair can be left for a while, like low-relief figures in a marble frieze, while Goll's origins are examined more closely.

The Origins of Goll

'One has only to go upon the track of Fenian folklore among the Connacht peasantry of today,' wrote E. MacNeill in 1908, 'to find that Goll is the foremost hero of every tale.'[19]

He is sometimes described as a giant of the Fir Bolg, the mythical Men of the Bag, a subject race who, according to Irish legend, were made to carry soil in bags from fertile valleys to the tops of rocky hills for the benefit of their oppressors' farms in ancient Greece. By converting their bags into leather coracles, they escaped and sailed to Ireland, where they were again defeated, this time by the Tuatha Dé Danann at the first battle of Moytura, thought to have taken place at Cong in Co. Galway. After their victory the Tuatha permitted the Fir Bolg to remain in Connacht.[20]

In the seventeenth century many of the inhabitants of Connacht traced their ancestry back to the Fir Bolg. Goll, their paragon of valour, has one eye in the earth bag because he was of the underworld. The other, visible to mortals as the westering sun, gave him his alternative name, *Aed*, 'Fire',[21] and helps to explain why he is described as Red-Maned. Myth's even-handedness establishes that Goll lost his first eye at the Battle of Cnucha, at the sunrise end of the Great Road. The fate of the second hung on the outcome of a Connacht fight.

Keeping at least one eye on (and in) the bag where the secrets of soil's power to generate life were stored, Goll could be said to be visiting a god of the underworld called Conn, the Conn with whom the people of the province of Connacht, as 'descendants of Conn', identified.

Conn also means 'head', suggesting a link with the Celtic cult of the severed human head, as the repository of inspired knowledge.

There is clearly some overlapping of function between Goll and Conn, though as a duo they broadly correspond to the demi-god and god layers of reality, so carrying the descending sun into the deepest recesses of the imagination. This is not to forget that some commentators call Goll himself 'a sun deity who was also Lord of the Underworld'.[22]

Dumézil's research enables us to see Goll's battles as an essential death-dealing element which helped to keep the believing community alive, and to place the Irish accounts in an Indo-European tradition. Once again, Ireland presented a near-universal scenario in terms peculiar to itself, and showed how the specialized art of war was interwoven with the administration of the sacred, and the cultivation of fecundity, to give a true account of a violent natural order, and of the harmony within its conflicts.[23]

The War Goddesses

One of Finn's captains, MacLuighdech, called his war-horse Badb, and so flew to battle on the wings of the hooded crow. This aggressive carrion-eater, 43 cm long, is known in Ireland as the hooded Royston, or scare-crow, and as a manifestation of the war goddess, Badb. Her grey back and belly divides a black head and tail, giving the bird a *caille*, or hooded appearance. Her loud 'Kraa-Kraa' voice, laboured flight, and menacing hop-hopping on the ground, and her attendance over unburied corpses of every kind, helped to establish her reputation. The word *badb* conveyed the 'rage, fury and violence' of the goddess. Not many years ago, sturdy men would abandon projects for the day if they heard her call, wrote Hennessy,[24] since it prophesied slaughter or misfortune:

> The red-mouth Badb will cry around the house.
> For bodies it will be solicitous.
> Pale Badbs shall shriek.
> Badbs will be over the breasts of men . . .

says the battle story, *Bruiden Da Choca*.[25] (The 'house' stood on the Eiscir Riada, at Breenmore Hill, thirteen kilometres east of the Shannon – a hill-top fort with extensive views into Connacht.)

The Hooded Crow, Corvus Corone cornix, was regarded in Ireland as the war goddess, Badb, harbinger of death and devourer of battlefield corpses

In Ireland, Badb merged with her sister Mórrígu (Great Queen), and both could take on the features of a human hag:

> Over his head is shrieking
> A lean hag quickly hopping
> Over the points of their weapons and shields
> She is the grey-haired Mórrígu.[26]

Dusk's grey cloud-feathers, and the black gloss of midnight, were awaiting Goll's sunset army, as it retreated into the arms of the terrible mother. Badb is an Irish Kali (the Hindu 'terrible goddess'). Her other sister, Nemain, destroyed her victims by driving them mad.

The war goddesses may be said to embody the horrors of the eating and being eaten to which all life is committed, and which finds mythic expression in the life and death of the sacrificed god-hero.

The Connacht Campaign

On the west bank of the Shannon, Goll fought a losing battle on the side of the dying day and sinking year. Through him, Connacht myths are able to speak of the clash of elemental forces in superhuman terms.

This is what MacNeill calls 'the oldest form of folklore – nature myth, where the mysterious forces of nature are deified, and the phenomena they produce appear as the wars and quarrels...of the gods, – the struggles between light and dark, summer and winter, fair weather and storm'.[27]

Consequently, the folk tales of Connacht, though absurd in detail, are rational in overall effect, in that they integrate human hopes and defeats into a much bigger drama. In this they differ from a modern rationalism, which is so rational in detail, yet unreasonable to the point of madness in its broader consequences. They were involved with war *in* Nature, as distinct from war *on* Nature. For all our skill in measuring, we are now frequently surprised by 'unforeseen side-effects', whereas in antiquity there *were* no side-effects, since everything was presumed to be interconnected. Goll stands at the hub of a narrative of defeat touching every aspect of life. Therefore the societies which told his story were unlikely to be ambushed by unknown forces.

Finn did not kill the sleeping Goll on the Shannon river bank, but sheathed his sword. Here, as on several other occasions, a companionship amounting almost to identity took over. As different aspects of a single solar reality, they had even fought side by side at the Battle of the Sheaves.[28]

Nevertheless, in Connacht Goll *did* retreat before Finn, and though offering fierce resistance, behaved as if he knew he must lose.

Yet when Finn and his men are ensnared by the three Hags of Winter before the caves of Keshcorran, Co. Sligo, it is Goll that comes to the rescue. Winter-in-Connacht was Goll's natural territory. Finn had seen

Three phantom sprites come out of the side of the [Keshcorran] hill. Devilish was the guise of the women. They spell-bound my companions. Three black unsightly mouths, six white eyes never closing, three red bristling heads of hair, six twisting legs under them, three warlike swords, three shields with their three spears – it was not an easy task to gaze on the women or their gear.

Rough grey iron of wizardry they had mounted on poles, giddiness and faint sickness came over Finn and the Fian at the sight of them.

They reduced Finn to 'a withered quaking ancient', and left seven battalions of Fian in the same plight 'around the door of the bone-strewn Ceis. . . . bound and cast into a house underground'.[29]

One of the hags was called Camog (meaning a small bag, which suggests that she was related to Goll, being a goddess of the Fir Bolg or Bag Men). Cuilleann (Holly) and Iornach (Spindle, or Skein of yarn) were her companions. This trinity of Neolithic Winter deities tied up the invaders with cobwebs. Goll, in turn, bound up Iornach, 'fast in fetters', and forced her to return Finn and his men to their proper shapes. Then 'right speedily', Goll burnt the hags' abode. 'I left black ashes that house at the foot of the Ceis.' When Iornach escaped, and challenged Finn in single combat, Goll intervened again, and 'by clean force I cut her head off with my blue blade'.

Finn, once freed, ruthlessly turned on and killed Goll's grandson, Fedha son of Cainche, whose name means 'songbird' (an act which might represent the silencing or migration of fledgling songbirds at summer's end). 'Without him I am lonely,' said Goll, who then abandoned all hope of friendship with Finn, and resumed the fight against his armies, but by rescuing Finn from the Hags of Winter, Goll had sealed his own death sentence at Finn's hands. Goll was a selfless hero.

War and Sport in Connacht

From the remotest times, the sports field has been the battleground of mythic truths. In modern Leinster-Connacht relations the stylized Neolithic pattern has re-emerged, having cast off the brutality of actual inter-provincial warfare, so much a feature of Irish life from the Iron Age onwards,[30] which perhaps still imparts intensity to sporting contests between East and West.

The Caves of Keshcorran, Co. Sligo. The gratuitous malevolence of the three Hags who inhabit the caves is well known. Finn was ensnared by them. They see every traveller as potentially a speck of dust, trapped in the eye-socket of a geological formation. They are the triple goddess, queen of destruction

For example, in AD 1990, '*Magnificent McGrath fails to save unlucky Sarsfields*', declares the *Connacht Tribune*, describing how a Connacht team lost to a Leinster team, for a place in the All-Ireland club semi-final. 'The match was played in front of a fanatical Ballinasloe crowd of 4,000, and at an extraordinary pace in difficult underfoot conditions.' The hero was not Goll, but McGrath.

His display will live long in the memory . . . it was as near perfection as made no difference. His inspiring leadership deserved a better fate.

McGrath's exhibition of hurling was undoubtedly one of the best ever seen on a Galway GAA field. He seized on to his responsibilities with an authority and vengefulness which was quite extraordinary in its intensity. But oh, how that commitment was so gracefully complemented with the more subtle skills of the game. McGrath's superb handling, lithe turns, darting runs and unerring accuracy were all condensed into one moment of second-half hurling magic in the 48th minute when he emerged from thickets of ash near the left sideline to stroke over a magnificent point from 60 yards.

Not till the dying minutes did the Leinster side finally deliver the fatal blows to a side almost unable to stomach defeat. Final Score: Sarsfield 0-12, Ballyhale Shamrocks 2-8.[31]

A mythology which ignored war would soon be overwhelmed by the forces it had failed to recognize. The wisdom of Goll and Connacht concern the ability to engage in war and absorb war's impact to the benefit of the country as a whole. Ultimately, the Connacht myth brings the mortally wounded hero to that womb of the goddess available to every inhabited island – the depths of the sea.

This denouement follows the plot of the setting sun, as it rolls, fat and bloody, down Connacht's huge cliffs towards oceanic infinity. The Connacht road leads eventually to the rainlashed, ocean-whittled and wind-scoured austerities of Connemara and the Nephin Beg mountains.

Here abundance gives way to imposed austerity, and the wedding feast shrinks to the last iron rations. Yet in this renunciation, a strange beauty arises, recorded by travellers to the far West. There the bones of mountains are dressed in a new kind of light, coming from beyond the land's end.

Driven across the province, Goll finally perched on a bare crag on the cliffs of Iar, or west Connacht, with the ocean as his only future. 'Wide is the sea around us, and I on the narrow crag: hunger for food is betraying me, and thirst is overmatching me . . . still more it takes the beauty from my cheek to have to drink bitter strong brine.'[32] Connacht has always been the land of brave losers, especially in its remote and mountainous west.

From his last toe-hold on the cliffs, Goll claims to have killed thirty hundred of the enemy, including Dubh Lughaidh – 'Black Want'. He had been refused help at Emain Macha in Ulster, and at Tara in Meath, because those kings had been too frightened of Finn's revenge. Then (a bitter blow) the royal palace of Rathcroghan in his own province had shut him out for the same reason. Only his wife and the piles of men he had slain remained with him. After thirty full days without food or sleep, he cried out, in despair: 'I was the deed-vaunting champion: I have a waist of bone. I was golden-weaponed Iollan [expert]. Tonight I am Goll the unsightly.'

He recalled that 'from Hallowtide till May I supported the entire Fianna', and 'the chase of Corann of the hillocks was held by us without refraining.'[33] (Corran means 'hook, or pruning hook', which suggests that Goll's struggles included a role in driving the momentum of the farming year before him.)

Rather than he should starve to death, his wife advises him 'to eat of those bodies at thy side, [and] drink of the milk of my breasts.'[34] He refuses, but asks his 'clear one of rosy cheeks, to prepare to depart the morn before my slaying'. He speaks to her as if she is the sky,

(Opposite) The Atlantic cliffs of Connacht. Here a defeated and starving Goll faced his one-eyed death, as the sun sank into the oceanic abyss. Red, evening, west, autumn, and death go together in many cultures, where natural and social realities are synthesized in supernatural tales. Inset: Goll lives again in 'Magnificent McGrath's' unavailing 1990 performance for Connacht's Sarsfield against Leinster hurling opponents

whose pink beauty, he knows, will soon fade once he, the light of her life, has dropped into the ocean. Preparing himself for that reversed birth, he asks her to take away his tunic.

Considering her own fate she cries out: 'O Goll…alas for those whose friends are few, which way shall I take?' With the stoicism that holds the natural order together, he replies: 'Seek the camp of Fionn of the Fianna; wed there, gentle one of red lips, some good man worthy of thee.' She is to go to his enemies and accept the new sun of the east into her vast spaces, so to enjoy the dawn of another cycle.

Goll's destiny was to slither down the rocks through lank seaweed, and to drop into the western ocean. *Acallamh na Senórach* says that he died after he had retreated 'to Carrac Guill in the West', which was presumably an ocean-girt rock-stack off the Connacht coast. There he was beheaded by Dubh Dithre's son, Mac Smaile (*Dubh* – 'black', *dithre* – 'feeble, spent, exhausted'). This was the same Mac Smaile who had reaped with the Fianna at the Battle of the Sheaves. *Smál* means 'embers or ashes'. Thus was Goll, light of the western fire, the setting sun, smothered, till his blackened head rolled powerless beneath the waves of midnight. In a sense he died by his own hand, since ash is the product of fire, just as the word *golighe*, or 'setting of the sun', carried his name and his remaining eye out of sight, in a dignified exit.

Brâzil

Following his death, Goll may have gone to the phantom Island of Brâzil. It was believed to lie off the south-west coast of Connacht, and was named after Bres, the son of Ériu, fathered by the Fomorian sea god, Elatha. Consequently 'Bresil' was a magic realm, neither sea nor land, yet both. Brazil, South America, was named after it.

In the early twentieth century Aran Islanders in Galway Bay continued to believe that *their* Brâzil was visible once every seven years. They called it The Great Land. The antiquarian T.J. Westropp wrote:

I myself have seen the illusion some three times in my boyhood, and made a rough colour sketch in 1872. It was a clear evening with a fine golden sunset. Just as the sun went down a dark island suddenly appeared far out at sea, but not on the horizon. It had two hills, one wooded. Between these, from a low plain, rose towers and curls of smoke.

Westropp's brother and several friends were equally amazed by the sight. One cried: 'I see New York!'[35] (In its position at the west end of Eiscir Riada, Brâzil is the counterpart to that eastern construction of the human imagination, Dublin.)

To earlier generations the Brâzil mirage was also known as the Isle of the Living, the Isle of Truth, of Joy, of Fair Women, and of Apples.

In the seventeenth century, Captain John Nisbet of Lisneskay, Co. Fermanagh, claimed to have landed on the island and found cattle, sheep, horses, black rabbits, and a strong castle. He knocked on the door in vain. At night he and his eight companions returned to the shore, and lit a fire. Then a hideous noise ensued, and they fled to the boat.

Returning the next day they found an old Scottish gentleman and servants on the shore, dressed in outdated clothes and of old-fashioned speech, who claimed to have been imprisoned there by a necromancer. They confirmed that the island was indeed O Brazile.

In John Purdey's Atlantic chart, published in 1830, its position was given as 51°10' North, 15°30' West. Not until the 1865 edition was it struck off.

Croagh Patrick

Whether or not Goll was resurrected in an offshore Otherworld, Connacht mythology, like that of every province, sought a suitable place on the mainland to re-enact its own rebirth. Connacht's nativity occurred annually at the start of harvest at a conical mountain, tipped with white quartz. It is called The Reek, or Croagh Patrick, and anciently Cruachán Aigle, perhaps from *aige* – 'act of celebrating or holding festivals'. It stands 762 metres high, overlooking the Atlantic and Clew Bay, Co. Mayo, – the salty bag from which came the Fir Bolg farmers, mythic ancestors of the entire Connacht population.[36]

From the mountain top one can see hundreds of islands in the Bay. Traditionally there are said to be three hundred and sixty six, enough for a year and a day.[37] They were known as *Insule Fortunate*, 'The Fortunate Islands', on maps and in Irish as Insi Modh, from *modh*, 'a measure', of time, or of grain, and may have been regarded as the progeny of the mountain.

Every year at Lughnasa, people came to witness the mother goddess give birth, though until the mid-nineteenth century only women were permitted to climb the steep 250-metre-high scree slope which led up to the summit of the mountain top. The Rev. James Page reported: 'None but those that are barren go there, and the abominable practices that are committed there ought to make human nature in its most degraded state blush.'[38] As Philip Dixon confided, these included sleeping on Lughnasa Eve in the summit 'bed' of the goddess.[39] In this way barren wives empathized with, and eventually hoped to participate in, the birth process. A strong belief persists in the locality that 'the Friday of Crom Dubh – the harvest god – in July, is the correct day for performing the pilgrimage, and many people living around the mountain . . . go up on that day.'[40] This remains true in 1990.

Folklore describes the struggle between the attempts of St Patrick to overthrow both the harvest god and the ancient mother goddess of The Reek, which has now been converted into the holiest mountain in Christian Ireland. On the first Sunday in August, 60,000 people annually ascend the peak to honour the saint. However, in the Irish manner, they often come in a mood of 'double coding', rather than to celebrate a total Christian victory. For example, the first cairn on the climb, where prayers are said, is known as The Bed of my Benen

(Leacht Mo-Bhionnain) – 'the boy' of Patrick. Underlying that title the new-born infant of the ancient goddess cries out for recognition.

St Patrick's struggle against the goddess of the mountain reached a climax when she confronted him as a great bird, Corra, and as a monster serpent, alias 'The Devil's Mother'. He allegedly drove her from the mountain. She escaped to Lough Derg, Co. Donegal, where the saint encountered her again at his 'Purgatory Lake' (Part One).

Yet as Thackeray discovered in 1840, her spirit lived on at Croagh Patrick. After the business on the mountain came the dancing and love-making at its foot. Fifty tents were set around 'a plain of the most brilliant green grass', where they sold 'great coarse damp-looking bannocks of bread...a collection of pigs' feet...huge biscuits, and doubtful-looking ginger beer. There were also cauldrons containing water for 'tay', with other pots full of pale legs of mutton...The road home was pleasant; everybody was wet through, but everybody was happy.'[41]

In terms of the pre-Christian annual cycle, Cruachán Aigle is a peak where the pot or *crochan* of harvest milk finally comes to the boil, having been first warmed at Rathcroghan in the midsummer kitchen of Medb, the provincial goddess, who was based 88 kilometres due east (see p. 237). Six months prior to that, at midwinter, the mythic pot or *crochan* had been divinely manufactured under Croghan Hill, Co. Offaly, on the Eiscir Riada (see p. 230), which, in turn, stands 88 kilometres from Rathcroghan.

The Shannon Axis

The mythic structure of Ireland was an amplification of symmetries discerned in nature. Thus the chief north-south axis of the country, based on Ireland's longest river the Shannon, was believed to terminate in an outpouring of supernatural wisdom comparable to the Eiscir Riada's Brâzil (map, p. 8).

The *Dindshenchas* describes how the river known to humanity, personified as a maiden, goes in search of this under-sea spring of sacred knowledge, for lack of which her reality is incomplete. 'The maiden right active, Sinann, radiant, ever-generous, bright streaming Sinann, yellow-haired Sinann of the Tuatha Dé Danann, yearned for, and sought after, the secrets of magic wisdom.' She had acquired all other accomplishments, but lacking that form of knowledge, she travelled 'to a spring not sluggish, under the pleasant sea in the domain of Connle or Condla to gaze upon it'. This submarine spring of Connla lay in an Otherworld, under the poet's music-haunted hazel tree.

> Connla's well, loud was its sound
> beneath the blue skirted ocean;
> Six streams unequal in fame
> rise from it, the seventh the Sinann.

There Shannon literally found herself, in the fountainhead of wisdom.

Croagh Patrick, Co. Mayo,
now the holiest mountain in
Ireland. The path is worn by
sixty thousand pilgrims, some
opting to go barefoot, who
stride and stagger to the top
during the last week of July.
Their walk converts a pagan
First Fruits Festival, still known
as 'The Friday of Crom Dubh',
into a Sunday mass on the
summit

At the Lecht Benian station
(left), two supplicants walk
briskly round a site honouring
'Patrick's boy', his attendant.
They repeat the set prayers
seven times. Then, with a quick
dab of the hand, from cairn to
head, impart the rocks' power
to themselves

169

Sagacity was disseminated from the well when the ripe hazel nuts, on falling into the water, were swallowed by sacred salmon, who carried the 'ideas' upstream. Alternatively, the milk from the nuts was converted into the air bubbles seen to rise along the Shannon's course. These were the *bolg fis*, 'bubbles of knowledge', or *bolg imbais*, of 'inspiration'. The priority given to the hazel nut in Neolithic ritual deposits proves the antiquity of its supernatural associations.

The Shannon as known to modern geography rises 'in an upland basin walled by the precipitous gritstone scarps of the Leitrim plateau',[42] in northernmost Connacht. The *Dindshenchas* explains how it migrated there from Connla's Well:

> The well fled back [to the land], (clear fame
> through the murmur of its musical lore!)
> before [i.e. ahead of] Sinann, who visited it
> in the north, and reached the chilly river.[43]

Like a salmon, the source sped upstream to the Pot, its earthly source.

From Connla's Well to Shannon Pot is a 320-kilometre journey between worlds, and between different ways of knowing. Thanks to Sinann, the wandering river goddess, the Two became One along Ireland's north-south water-spine. She gave her life to achieve their integration.

Shannon Pot is a steep-sided, clayey, oval hole, twenty-two paces long by fifteen wide, set in a melancholy landscape of boulder-strewn, rushy pastures, and close to a ruined farm, nine kilometres north-east of Dowra. This underground river-exit, coming from a hidden watercourse in the concealed limestone, is sometimes as placid as a mirror, and yet after heavy rains, boils and bubbles like an overheated cauldron. To that spot 'the comely lady' Sinann came and was drowned. She merged with her own water, having no life outside it.

Every province wanted a share of the Shannon's merit, and sent their poets to 'Contentions of the Bards' to compete in verse for her hand. Following a fifteenth-century contest at Killaloe the judge, himself a poet, awarded the river to Ulster,[44] the only province through which the Shannon does not run. Yet the Ulster-Shannon link is emphasized again by Geraldus, in his twelfth-century account: 'A branch [of the river] divides *the furthest districts of Ulster* from Connaught, and after various windings falls into the Northern Ocean... Thus flowing from sea to sea, it separates the fourth and western part of the island [Connacht] from the three others.'[45]

This imagined northern outlet persists in folklore to this day among people living around Shannon Pot. They believe that an underground stream connects it to the river Claddach, seen emerging at the Marble Arch cave system in Ulster. From there the water flows into Lough Erne, to enter 'the Northern Ocean' at Ballyshannon on Donegal Bay. This 'extended' river was thought to play a part in the agrarian cycle, and in farms an old belief is still recalled, that chaff thrown into the water at the Marble Arch cave will re-emerge at Shannon Pot.[46]

Erne Weddings

Ess Ruaid (Falls of Assaroe)

Traditionally regarded as the province of wisdom, through its myths Connacht articulates the principal east-west *and* north-south mythic axes of Ireland into its own boundaries. It thus gives structure to complex issues.

In a sense, all the myths of Ireland are concerned with boundaries, for at the frontier, what is divided is also brought together, face to face. Near provincial borders dangers and opportunities arise of every kind. There, supernatural and natural changes can be expected, requiring dramatic exposition and regulation by the story-teller's art. Hence the significance of the Falls of Assaroe at Ballyshannon on the river Erne, close to the Connacht border with Ulster (map, p.8). *Ess Ruaid*, their Irish name, means 'Red Cataract'. The mythical Northern Shannon[47] and the real river Erne here jointly enter the ocean.

In contrast to Eiscir Riada, which emphasizes martial encounters, at Ess Ruaid and along the Erne it is mainly the opposite sexes who confront each other, especially during *gam* (November), the month of weddings.

Ess Ruaid previously held the fate of the nation suspended in its glassy roar, though now it has been obliterated by changes in water level, following the building of a hydro-electric station.

Sometimes referred to as The Salmon Leap, The Falls drew together sunset, fire, water, humanity, fish, and vegetable life forms. In the seventeenth century O'Clery reported: 'The Irish people . . . speak of the salmon of the Red Cataract, and say that when the sun goes to the west, and shines on the Red Cataract, the water turns reddish, which seems to arise from a red weed growing on the rock inside the waterfall.'[48]

Pre-Christian sanctity attracted Christian attention, and the twelfth-century Assaroe Abbey was built immediately above a natural cave containing two bullauns of triangular shape, sitting side by side on an altar-like ledge of rock.[49] At least six centuries earlier, St Patrick had desired to 'set up at Ess Ruaid . . . in the place where are *Disert* and *Lecc Patraic* [his cell and bed]', but a local leader, Coirbre, resisted the saint and ordered two of his men to drive Patrick away.

'Not good is what you do,' said Patrick. 'If a dwelling were permitted me here, my city with its Ess-Ruaid through it would be a second Rome of Latium with its Tiber, and thy children would be [my] successors therein.'[50] The saint then cursed the north, or Ulster side of the river belonging to Coirbre with barrenness of fish. Then on *Sith Aeda*, the tomb of the drowned pagan King of the falls, Patrick prophesied the birth of St Columcille.

To pagan and Christian alike, in medieval times 'the Falls of Assaroe' were used proverbially to denote eternity and everlastingness. At that time they were employed to run the turbines of a supernatural cycle, discharging as myth. The technicians were the gods and demi-god heroes who laboured and often gave their lives to connect humanity to the cosmic power grid which they embodied.

The deliberate obliteration of the Falls prompts the question: has convenient access to light and heat rendered human imagination obsolete over wide areas where it was formerly active? Perhaps the consumer has been inoculated against a mythic engagement with Nature, now that sources are systematically converted into resources.

Yet the mythic inclination was always to accept what came to hand, including electricity, and in today's gathering dusk the flick of a switch may equally serve to re-illuminate lines of print, enabling them to leap again like salmon from the *Dindshenchas* pages. Ess Ruaid roars when remembered, and the act of remembering affects the future of real rivers, since their fate depends on how they are perceived.

Aed

The *genius loci* of Ess Ruaid was Aed, a word meaning 'fire'. He was the fire prince (or King) of Royal Ess Ruaid.[51] As Aed Ruad (Fire Red), son of Badurn, King of Ireland, he was drowned there while gazing at his image and swimming the rapid. His gravemound, Síd Aedá, is on the rapids' brink, and 'his body was born into the elfmound there'.[52] (This tumulus, on the north bank hilltop, was obliterated by the construction of a fort in 1798, designed to repel Napoleon. An Episcopal church now occupies the site.)

Aed is described as 'rich with a good father's wealth', and as Argatmár's grandson. (*Argat*, 'silver', gave him a lunar pedigree on his mother's side.) Another story recorded in the Middle Ages says that a soldier came to him, a match for a hundred men, and was persuaded to stay for one year in return for a hundred men's wages. When the year was over, Aed refused to pay. Enraged, up rose the hireling, 'fiercely holding his tall spear-shafts', and 'roused his sureties' against Aed, who was bathing in the rapids. 'Though thou set the sea against me', said the comely High-King of Erin, 'thou shalt never get from me aught but the same as any soldier.'[53] The King 'broke upon the soldier the stars visible and invisible', an enigmatic phrase that expands the scope of the story to include an otherworld firmament.

Ess Ruaid (Falls of Assaroe), river Erne, Ballyshannon. They are named after the god or king, Ruad, 'Red'. As a one-eyed salmon, Goll swam here

But the soldier would not be intimidated, and 'incited sea, wind, sun, ether and firmament' against the King, to avenge Aed's betrayal of the elemental powers on which his reign depended. Aed had flouted the rules of fair exchange, and was therefore drawn back to extinction.

The anonymous spear-carrying soldier whose *láigen* (spear) may indicate that the forces of Leinster had driven to the Western ocean, lured Aed by means of the 'sun's sultriness' to enter the rapids and bathe...' 'till Aed was drowned therein, by a miracle of sea and mighty wind. Hence Ess Ruaid, [or] Aed Ruaid's Rapid is said.'[54] Justice was done by solar fire on royal fire.

The Assaroe stories continue to describe a fire god's annual death in an archaic nature religion, at the hands of a virile rival from the east, Finn or his surrogate. Nor was it an *absolute* death, but rather a re-arrangement of form comparable to the return to the solar furnace of a flaring prominence. *Aed* (fire), and *goll* (one-eyed sun) were interchangeable names, and when the sun dropped below the Atlantic horizon beyond Donegal Bay, its 'death' was presumed to be only an aquatic metamorphosis, enabling Goll to turn into a mythical salmon, who swam back to the Falls as Goll Essa Ruaide![55]

Goll as Salmon

So The Great Silver (Argatmor) makes his inspired leap from the Otherworld depths, back into the river systems known to humankind. This legendary fish unites Goll and Aed at the Falls, and links both of them to the Connla Well salmon, at the mythical southern end of the Shannon system.

... That is a well at which are the hazels and inspirations[?] of wisdom ... the hazels of the science of poetry, and in the same hour their fruit, and their blossom and their foliage break forth, and these fall on the well in the same shower, which raises on the water a royal surge of purple. Then the salmon chew the fruit, and the juice of the nuts is apparent on their purple bellies. And seven streams of wisdom spring forth and turn there again.[56]

At Connla, so at Ess Ruaid, the spots on the salmon's sides, its natural markings, were interpreted as the sign of supernatural origins, coming from within.

The Goll-Salmon, leaping up the Falls on its annual spawning journey, epitomized the divine economy at work, just as the supernatural may be regarded as a countercurrent sustained within the ordinary flow of natural forces.

On the river bank, who but Finn should be seen, roasting a salmon? According to Connacht and Donegal folk-tales, he was cooking it over a fire for a one-eyed giant, but burnt his thumb when touching a heat blister which had risen on the side of the fish. Then, sucking his injured thumb to cool it, Finn found that all knowledge was revealed to him, including how to set about killing the giant. The giant was probably Goll in terrestrial form, and another form of a legendary, one-eyed fish, 'Goll below the waves'.

Egyptian mythology tells how the god Horus lost an eye, and gave it to the dead Osiris to eat, the latter thereby being equipped with a soul. 'From Ireland and from Egypt we seem to be listening to far-away echoes of one and the same primitive story, of sunrise and sunset. The tearing out of the eye appears to be connected with the creation or re-creation of sun or of moon.'[57]

The primordial nature of the Ess Ruaid salmon sacrifice is emphasized by the founding father, Fintan, who, in salmon form, lost an eye, and was also known as *Goll Essa Ruaid*.[58] This confirms the Assaroe events as belonging to the earliest strata of Irish mythic imaginings. The archaic tale swims on, disregarding priestly claims to exclusive fishing rights. Similarly, the river of scientific myth may remain open, providing Nature is allowed a close season for the recuperation of her stock.

Lady Ruad

Another Ess Ruaid story concerns an Otherworld female called Ruad. That at least 'was her name in her first husband's time',[59] a statement which alerts us to the possibility that she was a goddess, choosing a new husband annually, at Samain. Her lovers had included Aed-

Srónmár, 'Fire-Bignose', to whom she had given 'great love'. This reference sets a Hallowe'en tone of an eternal maiden seeking a virile mate, as at Rannach Crom Dubh. Her *ruad* is the virgin's blood, ready to be spilled in the river. *Ruad* means 'dark red', the colour of 'bloodstains', and, O'Rahilly asserts, is one of the names of the god Dagda, of whom Lady Ruad was probably the partner.

Lady Ruad arrived alone in the estuary, below the Falls. She had travelled in a bronze boat, with a tin sail. The boat belonged to Abcán, the dwarf poet of the Tuatha Dé Danann, and the sail could be the white lunar sickle of a maiden desiring fulfilment. The preferred metals are pre-Iron Age.

She had come from the northern ocean, 'with Ireland on the larboard side'[60] leaving behind the pure sagacity which can be found in the sea, her inheritance. 'When she went with Gaeth (*gaeth*, 'the Sea'), son of Gaes Glan (*gaes*, 'intelligence', *glan*, 'pure'), her previous dwelling is described as *Mag Maen*, 'The Great Plain of Dumbness'.

Once again, it is clear that myth involves an arousal to speech, or song.

After the silence of the Western deep, Lady Ruad yearned to hear voices. Therefore 'the Tapered-fingered came on a path of happy love', and, as a goddess of love, 'That fair and modest maiden happened upon the famous bay below the Falls, . . . and she asked in no uncertain wise that the river should be her freehold, [saying] "This is the brightest inver [estuary] in Erin."'

'Then Aed saw her from the seat he occupied, but he knew not who the girl might be, and she knew not what land she was in.' Across the estuary, 'from a burden of sea-maids', she heard the mermaids' melody. 'Then she fell asleep at the music, among the streams of the eddying bays, tumbled over the bow of her boat, and was drowned, [and therefore] never reached the hero her love.' Or, 'she leapt overboard, not mastered by a spell, but by the doleful music of the fairy mounds. So from her comes the name Ess Ruaid with its greatness.'[61] (As a language word, *ess* means waterfall, boat, *and* death.)

One can interpret her death as Christian alteration of an oral tradition, with the new cult of virginity replacing a pagan love match. Yet if Lady Ruad is salt water, her 'drowning' becomes a lying-in-wait for the inevitable fall of her lover (the cataract) into her arms, in a union audible and visible to all.

From the long reaches of Upper and Lower Lough Erne, the sluggish river Erne creeps in silence till, falling through space, it roars into the receptive body of the ocean, personified by Lady Ruad. Myth tends to grow at places where the hidden voice is heard, and where stored energies are unleashed in divine encounter. That Aed was of a sacred pantheon is confirmed by an alternative title of the Falls – Ess Duind, named after Donn, god of the Underworld, Son of Duban (from *duban*, 'aroused up'), son of Bile, from *bile*, 'tree'. This family tree brings the Ess Ruaid events into alignment with the *axis mundi*, thereby 'centering' the island at the start of a new year, and at the place of the festivities.

The desire of the goddess, and the arousal of the god, provided the underlying theme. The arrival of the craft under the Falls signified the *hieros gamos*, or divine wedding; consequently the cataract ran red.

A fragment from the Yellow Book of Lecan makes it plain that the Dagda, greatest of all the Irish gods, wished to identify with Aed at his marriage. Therefore the Dagda says: 'I *am* Aed Abaid of Ess Ruaid, that is the Good God of wizardry of the Tuatha Dé Danann.'[62] Lady Ruad, we may take it, was his bride, and their union brought land and sea together.

Diarmaid at Ess Ruaid

At the end of every year, towards the Falls of Assaroe galloped Diarmaid, consort of Gráinne. He came mounted backwards on the boar to which he clung; their destinies were tied together in a death ride. 'When the beast reached Ess Ruaid it gave three swift leaps across the Fall, hither and thither, [but] it could not put Diarmaid off.'[63] Nevertheless, these jumps signalled Diarmaid's end.

His year and a day with Gráinne was nearly over. He had suspected that her attention was already turning elsewhere, and had taunted her about her feelings for 'the youth in the green garb' – the hidden prospect of spring, waiting to push him aside. Co. Roscommon folklore rumours that Gráinne was having an affair with a giant called Cuithach (*cuithach*, 'hurtful, destructive').

When first threatened by the boar in North Sligo, Diarmaid had struck at it with his sword *Fearless*, but the weapon broke in two; a sign of weakening sexual potency.

Then the hero, still on the boar's back, was galloped to a mound on top of Ben Bulben overlooking the Sligo coast, there to be thrown off and gored by the beast, till the hero's bowels and entrails 'lay about him'. Yet Diarmaid summoned up the strength to pierce the boar through the navel, and killed it.

Finn (who had been hunting Diarmaid all year, ever since he had run off with Gráinne from Tara in Leinster), then came up to gloat. 'I like to see you so,' said Finn, 'and I regret that all the women of Ireland are not looking at you now, for your beauty is turned to ugliness and your good form to deformity.'[64] Diarmaid's fabulous spear, *Ga Buidhe an Lamhaigh*, which combined martial, solar and phallic virtues, was useless to him. Prior to the battle with the boar, Gráinne had advised him to put it aside and to take instead *Ga Dearg Duinn*, the 'red, ruddy, or blood-coloured spear', better suited to his

Sacred weapons were mythic characters in action. An Iron Age spear-head from Boho, Co. Fermanagh (left), was perhaps conceived as the solar goddess Gráinne. The hilt of an Iron Age sword, from the river Erne at Ballyshannon (centre), may have represented Diarmaid or Aed. God as shaft or blade entered female ferule, or sheath. A votive Iron Age sheath from Lisnacroghera, Co. Antrim (right), as female 'swallower', has 'Caoranach' (serpent) eyes

imminent death; but he had not done so, preferring to keep faith with the gold weapon of happier days, such as those he had spent with her around Lough Gur. But in Co. Sligo, the boom of Ess Ruaid spoke of Gráinne changing her partner, and so he died.

It becomes clear that Ess Ruaid played a role in more than one myth-cycle concerned with love, death, and phallic sword.

Fishermen dredged up a sword from Ballyshannon harbour in 1916. The iron blade encrusted with lime and shells was a metre long. Its bronze hilt was in the shape of a man, with outspread arms and legs in La Tène style, *c.* 100 BC–AD 100.[65]

In Britain and Ireland swords and daggers were often thrown into river estuaries as offerings to the goddesses of waterways. The male head and body of this hilt may have been locally regarded as Diarmaid, or Aed, though it was probably made in Gaul.

Throughout north-west Europe the symbolism of sword and scabbard expressed sexual union.[66] Gaelic *faigen* or *faigeann*, means scabbard *and* vulva, while 'sheath', *truaill*, is also 'vagina'.

The phrase '*Banba an Truaill*', quoted by Cormac, brings the scabbard-vagina within a Goddess-Banba image. An accepted poetic term for Ireland, Banba, when combined with Truaill gives a nation-wide context to the cult of sword and scabbard as a sacred love-rite between Ireland and king. The Ballyshannon hilt therefore equips the affair of Aed and Lady Ruad with the necessary tool, and turns the art of war towards love.

In prehistoric Britain and Ireland the vagina-scabbard was often portrayed in snake form, as the great female swallower, analogous to Caoranach of Lough Derg. The bronze sheath from Lisnacroghera, Ulster, has a snake-shaped chape, or end, with 'eyes' studs and a pair of engraved 'eyes' at the 'mouth' opening. This piece was deposited as an offering in water and so can be seen as a return of 'Caoranach' (or her sea serpent sister) to her natural watery habitat.

Partholón and Inis Samer

In the widening river Erne, two hundred yards downstream from the site of the Assaroe Falls lies a small, fish-shaped island. Now called Fish Island, its Celtic name was Inis Samer, the Isle of the lapdog Samer. There lived Partholón, the mythic 'King' who, in *Lebor Gabála*, led the settlement of the country. He set up house within sound of the Falls with his wife Delgnat and his servant Tobar.

Macalister identifies Partholón with Bith (Cosmos). Bith's cairn, it will be recalled, was erected on the Ulster-Connacht boundary at Slieve Beagh, 68 kilometres from Inis Samer (p. 58). The name 'Partholón' is thought to be a version of Bartholomew, and both forms may be the outcome of a Christian scribe's attempt to insert the name of the only apostle for whom claims of noble blood have ever been made, into a pagan cycle.[67] In an Irish mythic context, *Bartholomew* and *Partholón* are equally anomalous as names, but can be explained as active versions of *Bith*. Partholón was said to have come from Sicily, where sons were traditionally reputed to murder their aged parents, so alerting us to an elemental cycle.

'His story, like Bith's, is connected with the creation or recreation of the sun or of the moon, with their death at setting and rebirth at rising, involving ritual combat. He combines these echoes with the function of a vegetation god who must die under the strokes of the winter-daemon.'[68] Queen Delgnat's eventual desertion of Partholón in favour of a younger mate is the standard mythic way of expressing the ruthlessness of the seasonal drama.

As the ultimate river of Harvest Home, the Erne was, in Partholón's estimation, 'the most fruitful which he had found in Ireland'.[69] From his house in mid-stream, he then 'went a-hunting and a-fishing' and he left his wife and his henchman Tobar to guard the island. The woman bade the henchman pair with her. He refused. The woman called him a coward. At last, he consented 'because the woman was reviling him. From that indecency and folly, which those two wrought, the name clave to the creek, *Da Econd* [of the two fools].' Thereafter thirst seized them and they:

Inis Samer (Fish Island), Ballyshannon, where Delgnat, Partholón's wife, made love with Tobar, and Partholón killed her dog, Samer, This Summer's end (Samain) myth describes an old god ousted by next year's youth

drank of the measures [vessels], and tubes of Partholón, [who] came to the house at the end of the day and perceived the taste of Tobar's mouth and that of Delgnat upon the tube and so became aware of the misdeed; great wrath seized him, and so he killed his wife's lapdog, which was called Saimer, whence Saimer's Island has its name. . . . so this was the first jealousy and the first lust in Erin. Thereafter the servant escaped, fleeing at random, and was eaten by dogs and birds.[70]

Beneath the tone of monastic misogyny which has coloured the written account, a pre-Christian structure survives, as does the Arcadian mood of the accompanying verse, in speaking of the lovemaking isle:

> The place where it was done,
> after its fashioning certainly –
> great is its sweetness that was there that day
> in the land of Inis Saimera.[71]

The gold tubes used by the lovers on the island are matched by the wheatstraws employed in Welsh oath-swearing rites, while the cup or bowl has been acknowledged as the vessel of the feminine by most cultures. In this instance, the name of the male lover, Tobar, attached itself to the vessel, for as a language word, *toba* can mean 'drinking vessel'. *Tobach*, 'the act of reaping', produced the necessary straws. That the initiative is taken by Delgnat 'is entirely in keeping with the archaic pattern'.[72]

Equally, the queen is not cowed by Partholón's protests, but answers, in Keating's seventeenth-century rendering: 'Do you think that it is possible that woman and honey be near one another, new milk and a cat . . . or a man and a woman in private without their meddling with each other?'[73]

> Master, fair one, Partholón!
> when longing for a pairing comes, it is not easy to subdue it.
> See thy speckle-coloured cattle-herds
> in their tight bond they have desire!
> See thy sheep of fair garb
> that tarry not for a pairing master!
> Foaming milk of thy horned cow, be it not trusted to a kitten.[74]

Macalister regards her verse as 'primarily a fertility spell', and the king's slaying of the dog as a surrogate offering for himself.

Frazer has collected numerous instances of comparable substitutions. The sacrifice enabled Partholón to live out thirty years of occupation as a culture hero, introducing the arts of cattle-rearing, building, cooking, brewing, duelling and guesting – offering hospitality. He was also credited with clearing four plains, and creating numerous loughs and rivers.[75] Then he divided the country between his four sons, using the Eiscir Riada as the east-west boundary, intersected by a north-south frontier, running from Ailech Neit (the hill near Derry, on which stands the imposing fortress of Grianan Ailigh overlooking Lough Foyle), to Ard Nemid, an isle in Cork Harbour, Munster.

To recreate the four quarters was a feature of many divine plans – a desire passed from god to god, and the joint effort of deadly rivals. Thus we learn of Partholón and Delgnat's attempt at the grand design, that 'Ita was their hireling, or Toba was his other name'. *Tobar* means 'source, spring, well'; *Ita*, 'corn' (*Ith*). Partholón's rival was therefore himself, when young. 'Ith, like Tobar, is a sort of rebirth of Partholón.'[76] But Tobar never ascends the throne. Instead he disappears *into* Nature via the digestive tracts of wild beasts.

As for Partholón, a folk practice reported from Co. Waterford shows that his spirit as an end-of-harvest god continued to stalk the fields of Ireland into the nineteenth century:

The Day of Parthanan comes a short time before the end of Harvest, and everybody tries to have his crops mown before then, because on that day Parthanan is said to go round threshing every grain from corn still standing.

To deny him these pickings, men would hastily roll over and flatten the unmown remainder of their crop.[77]

Partholón and Nemed

In Ireland there was a strong 'family resemblance' between the sons of supposedly different mythic invaders. Nor were such similarities regarded with dismay, for in the age of myth, 'originality' involved the incorporation of origins, just as the sapwood of a tree incorporates in heartwood the secret of its strength. Consequently, The Four Sons of Nemed, described in *Lebor Gabála*, are remarkably similar in their names to the 'four sons of Partholón'. Ultimately, they were all children of Bith and the birth-giving goddess Cesair.

Commentators detect an overlap verging on synonymity between Partholonians, Nemedians, and Fir Bolg, as recapitulations of a common agrarian mythic cycle.[78] Read together they make muddled 'history', but are valuable pointers to a 'very ancient stratum of tradition . . . highly suggestive of primitive myth'.[79]

Samer's End and Lough Erne

The river Erne in which Inis Samer lies was previously known as the river Samer or Samhair. This archaic title deepens further the involvement of Lady Ruad and Aed (along with Delgnat, Tobar, Partholón, and Saimer the dog), in versions of a Summer's end drama, which stretched upstream to incorporate Lough Erne.

Lough Erne 'first showed its troubled waters . . . on a radiant evening in harvest',[80] when 'the noble Erne [who was] chief among the maidens in Rathcrúachan [the síd of Medb, fairy queen of Connacht], fled with a troop of women to the plain where now Lough Erne lies'. They had been frightened by the emergence from the Caves of Crúachan of the 'grisly shape and rough brawling voice of the giant Olca Ái. One version of the story says that although Olca Ái's purpose was 'to contend against Armargen the Black-haired', Olca incidentally 'shook his beard . . . and gnashed his teeth' at the boys and girls of the country, '[so that] they went mad, and ran towards Ess Ruaid'.[81]

Meanwhile, the queen-goddess Medb had given the potent symbols of her divine sexuality, her 'comb, and casket unsurpassed',[82] to Erne, 'chieftainess of the girls of Crúachan', and they were in the maiden's possession when she was drowned with her party, under the waters of the new lough, 'the blameless vast noble lough Erne', with its 'pure light portion', which even the Christian god exalts, says the poet.

The effectiveness of the casket given by Medb to Erne depended upon a male response, which may be visible today in the notable concentration of stone effigies sited on islands in Lower Lough Erne. The row of eight statues on White Island are thought to have been carved before AD 900 and include a broadly smiling female, naked except for a very short cloak. She sits in a knees-apart manner, reminiscent of a sheela-na-gig, and has sometimes been classed as such. Her lack of breasts indicates a pre-maternal state and was probably the sculptor's way of distinguishing between maiden and mother. Next to her (now set in a twelfth-century chapel wall) is a heavier female carrying a box or perhaps a casket – even *the* casket of Medb; this second figure has the same rounded cheeks as her partner, and the hint of a smile. She may represent the maternal aspect of the libidinous maiden. Both have a pedigree traceable to the Old Stone Age in mainland Europe.

On nearby Lusty More Island a 1.2-metre-high megalith, carved as a woman, is 'grasping something in each hand',[83] as she opens in sexual readiness.

At the west end of Boa Island is a pillar statue of seventh-century date, 70 cm high, generally regarded as depicting two gods, back to back, with crossed arms.[84] The cases of Diarmaid and his rival, the youth in the green garb, and of Partholón with Tobar, supply the narrative theme of a male pair whose destinies are entwined, as the goddess abandons one male consort for another at Samer's end. One head of his 'Janus' image wears a forked beard. Both have arms crossed, and share a broad belt, and 'hair', plaited in a 'corn dolly' manner.

At Crúachain, sacred capital of Connacht, the emergence of the underworld libido was shown and felt in the bull-like figures of Olca Aí and his partner and rival, Armargen the Black-haired (*Olca*, 'he who wrongs a saint', with *aí*, 'poetic inspiration'). These powers are comparable to the Lios bull at Lough Gur. It was at Samain that Medb gathered the forces of Ireland and set out from Crúachain to seek the Brown Bull of Cualgne in Ulster to match against her own Whitehorn. The maiden Erne's paternity further strengthens the bull link, since her father, loud-shouting Borg-Ban, was also known as Good Borg the Bellowing,[85] which has a very bovine ring.

Overlooking Lower Lough Erne, a stone circle erected c. 2000 BC on the Co. Tyrone shore at Kiltierney still displays the horns of Good Borg in the 'recumbent' (skull) and two uprights which form a group on the west-north-west side of the eight-stone ring.[86] Facing her father's stonehorns across the circle is 'Erne' herself, represented by the carved bullaun stone, deliberately hollowed to collect water which, until very recently, was used in matters of female fecundity. The vulva-shape of this megalith is noteworthy (p. 184).[87]

An Iron Age bronze brooch, excavated from a nearby cairn, shows the open vulva together with coiled serpents in a different form. Both the stone and metal images have antecedents traceable to the Palaeolithic.

Whether called Erne or by some other name, the emergence at Samain of the New Year maiden from Queen Medb's síd is a recurring feature of Irish myth, and lived on in the traditional behaviour of young women at Samain. The following oral account by a Co. Donegal woman is of her mother's mid-nineteenth-century experiences.

Gold casket with solar symbols, 6 cm diameter, c. 800 BC, from Ballindemensig,
Co. Kerry. The casket given by Medb, daughter of the sun goddess, to Lady Erne,
may have been of this widespread Irish type, invariably made sealed up. It suggests
the unknowable Grianan or 'creation house' behind the face of the sun

(Below right) Sculptures of White Island, Lough Erne, 60 cm tall, late Iron Age.
The Boa Island Janus figure (below left), 75 cm tall, fifth century AD, may show
rival gods of consecutive years, obliged to share a threshold, and to demonstrate the
reversability of Time itself, for Summer's end was twinned with New Year's day

Hers was the last generation of young girls in the district to spend the summer herding on the mountain pastures before returning a few days before Samain to the company of the young men in the lowland farms. At that festival she 'came out' from the mountain cave, following the archaic behaviour track: 'The girls were delighted to be coming home after such a long stay in the hills, and they had a very merry time for a week after their return. Their people and the neighbours made them very welcome and it is they who were in good health and heart on their return – strong, healthy, ruddy, full of blood, with not a care in the world except to have a fine time.'[88]

Carved bullaun *stone, Kiltierney megalithic ring, near Lough Erne, Co. Fermanagh. To cure infertility, women drank from its pool till* c. AD *1930*

Flood, Fish, Word

Indulgence of appetites on the human level was patterned on the presumed behaviour of the gods. Gluttony and sexual desire meet in the Dagda and his young mistress, daughter of Indech. In Connacht they feasted on each other and on the fruits of earth and ocean; but she was a Fomorian princess and so, like Lady Ruad, represented the power of her Oceanic father.[89]

Winter Flood

The orgiastic flood of Samain quickly took on the threatening quality of wintry inundation, engulfing whole territories, and giving another twist to the Lough Erne story: 'Once the land under the Lough was the territory of a tribe called the Ernai who were drowned there when the Lough was created, and thereafter the lake burst *throughout the land of Erin*, and this is truer,'[90] says the Edinburgh *Dindshenchas*, where the lough is presented as the model for a national submergence.

At the onset of winter, gales and a drop in evaporation with falling temperatures, together with increased tides, were to be expected, as medieval 'Winter' poems record: 'The sea is running high...the voice of the barnacle goose sounds frequently...wild waves run...each least lake grown full; a full lake each puny pond.' 'Ireland's fish wander the more,' says the poet of 'Winter Cold'. 'Each fine furrow is a river, and a full pool is every ford. The size of a great sea is every angry lake...each lashing lake – a sea strong.'[91]

The Gaelic word *turboch* denotes lands that become winter lakes, and what the traveller Lithgow wrote in 1619 is applicable to the modern winter landscape, despite many drainage schemes:

And this I dare avow, there are more rivers, lakes, brooks, strands, quagmires, bogs and marshes in this country, than in all Christendom besides; for travelling there in winter, all my dayly solace was sinke downe comfort, whiles boggy-plunging deepes kissing my horse belly, over-mired saddle, body and all; and often or ever set a-swimming in great danger, both I and my guides of our lives; that for cloudy and fountayne-bred perils, I was never before reduced to such a floting laborinth...in five moneths space, I quite spoyled six horses, and myself as tyred as the worst of them.[92]

The sense of an entire country swamped was confirmed for him by finding that even *within* houses 'in foule weather scarcely can they find a drye part, whereupon to repose their cloud-baptized heads'. The ancient Irish word for winter was *Gaimrad*, from *Gam*, marriage; for in winter the elements of earth and water were conspicuously intertwined.

Annual floods were assimilated on the mythological level; for example, when two horses, belonging to Macha, daughter of Aed of Ess Ruaid, are released from her síd, 'A stream broke forth after them, and there was much foam on that stream, and the foam spread over the land exceedingly.'[93]

The *Dindshenchas* of the Plain of Louth states: 'The sea covered it [this plain] thirty years after the flood, hence it is called 'darkness of the sea', or 'it is under the sea's roof'. Or there was a magic sea over it, and an octopus therein, having a property of suction. It would suck in a man in armour till he lay at the bottom of its treasure bag. The Dagda came with his 'mace of wrath' in his hand, and plunged it down upon the octopus chanting these words: "Turn thy hollow head! Turn thy ravening body! Turn thy resorbent forehead! Avaunt! Begone!" Then the magic sea retired with the octopus.'[94]

In the myth cycle, the annual saturation of Ireland brought the entire country through the flood of coition, leading nine months later to the harvest birth event. The Samain affair, typified by Delgnat and Tobar, is the origin of the next amniotic sea, a gestation with which every part of the country identified, and so shared in the accumulation of 'pre-natal waters'. They spread around Lough Erne, and along the Shannonside meadows, filtering across the Midland Plain, singing the quiet music of re-saturated bogs, whilst roaring in fury down every mountain gulley.

The *Dindshenchas* carries the idea of national inundation to the primordial time of Bith, father of Cesair, and the first 'man' ever to settle in the country. Fleeing here, forty days before Noah's Flood, his hope of escaping the world inundation were disappointed. The waters 'overtook him on Sliab Betha [Slieve Beagh], and he was for a whole year beneath the waves, and then the sea gave him up again, and he was found dead on the mountain.' That mountain overlooks the Erne Valley, and Bith's experience may be regarded as the prototype for Aed's submergence in the arms of the inrushing sea goddess. In terms of Bith's role in the Ulster-Connacht dialogue, some ancient sources call his mountain 'one of the hills of Connacht, Sliab-Betha ever fresh'.[95] In both provinces, repeated floodings brought the old gods to life again in story-telling, as in physical fact.

Ireland does not claim to have *invented* the link between topographical flooding and feminine secretions. Rather, in the prehistoric world, hydrographic changes were often related to aspects of human reproduction. For example, in a story from ancient Persia, known to Herodotus, the mother of Kyros had a dream many months prior to his birth. Falling asleep in a sanctuary while tending goats, she dreamt

One-legged Sciapods of Eurasian fable
reappear as Irish Fomorians, erupting
from oceanic chaos to raid surface reality

'that so much water passed away from her in giving birth that it became a large stream, inundating all Asia, as far as the sea'.[96]

The belief, widespread in Europe, that conception took place by immersion in water, also served to unite the month of human marriages, Gam, with the regularly observed flooding of the Irish landscape at the start of winter. Then the whole island 'died' with the passing of the old year, and was conceived again in water, prior to its eventual rebirth during the following summer.

The Formorians

Perambulations from Connacht take us into the formless north-western ocean, where, in the uncertainties beyond sunset, wave after wave of mythic rivals are seen to lose their grip on Ireland.

Through the agency of the migrating divine salmon, and of other gods, Connacht myth also surges northwards, to the furthest reaches of Ulster, thereby completing a sunwise national cycle. So, the mythic monster is seen to swallow its own tail (and tale).

In Ireland, the supernatural beings most closely identified with inundations were the Fomorians. Folk etymology interprets their name as *Fo*, 'under', with *muir*, 'sea'.[97] Living mainly in the ocean, or on offshore islands, the Fomorians were regarded as coeval with the world itself. From their base on Tory Island, beyond the extreme northwest tip of Donegal, they regularly invaded the mainland.

They were often portrayed as one-legged, one-armed giants, or in the words of *Lebor Gabála*, 'men with single noble legs, and with single full hands', a condition midway between man and sea-serpent.

They represented the human admission that beyond the walls of organized beings and specific consciousnesses lay a sea of mutations. Fomorians laid claim to the solid land of Erin, knowing that without their contribution it would soon atrophy into a rigid state. They were particularly active at the onset of winter, when the crack between the ending of one year and the start of the next was wide enough for the forces of chaos to slip through, to alarm the population with a flood of darkness from the north-west, and to remind the individual of black forces concealed within the psyche.

187

At that season the Fomorians are reported to have claimed their annual tithes from the Irish at Mag Cetne, on The Plains of Tribute, which lay on the south side of the Ess Ruaid Falls, stretching towards the river Drowes along the coastal plain of north Sligo, and referred to in the Annals of Connacht as Mag Cetne of the Fomore. 'The extent of that tribute', wrote Keating, 'was two thirds of the children, and of the corn, and of the milch kine of the men of Ireland, to be offered to them [the Fomorians] every year on the eve of Samhain.'[98] In addition three full measures from every household in Ireland of the cream of milk, of the flour of wheat, and of butter to be brought to Toirinis (Tory Island), and a female steward who was called Liagh (*liach*, ladle) enforced the tax throughout Ireland.

Drownings were another aspect of the *Gamraid* ceremony – the marriage of young men to Indech mac Dimnann's daughter of Ocean, and the Dagda's lover. Bereaved mothers around the coasts of Ireland accepted these repeated claims with numb resignation.

Low-lying coasts were particularly vulnerable to Fomorian attack. The *Dindshenchas* for Mag Muireisce in Co. Sligo, 'that was visited by the strong rushing wave', speaks of a tumult of life-forms spewed directly from a sea monster, in an anarchic manner.[99] Other accounts recall 'a warm flood, an inundation of dead fish', and a time when 'the sea belched forth with thousands of children throughout Erin's four lands' (provinces).[100]

The only mythical group *not* to have been attacked by the Fomorians were the Fir Bolg, with whom they had much in common. For example, after the Fir Bolg had been defeated by the Tuatha Dé Danann in the First Battle of Moytura (Moytirra), at Cong, Co. Galway, the losers dispersed to 'certain outlying islands and other remote places'.[101] Their ocean nature is reflected in the names of coastal bays in the north and west incorporating 'bolg' – 'sea belly'.

The Nemedians

The mythical Nemedians were also unwilling to pay Fomorian tithes. Instead they attacked Tory Island to destroy the 'enemy' tower. The Fomorians then brought up reinforcements from Africa. During the ensuing battle neither side noticed the sea 'coming up under them', with a gigantic wave... filling up every side around them, and all but one boatload of Nemedians were drowned.'[102]

> The men of Erin were all at the battle,
> After the Fomorians came;
> All of them the sea engulphed,
> Save only three times ten.[103]

This last boatload sailed away, watched by the Fomorians who returned to their native watery depths from where, for hundreds of years, they nursed an Ireland cleansed of all human inhabitants back to health.

Perhaps that, too, is a cycle of events about to be repeated.

*Mam Ean, Co. Galway, Lughnasa pattern (Fair), by W.H., Bartlett, 1842. The
people gathered there are 'doing the rounds' of holy cave, spring and lough.
Connacht people traced their mythic origins to the soil-engrossed Fir Bolg, or Bag
Men, who were defeated by the clever Tuatha Dé Danann, and thereafter confined
to Connacht*

Each new group of mythical invaders was confronted by the
Fomorians. Neither men nor gods could escape the dialectic. Of the
Danann's battle with the Fomorians, Gray says that 'it stands at the
centre of Irish mythology'.[104] It is the stuff of eternity. Today the place
of the battle, Moytirra, Co. Sligo, is a scattered community of small
farms on a thin-soiled limestone plateau, overlooking Lough Arrow
in Co. Sligo, where huge blocks of limestone rest as the ice sheet left
them, scattered across the terrain. The five-metre-high Eglone stone,
an erratic of magnesium limetone, stands erect. Others, like mortally
wounded soldiers, lie around in the rushy pastures together with the
remains of megalithic court tombs, dating from the early third
millenium BC, in a timeless landscape. Nor is the battle forgotten by
the present inhabitants, who are proud to occupy land of such
significance.

The Dagda's tactic at the Second Battle was to deny water to the
Fomorians, the element they loved best.

And the Dagda asked the cup-bearer what power he wielded. He answered
that he would bring the twelve chief loughs of Ireland into the presence of
the Fomoire, and they would not find water in them, however thirsty they
were. [Lough Derg, Luimnig, Corrib, Ree, Mask, Strangford Lough, Belfast

189

Lough, Neagh, Foyle, Gara, Loughrea, and Márlock were named.] They would then proceed to the twelve chief rivers of Ireland – the Bush, Boyne, Bann, Blackwater, Lee, Shannon, Moy, Sligo, Erne, Finn, Liffey and Suir – and they would all be hidden from the Fomoire. Druids promised three showers of fire upon the Fomoire, and to lock their urine into their bodies, and into the bodies of their horses. The Dagda said, 'The power which you boast, I will wield it all myself.' 'You are the Dagda ['the Good God'] said everyone...'[105]

At the end of the battle the vanquished Fomorians returned to the sea. However, several of the protagonists, Bres and Lugh for example, had parents coming from *both* camps.

The purpose of the battle was to illuminate 'the principles fundamental to the ordering and maintenance of human society', including 'the contractual and magical aspects of sovereignty', writes Gray.[106]

Tuan

After Partholón's tribe was wiped out by plague, the work of reconstruction fell on the sole survivor, his brother's son, Tuan. *Tuan* means 'wholeness'. How could he live up to his name, and father a new and healthier human race?

Irish mythology implies that the recovery of good order involves the sacrifice of human separateness from the rest of the living world. Only by empathizing with, and thus *becoming*, the 'lower' species can humanity hope to return from spiritual, moral and physical death.

Thus for nine hundred years Tuan lost his human form, 'And these are the shapes he was: a hundred years he had in the form of a man, three hundred years in the form of a wild ox over waste places, two hundred years in the form of a wild stallion, three hundred years in the form of a solitary bird, a hundred years in the form of a salmon.' In that shape a fisher took him to the queen of Lord Red-neck, the Ulster King. The queen desired the salmon to mate with her. 'So he was urged of her, and of her Tuan was conceived at last.'

As with the Last Supper, union with the godhead sometimes involved eating:

> When she saw the pure salmon
> the queen desired him.
> So that was assigned to her, a good course,
> and she ate it all by herself;
> the very noble queen became pregnant,
> and thence Tuan was conceived.[107]

Either way, the work of restoration depended on feminine invitation, but since there were no women left alive, the queen of Lord Red-neck must have been a goddess, wife of a god. When a goddess and shape-shifting man come together, a new human race may be initiated.

Thus Tuan-the-fish fathered Tuan the first human child, in the síd of Grianan Ailech near Londonderry, the northern marker of Partholón's division of Ireland. Fishy Tuan reclaimed the female womb as a symbolic universal ocean. The human child born from that deep could then arrive in the land-world with the knowledge of submarine wholeness, and was therefore fit to recreate comparable conditions on earth. A new human order could then arise, having a purified bloodstream modelled on the salmon's habitat. His river connected earth to sea, Fomorians to sky deities, and fish with people. Renewed hope flows from the story.

Fish, tongue, and mythic word

The annual migration of salmon through Atlantic Irish waters from west to north provides a natural context for the linkage of Ess Ruaid and Grianan Ailech salmon myths. They collaborate to make the sound of a new utterance, and a renewed cycle. Hence, it is the queen of the far north who touches the salmon with her tongue.

In many Indo-European languages, the final part of several words meaning 'tongue' also serve as terms for 'fish'. This fish-tongue amalgam can be assigned to a very early date, with 'tongue' being derived from 'fish'.[108] (In Achill Island, Co. Mayo, the sole-fish is called *teanga cait*, literally 'tongue chaff'.)

These coincidences may arise from the mythic need for *verbal* conception, whereby a tongue, sounding in the bowl of the mouth, is involved in every divine birth, since *the story must be told* before any parturition can be seen as sacred. A deity is born when word of mouth and delivery from the womb are twinned together.

In nature the male salmon comes from the sea during late winter in good, fat, condition. Travelling up Lough Foyle it enters the river Derg and so arrives at the brink of Lough Derg and St Patrick's Purgatory. The ability, persistence, and strength of salmon in surmounting waterfalls and other obstacles during their ascent is well known. Big salmon can jump about three metres in the air on their way to the spawning place – usually a gravel-bottomed reach of moderate current selected by the female in late autumn. She excavates the gravel by vigorous movements of her tail, to make a hollow thirty centimetres deep, and a metre long. During the spawning, the male lies alongside the female. Roe and milt (sperm) are shed into the 'redd', and covered together under the gravel. Then the female makes another gully upstream of the first.[109]

River and landscape act as a surrogate mother to this annual event. In this sense Tuan couples with Ériu-the-land-goddess every year. Each year humanity is offered a fresh start by their example, as the headwaters of the river Derg lead from a purgatory of estrangement towards the lost love of Earth.

The whirlpool of the natural cycle is the shrine where all the gods have their being, under the sign of the fish.

Part Five **MIDE**
The Spreading Centre

The Centre Stone

Mide and Ériu

The Irish word for province, *cóiced*, also means a fifth; yet the ancient and continuing division of the island into the *four* provinces of Ulster, Munster, Leinster and Connacht seems to leave no room for a fifth part.

The discrepancy has sometimes been explained by recalling that at certain historical periods Munster was subdivided into two, so turning the four provinces into five.[1] Yet many scholars think that the elusive fifth stands for something more fundamental.

The likelihood is that ever since the Stone Age (and despite numerous boundary changes in detail), Ireland has been subdivided into four provinces, held together by a mystical fifth, territorially elusive, yet vital to the cohesion of the whole sacred array.

The fifth province was called Mide. The four-plus-one pattern, of which Mide formed the centre, could be seen as the predictable outcome of Ireland's compact shape. Malin Head in the far north lies 400 kilometres from the south coast of Munster, compared with a maximum island breadth of 340 kilometres. This makes a quadrilateral division around a shared centre point, a convenient practical arrangement.

But since the mythic view of reality declares that efficiency is the outcome of magical accord between the seen and the unseen, there is more to Mide than simple geometry.

In Mide, people could encounter the gods on the most sacred ground. Like a good idea, its space was small yet extendable. As a national 'head and brain', it co-ordinated intelligences from the other provinces.

Human spatial awareness has always been profoundly affected by the cardinal directions of the human body, to the furthest horizons of terrestrial and spiritual possibilities. Ancient God-filled space normally displayed the symmetries of the worshipper's frame, just as the

---

(Previous page) The Great Yew, Crom Castle. Seen from Mide, Ireland was inseparable from the limbs of deity

*Aill na Mireann, the 'Stone of Divisions',
symbol of the four provinces and their unity in
Mide. The stone was also called* Umbilicus
Hiberniae, *the 'Navel of Ireland', and 'The
Stone of the Cat'. As Mide, the fifth province,
it is seen here from south (top left), north (top
right), east (bottom right) and west (bottom left)*

envisaged gods often took anthropomorphic form. The left-right balance (Ulster-Munster), of human eyes, ears, nostrils, nipples, testes, arms, legs, and sets of fingers and toes, disposed evenly on either side of a central axis, is bisected at right angles by the equally physical reality of back (Connacht) and sunrise-facing front (Leinster).[2] From Mide, the qualities specific to the mythic space of each of the surrounding four provinces were differentiated and co-ordinated into a divine island metabolism.

Dumézil confirms that 'the natural concept of four cardinal points and a centre is found widely on every continent', and forms the basis of many cosmologies.[3] The Indian *Rig Veda* speaks of the five directions as North, South, East, West, and 'Here'. In ancient Ireland, Mide was 'Here' to everyone. It was held in common.

Mide, the notional centre of Ireland, was conceived as a point where an umbilical cord attached the country to the womb of the gods, who endlessly created and sustained its existence from above and below. Yet Mide was a real place, namely the Hill of Uisnech or Uisneach, now in Co. Westmeath. It was also identified with the large boulder called Aill na Mireann, standing on Uisnech's south-west slope, *and* with the various archaeological sites visible on the hill.

The extensive view of the Irish midlands gained from Uisnech may also be regarded as integral to Mide, but not in the sense of the political annexation which King Tuathal Techmar attempted (and for a while sustained) in the second century AD. Nor should mythic Mide be confused with the modern counties of Meath or of Westmeath.

Seen from Mide, the energies of the four provinces could be woven by enlightened observation into a web of radial and concentric 'place-events'. From Mide, the array of distant hills and mountains, and the solar and lunar risings or settings which coincided with their summits, were the stuff of a god-given mandala. This served to reveal Sacred Ireland in its entirety, and set it within the orb of a divine universe, rendered synonymous with the eyeball of the human worshipper.

The Irish word *mide* means 'neck', and the fifth province may be regarded as the means of joining head to body, idea to thing, and body to soul. Mide was almost nothing, yet everything. It was the making of a divine island, called by the name of a living goddess, Ériu. In her name every province had a place. She was their collective origin and product, the comprehensive landlady, who built, owned, named, and lived in the island-home.

The Stone of Divisions (Aill na Mireann), and Omphalos

The entire fifth province can be condensed into Aill na Mireann, the Stone of Divisions. This fissured and fragmenting limestone boulder stands on the south-west slopes of Uisnech Hill thirty metres below the summit, where it was deposited during the last Ice Age as a glacial erratic, before the first human beings arrived in Ireland. Its grey mass, nearly five metres high, traditionally symbolized Ireland, united in its divisions.

The Yellow Book of Lecan describes how the god Fintan, son of Ocean, returned to Aill na Mireann: 'It is long since I drank a drink of the Deluge over the navel of Uisnech', says the god, implying that the Flood of prenatal waters were also centred over Ireland's 'mother' stone. Fintan's task was to re-establish the Stone at the core of national life, after Tara had threatened to disrupt the pattern.

He was asked: 'O Fintan, how has our island been divided?' He replied, 'Knowledge in the West, Battle in the North, Prosperity in the East, Music in the South, Royalty at the Centre.' At Aill na Mireann, the attribute of the provincial directions combined into a synthesis, where 'royalty' was the display of the divine on earth.

'The points of the great provinces run towards Uisnech, they have divided yonder stone through into five,' explained Fintan, 'And he assigned a ridge of it to every province in Ireland.'[4]

The stone's central role continued to be acknowledged in the present century, when, in the struggle for Irish independence from British rule, a hole was sunk into the top to receive a flag-pole around which political meetings were held. (Traces of the rotting stump remain in the stone socket; but of the four provinces, only three accepted the revived symbolism, and to this day, six of the Ulster counties stand aloof. Of old Ulster, only counties Donegal, Cavan, Monaghan and Louth are incorporated into the Republic.)

In *Finnegans Wake* Joyce calls the stone 'Mearing Stone'[5] – an archaic English term meaning 'boundary stone', and chiming, if not rhyming, with Aill na Mireann. In fact the stone has several names. Local people in the 1930s called it *Carraig a' chait*, The Rock of the Cat, from its supposed likenesss to a cat crouching to pounce on a mouse; but this title, O'Donovan believed, was a corruption of *Carraig Choithrigi*, found in the Book of Armagh, meaning the Rock of Division of the Sovereignty, from *coite*, 'slice, bit'; and *rige*, 'kingdom, sovereignty, act of reigning'.[6]

The name which appears on the Ordnance map, Aill na Mireann, is close to this in meaning: *aill*, 'a cliff, a rock'; *mireann*, 'a portion, a share', expanding in Old Irish to *mireanna*, 'portions, shares, morsels, food, and parts of a country'. Old Irish also enlarges the stony *aill* into the form *aille* – 'the act of praising, or giving thanks'.

The ancient ring bank, eight metres diameter, which surrounds the stone and sets it in a saucer-shaped hollow, confirms that it was the centre of attention. Great chunks of the rock have split, and wedged themselves into a heap against the south-east side. The weathering on these pieces shows that the collapse probably happened prior to the first human arrivals. No one now accepts O'Donovan's view that they were 'erected into a splendid cromlech'.[7] Yet chance has left a tunnel through the blocks at ground level, running east-west, and offering a symbolic access to the abyss big enough for an adult to crawl through, and perhaps used in rebirth ceremonies.

Irish myth suggests that the subdivision of Ireland from Aill na Mireann was re-enacted by successive waves of settlers who wished to claim divine sanction for their invasion. Thus Giraldus wrote of the 'Five Sons of Dela' (alias the Fir Bolg), that on 'coming to Ireland from Greece...their bounds met at a stone...called *Umbilicus Hiberniae*, the navel of Ireland, because it stands in the middle of the country. Each of the five brothers had a small portion of Meath abutting on the stone just mentioned, in as much as that territory had from the earliest times been the richest part of the country, having a level plain, and being very fertile and productive of corn. Hence none of the five brothers wished to be shut out from it'.[8] Many parts of Ireland, Co. Wexford, for example, are much more fertile than West Meath, but the prestige of Uisnech ensured that the reputation of its agriculture rose with the omphalos.

The omphalos tradition is deeply rooted in European and Near-Eastern culture, and it is likely that the earliest Irish brought with them from the continent a belief in the omphalos as a centre of the universe. On the Eurasian continent, so in Ireland, the human navel was widely held to be the source of the human embryo, and (by extension) the divine omphalos-navel was believed to be the origin of the earth, born of a mother goddess, 'chicken and egg' together.

Even in countries like Israel, from which the mother goddess had been officially expelled, birth symbolism persisted around the omphalos. A Rabbinical text states: 'As an embryo proceeds from the navel onward, so God begun the creation of the world from its navel onward and from thence it spread in different directions.'[9]

The Uisnech Horse Temple

At the still centre of Ireland, one would expect the fastest forms of the sun deities to take a rest. Therefore at Uisnech the solar horses were stabled. According to the *Wooing of Étáin* manuscript, the horse god Eochaid Ollathair had a house on Uisnech, 'with Ireland stretching equally far from it on every side, to south and north, to east and west'. Eochaid's name is derived from *Éach*, 'a horse', and *O'llathair* means 'father of all'. This horse god of the central hill was synonymous with the Dagda, chief of the Dannans, 'who used to work wonders for the people and control the weather and crops'.

The prehistoric Uisnech stables of the Dagda as horse god may have been found by Macalister in 1929, at site 17, on the north flank of the hill, facing the same god's Ulster house at Grianan Ailech. In outward form, site 17 displays an outer circular rampart and ditch, 78 metres in diameter, with a raised inner hub, also surrounded by a bank, and with an internal ditch. Both rings have an entrance aligned to the north-east.[10]

Beneath the paved floor of the inner ring lie two sets of tunnels or *souterrains*. The southern souterrain was possibly designed to resemble

A ⊣ ⊢ B

B

Banks

Ditches

The Mare

The Stallion

N
↑

0   30 metres

'womb'

Stable of the horse deities, Site 17,
Hill of Uisnech, fifth century AD.
The wheel-shaped enclosure conceals
two elaborate sets of tunnels beneath
the paved floor. Their forms can be
recognized as monumental horse
deities, like the White Horse of
Uffington in Berkshire, England
(below). Round the inner enclosure
the divine 'mare' is pursued by the
Dagda-as-stallion. (Literary sources
confirm that the Dagda lived on
Uisnech.) A Saxon brooch of
'prenatal triplets', gilt bronze, AD
500, was found over the mare's
womb chamber

scale of feet   0   50   100   150   200   250

and *be* the Dagda as galloping stallion. He addresses his partner, the northern *souterrain*, shaped like a mare.

For Iron Age communities, the assumed integration of spiritual and physical life was brought to reality partly by means of gigantic images of the living gods. That was the tradition inherited from the Neolithic community, an orthodoxy unchallenged until the arrival of Christianity. In subsequent oral belief these buildings continued to be called giants and giantesses, reflecting their construction as supernatural beings.

When laid out on this scale, the hidden gods could be seen *and* entered; idea, icon, and physical experience were combined.

St Patrick at Uisnech

In the fifth century AD Uisnech was visited by St Patrick, according to Tirechán, who claimed that the saint 'remained beside Petra Coithrigi at Uisneach, intending to establish a church. He was opposed in this ambition by the two sons of Niall, Fiachu and Endae. Patrick began to curse them, but no sooner had he said "A curse...", than his follower Senchall interjected "...be on the stones of Uisneach". "Be it so," said Patrick, and ever since the curse fell, the stones of Uisneach have not been of any use, even as washing stones,'[11] i.e., stones suitable for heating washing water. The limestone of Uisnech *is* notably fissured and prone to fracture.

This incident of the joint curse is an indication of the awesome risks involved in damning *Aill na Mireann*, since the cohesion of Ireland depended upon the rock. Who can blame St Patrick if he was reluctant to assume sole responsibilty for the deed?

To indicate the success of Patrick's intervention and the arrival of a new vision, the saint was honoured with a well on the hill, surrounded today by cast-iron railings, made in England. Within the enclosure, a stout wooden lid and rusting corrugated iron sheets cover a concrete tank, with plentiful water, and many snails climbing the dank walls.

Uisnech and Stonehenge

Exchanges between Uisnech and Britain took another form in the medieval belief, reported by Geoffrey of Monmouth, that Stonehenge came from Uisnech. He wrote: 'They are mystical stones, and of a medicinal virtue. The giants of old brought them from the farthest coast of Africa and placed them in Ireland, while they inhabited that country. Their design in this was to make baths in them, when they should be taken with any illness. For their method was to wash the stones and put their sick into the water which infallibly cured them... There is not a stone there which has not some healing virtue.'[12]

Uthor Pendragon was sent to Ireland at the head of fifteen thousand men, in order to bring the stones to Britain. Having defeated the Irish king, Gillomanius, the British advanced on Uisnech, and came to The

Giants' Dance, the sight of which filled them with joy and admiration. However, the men were unable to shift the megaliths till Merlin personally 'placed in order the engines that were necessary, and took down the stones with incredible facility'.[13]

This fable is untrue, but since (as we shall see) Uisnech and Stonehenge were both centres of a prehistoric sun goddess religion, exchange of *some* kind between them was to be expected.

Uisnech was an Irish Jerusalem from which gifts, comparable to imagined fragments of the True Cross, were probably distributed to sanctify other places. Seen from Uisnech, the British Isles are the *Irish* Isles, for each sacred centre acts as a world focus.

Fintan and the Reunion of Species

When Fintan, who had featured in Cesair's creation myth, returned to Uisnech, he brought to the hill his own polymorphic ability to manifest as man, salmon, eagle and hawk – the last two creatures being noted for their keen sight. Through these changes he made inferences beyond human and superhuman exclusivity, to reconstruct a parliament of the species. In this sense every generation needs to rediscover Uisnech.

The Uisnech perspective, as recommended by Fintan, did not require the abandonment of self-centredness, but a return to a more ambitious definition of the term. In the same spirit, J. Leslie, in his recent discussion of the Anthropic, or Man-Centred Cosmological Principle, writes '*Psychocentric* would be a better description, since a vision which dealt only with human life would fall into triviality'[14] (not to mention ecological catastrophe).

Fintan speaks for the community of life as a whole, by combining a delight in differences with a demonstration of their unity. In this he supported the goddess Ériu – Ireland personified, who was prone to appear as a hag, a hooded crow, *or* a beautiful young woman.

Ériu and the Sons of Míl

Lebor Gabála describes how Ériu returned to Mide in order to negotiate with the invading Sons of Míl. Equally, *their* prospects of settlement depended on reaching an accommodation with her. Standing at the centre of her island-self, she held the title deeds of legitimacy, sealed by the continuity that she could confer on newcomers. Consequently, the Sons of Míl (usually identified with the gods of the Celts, invading after 500 BC) 'had a colloquy' with Ériu at Uisnech. She said: 'Long have soothsayers had knowledge of your coming. Yours shall be this island for ever; and to the east of the world there shall not be a better island. No race shall be there more numerous than yours.' 'Good is that,' said Amorgen, their poet; 'good is the prophecy.' 'No right were it to thank her,' said Eber Donn, eldest of the Sons of Míl, 'thank *our* gods, and our *own* might.' 'To thee 'tis equal', said Ériu; 'thou shalt have no profit of this island, nor shall thy progeny.' Then, turning to the others, she asked: 'A gift to me ye Sons of Míl, and ye children of Breogan, that my name shall be on this island.' 'It shall be its principal name', said Amorgen,[15] content to accept it as the established key to the island's sanctity, and the seed-bed of his hopes.

On the political level, it was customary for the claimant to the high throne of Ireland to 'marry' Ériu at a ceremonial *banais rígi*, or 'wedding feast of kingship'.[16]

Though militarily defeated, Ériu ensured that Eire remained hers. Hers was the mind and body within which kings and gods, including Lugh and Jehovah, came to life. It had been so since the start of human experience in Ireland, according to Macalister, who equates her name with Cesair, the 'bringer forth' of the land,[17] which was symbolized by the primary hill of Uisnech, and by the complementary birth mountain, Árd Éireann, on Slieve Bloom.

The contract collapsed only when the invading powers ceased to believe in the land's divinity, and came to regard Ériu as no more than an allegorical figure ripe for economic exploitation. This reduction is anticipated (and not without some affection) in the writings of Luke Gernon, a seventeenth-century English officer in Ireland. He wrote:

It was my chance once to see a map of Europe . . . described in the lineaments of a naked woman [and] in such a forme will I represent our Ireland.

This Nymph of Ireland, is at all poynts like a yong wenche that hath the greene sickness for want of occupying. She is very fayre of visage, and hath a smooth skinn of tender grasse. Indeed she is somewhat freckled (as the Irish are) some partes darker than other. Her flesh is of a softe and delicat mould of earthe, and her blew vaynes trayling through every part of her like ryvoletts. She hath one master vayne called the Shannon.

She hath three other vaynes called the sisters, the Seuer, the Noyer & the Barrow, wch rysing at one spring, trayle through her middle partes, and ioyne together in theyr going out. Her bones are of polished marble, the grey marble, the blacke, the redd, and the speckled, so fayre for building that their houses shew like colledges, and being polished, is most rarely embelished. Her breasts are round hillockes of milk-yeelding grasse, and that so fertile, that they contend wth the vallyes. And betwixt her leggs (for Ireland is full of havens), she hath an open harbor, but not much frequented.[18]

Prior to the mechanization of thought in seventeenth-century England, those who had come for conquest sooner or later entered into the body of Ériu's sacred word, name, and land, and in doing so, played out the role of the male gods. Like Geároid Iarla, they consummated the mythological marriage anew, sharing her bed, her food, and the grave of her outstretched form.

As traditionally understood, Ériu was an active not a static deity. Her name means 'the regular traveller', according to O'Rahilly, who points out that although she was primarily the deity of Ireland's plains, mountains, rivers and springs, her scope went beyond that to include the sun.[19] Her nominated husband was Mac Grene, meaning 'son of

Sun', and grandson of the Dagda, and she herself often bore the epithet '*ain*', as in '*Ériu ain*', and '*i nErind ain*', wherein she neatly effected a merger with Áine of Munster, and so brought a redoubled power to the Beltaine festival at Uisnech. There, as we shall see, she also acted as foster-mother to Mide, whose job it was to distribute the sacred fire, derived from the sun.

Ériu – Fódla – Banba

Ériu was one name of a triple goddess. Her 'sisters', Banba and Fódla, being synonymous with her, were therefore alternative names for Ireland.

In Ériu's colloquy at Uisnech, her sister-goddess Fódla or Fotla is sometimes named in place of Ériu, as participating in the bargaining with the sons of Míl.

As a language word, *fotla* (*fodhla*), 'explaining, revealing, and division', is related to *fodlach*, 'a division, a part', and to *fothla*, 'withdrawing, deducting, and abducting'.

Ériu and Fódla are complementary. Ériu is the 'whole' and Fódla is the 'parts'. They are both necessary to an understanding of Ireland, and both are required at Aill na Mireann, where the whole and the parts appear together.

Similarly, in marrying a male version of the sun god, Ériu (as the whole island) chose Mac Greine, the whole sun, *grian*. By contrast, Fódla wedded Mac Cecht, (*checht*, 'ploughshare'), to suit her distinctive cutting and dividing role.

At Aill na Mireann, Fódla-Ériu combined to reveal their interdependence. (Without subdivision there can be no characters, and thus no action. Without the whole, there is no shape to the play.) Hand-in-hand the divine sisters lay these inescapable truths on the stone, which reflects both their name-words in its outwards appearance; the rock is divided, yet whole.

Another aspect of the collaboration between the two, as described in *Lebor Gabála*, is that when one is at Uisnech the other appears on Slieve Mish, a mountain near Tralee in Co. Kerry, and vice-versa.[20] Since *mis* means 'a month', and its related *mistae*, 'menstrual flow', an Uisnech-Slieve Mish axis may be said to illustrate the fusion of Space with Time. The world of Ériu-Fódla was, it appears, a space-time continuum, where interchangeable terms operated.

Additional weight is lent to this possibility by Fódla's appearance at a third place (in another version of the same text), namely at Slieve Éblinne, also called Felim, in Co. Limerick. Since this mountain was (and is) one of a group of twelve clustered around, and so including the Mother Mountain, Mauher Slieve, a division of the year into twelve months may have been the intended reference.

While Ériu and Fódla were concerned with the establishment and subdivision of Ireland's surface, the third member of the trinity, Banba, seems to have had responsibility for the country's vertical axis. Banba married a sungod called Mac Cuill ('son of Holly'), which suggests a honeymoon in the midwinter underworld. There she was associated with the supernatural pigs of the síd, judging by the similarity between her name and the language words *banb*, 'a young pig', *banabh*, 'a suckling pig', and *banban*, 'a small pig'. Like her sisters, she was synonymous with Ireland in its entirety, which may help to explain why Keating gives Pig Island (Muicinis) as a name for Eire, following a tradition of worship imported from continental Europe. There, 'The connection between the Vegetation Goddess and pigs', writes Gimbutas, 'goes back to the Neolithic era. Sculptures of pigs are known from all parts of Old Europe. The fast-growing body of the pig will have impressed early agriculturalists; its fattening must have been compared to corn growing and ripening, so that its soft fats apparently come to symbolize the earth itself, causing the pig to become a sacred animal probably no later than 6000 BC.'[21]

The *Dindshenchas* implies that of all the creatures on earth, the pig was most desired at the Uisnech centre stone, and was brought there, in the form of tribute from every farmstead, to re-establish the vertical link between human farm and subterranean síd. 'So the right belongs to the gentle heir of the plain of Mide mirthful and bright, even a measure of fine meal with a white pig for every rooftree in Erin'[22] or 'a sack of corn with a pig from every housetop in Ireland.'[23] By implication this brings to Uisnech the third member of the trinity, 'White Banba', as *Lebor Gabála* calls her.

Mide Fire and Druids' Tongues

According to the *Dindshenchas*, Mide, foster-son of Ériu, was the first to light a fire in Erin. It was 'a mystic fire'. 'Hard by Uisneach he kindled it' reported Keating.[24] From his foster-mother's central hearth, for 'seven years good was it ablaze . . . it was a sure truce, so that he shed the fierceness of the fire for a time over the four quarters of Erin . . . and from that fire were kindled every chief fire and every chief hearth in Ireland.'[25]

In return for the sun-goddess-derived hearth-fire, without which domestic life would have been impossible, Mide and his successors asked for the tithe of flour and pork. Mide the god was concerned with the art of sharing, and the harmony that flows from its practice, as a matter of mythic truth.

But in the Iron Age, the Irish druids suddenly refused to pay the Uisnech pig tax, saying that 'the smoke of Uisnech has brought an ill mood to our mind, . . . Hateful to us is the fire that hath been kindled in the land.' 'Then Mide the untiring assembled the Druids of Erin into one house, and cut out their tongues (a harsh presage) . . . and buried them under the earth of Uisnech in mighty Mide, and sat him down over the tongues, he, the chief seer and chief poet.'[26]

As a metaphor, Mide's action implied that poets who oppose or are indifferent to the exchange of gifts between worlds are no poets, and

The sacred pig, introduced from
continental Europe, became the
Irish deity Banba, controller of the
vertical axis between underworld
and sky. (Scene of Fair Day,
Castlewellan, Co. Down.) Banba
was one aspect of the triune
goddess (Ériu-Fódla-Banba),
perhaps symbolized before 3000 BC
in this New Grange design (left)

had better fall silent. The purpose of language, as heard at Uisnech, was to articulate a sense of cohesion.

Uisnech Hill and the Fire Eye

Seen from any direction or distance the Hill of Uisnech fails to dominate. It stands discreetly tucked in among undulating countryside. The summit rises 181 metres above sea level, but is less than 80 metres above the nearby valley road from Athlone to Mullingar. Nor is the Hill's form memorably compact. Lobes run north, south and west, while three or four swellings compete with the 'real' hilltop for pre-eminence. Uisnech is grass-coloured, with a glint of grey limestone showing through here and there. Black and white bullocks romp about.

Yet looking *from* Uisnech, another kind of view can be had. In every direction, hills and mountains animate a horizon where fore-ground greens are dyed in easy stages to make oceanic blues. These hint at seas lying beyond the topographic panorama, and in a complete encirclement. At Uisnech we sail in the good ship Ériu. Sixty years ago Macalister wrote: 'It would be difficult to match in Ireland the range of prospect from the top. The view embraces the whole central plain, and the rim of hills which enclose it on all sides. Landmarks in no less than twenty counties are to be identified from the summit.'[27]

Yet in trying to reconstruct Uisnech as a centre of pre-Christian Irish gravity, Eliade's warning that sacred space should not be confused with the simple space of 'realistic' human observation should be remembered. 'In mythical geography, sacred space is *the* essentially real space, and in the archaic world the sacred is the only indubitable reality.'[28] Therefore the question remains, what was the view from Uisnech worth in sacred terms?.

Ancient Mide was encircled by peaks and hills which contributed varying elements (and in differing degrees) towards a complete web of sacred relationships. The ring of 'real' views was passed, via sight to insight, in a symbol-making process activated by ritual, and thereby turned into myth. In this way, the landscape became an authentic version of a divine life story, and Ériu breathed again.

At night, the process was probably assisted by beacon fires, lit in response to an Uisnech hearth. As Macalister observed, 'beacon-fires lit upon its summit could be seen over a quarter of Ireland, and in most directions the hills upon the horizons could relay the message of the beacon as far as the sea-coast. The claim of Uisneach to be the centre of Ireland is thus quite justifiable, even though it may not be mathematically accurate.'[29]

Consequently, by employing only two concentric beacon rings around the central Uisnech fire point, the entire country could be encompassed within a single intelligence, in a great 'fire-eye', glittering simultaneously on many a muddy estuary and pebbled shore, from sea to sea. Such a nation-wide double ring of bonfires would have

1 Granard, Co. Longford
2 Slieve Beagh, Co. Tyrone
3 Slieve Glah, Co. Cavan
4 Sliab na Caillighe, Co. Meath
5 Frewin Hill (Fremu), Co.
    Westmeath
6 Croghan Hill, Co. Offaly
7 Dunmurry Hill, Co. Kildare
8 Wicklow Mountains, Co.
    Wicklow
9 Cullenagh Mountain, Co. Laois
10 Mount Leinster, Co. Carlow
11 Croghtenelogh, Co. Kilkenny
12 Slieve Bloom, Co. Laois
13 Mauhler Slieve, Co. Tipperary
14 Tountinna, Co. Tipperary
15 Slieve Bernagh, Co. Clare
16 Slieve Aughty, Co. Galway
17 Slieve Bawn, Co. Roscommon
18 Slieve Anierin, Co. Roscommon
19 Ardagh (Brí Léith), Co. Longford
20 Cuilcagh, Co. Cavan

From Uisnech, hills and mountains in twenty counties can be identified. Beacons lit
on their summits, answering Mide fire, could unite the provinces in a two-way
ring of observances (below). A further outer array of hilltop fires is intervisible
between Ring One and all coasts

(Right) Megalithic 'fire-eye'
carved at Sliab na Caillighe,
the 'Hill of the Hag',
Loughcrew, Co. Meath

been a co-ordinated work of community art on a colossal scale. Each widely scattered group may be assumed to have assembled on their regional mountain to contribute a fire to the overall pattern, thus knowing, and being known by Ériu, the idea of Ireland.

Crawford's book *The Eye Goddess* traced the use of the eye symbol as one of the key images of the Neolithic across the Near East and Europe.[30] Eye symbols, engraved in the fourth millennium BC as part of the original iconography of several Irish monuments, show the presence of the 'eye goddess' in Ireland. Where a symbol was in general use as an image of divine vitality, its enlargement on to a topographic scale presented no difficulties in terms of understanding, any more than is today encountered in the proposition that a piece of coloured cloth known as the tricolour or Union Jack *is* the country which it represents. Once the visual 'gestalt' had entered common currency, the fact that the hills and mountains around the Uisnech horizon were at differing distances from the centre would have constituted no difficulty. Rather, a superimposed idea of *objective* vision is the illusion, for the eye prefers to interpret what it sees on the basis of patterned, shared experience, which finds symbolic expression in our 'mental maps'. Modern cartographers are well aware of the processes involved, and might recognize the Uisnech-based fire eye as 'an information field and a perception surface',[31] where the goddess Ériu was perceived to be at home, across the field of Ireland. Religious art tends to draw the most powerful of mental maps because *everything* depends on them. Ériu's bonfire map linked province to nation, home to island, and individual to godhead.

Confirmation of the ancient pattern comes from John Toland, an Irish-speaking scholar, born in the Inishowen peninsula, who, in 1740, recalled chains of fire-beacon sites, 'which being every one...in sight of some other, could not but afford a glorious show over a whole nation'. He states that at each site a *pair* of fires was lit (perhaps complementing the paired human eyes), 'one on the carn', or heap of stones, 'another on the ground', together evoking the rising sun.[32] These 'prodigious' fires were lit on May-eve, for the Beltaine festival. He adds: 'I remember one of those Carns on Fawn-hill...known by no other name but that of Bealteine, and facing another such Carn on the top of Inch-hill.'

Beltaine and the Uisnech Fire Temple

Keating, the seventeenth-century Gaelic historian, lends Uisnech weight to these bonfire reports by clearly specifying Beltaine as the time of the annual *oenach* or gathering at Uisnech: 'It was at Bealltine that this fair took place, at which it was their custom to exchange with one another their goods, their wares and their valuables. They also used to offer sacrifices to the chief god they adored, who was called Beil, and it was their wont to light *two* fires in honour of Beil in every district in Ireland, and to drive a weakling of each species of cattle that were in the district between the two fires as a preservative to shield them from all the diseases during that year.'[33]

'Beil' has long since been dismissed as his invention, but the twin fires, confirmed by folk practice, though losing their Uisnech-co-ordinated shape, flickered on in every village of the nation, and 'the more ignorant Irish still drive their cattle through these fires, as an effectual means of preserving them from future accidents', wrote Ledwich in 1804.[34] In Limerick City, May Eve is still called Bonfire Night.

Macalister's 1927 excavation of a hill-top sanctuary, 'the most important enclosure upon the summit of Uisnech, at the head of an ancient roadway', revealed a substantial layer of ash across the southern arc of a prehistoric ring ditch, which 'must either have been a relic of a perpetual fire, or else (and more probably) of a great bonfire lit at frequent intervals'.

This is strongly suggestive of a sanctuary site. Carcasses of animals had been burnt on the site, and vast quantities of their bones were scattered about promiscuously.[35] He interpreted these conflagrations and feasts as the Beltaine fires of Keating's seventeenth-century report, and as the national hearth mentioned in the *Dindshenchas* – 'the tangible traces of the great sacred flame, which made so deep an impression upon folk memory'.[36]

This near-circular sanctuary, 55 metres in diameter, was defined by a ditch 120 cm deep and 100 cm broad at the base, making a simple ring which nevertheless may have acted as the pupil to the eye of the *greater* fire ring, visible all around the horizon, linking distant mountain to mountain, just as Aill na Mireann symbolically incorporated all the rock of Ireland into its relatively small body. The sanctuary ditch was probably dug in the Neolithic, and certainly before the Iron Age. Filled with a brown soil (mixed along its western circumference with layers of 'black' vegetation), the ditch may also have stood for the marriage ring of Ireland's agricultural hopes to the divinities of fire. These gods may have been represented further as effigies, set in the massive post holes which, in pairs, addressed the ring's easterly sunrise entrance.

As the May-Eve twilight dropped into true blackness, we may suppose that the bonfire lit at Uisnech, and believed to be supernatural, initiated the far-flung circles of fire. Through them the goddess re-occupied and *saw* her whole land, and by the embers, promised to return next day with an entire summer's sunshine.

Old Irish *súil* means 'eye' *and* 'sun'. So, in a word, the gap between human subject and divine object disappears as a light-beam enters the eyeball. *Súil*, the divine intelligence, integrates with the eyes on earth of bird and beast and humankind and thereby enters the brain and heart. This is typical of mythic perception, where phenomena become distinct and separate only to re-unite in a god-given word. No wonder that the population stumbled up mountains through gathering darkness to have this good fortune visibly confirmed. There they heard the crackle of yellow furze turning momentarily orange as it leapt above the winter world of grey and black ash, to usher in the first dawn of the summer half. (The *Vita Tripartita* expressly states that on Beltaine Eve every domestic hearth-fire in Ireland was quenched. This imposed darkness further served to focus attention on Uisnech, from where, it was hoped, the sacred gift would rise again, later that night.)

The divinity of the fire-eye was confirmed in the ninth century AD by Cormac, who stated that *aed*, 'fire', and *dea*, 'goddess', were two faces of the same word, which he links to the Roman Vesta, goddess of fire.[37] The etymology is fanciful, says Murphy, but adds: 'it may well be that in the Old Irish period it *was* usual to associate *aed*, 'fire', with a god.'[38] What emerges is an integration of the elemental fire and the divine eye, as demonstrated in the Uisnech-centred national fire ring – a single leaping presence, appearing variously as flame, sun, and as the sparkle behind the concentric rings of the human pupil. Fintan, Uisnech's advocate, was one-eyed, and one meaning of Old Irish *aed* is 'eye' – the connecting link being 'the pupil', which is 'the fire of the eye', and cognate with Latin *aedes*, so validating Cormac's classical allusions.

Whitley Stokes found the primary sun deity, Áine, located *within* the name of the Beltaine festival, preceded by *belt*, 'white'. He wrote: 'The root of Belt-aine, as I divide it, is perhaps the same as that of Lithuanian 'white', *baltas*, plus *aine*.'[39] *Belt* could refer to the white lunar eye, so making a balanced title, where the May-Eve moon preceded the arrival of the sun syllable. This reflects Beltaine ritual, which emphasized the transition from night *to* day. The word of the principal Uisnech festival, Beltaine, may bring the eyes of night and day together.

The Sun Circle, Ériu's Web

Throughout prehistoric Britain and Ireland, it was by noting the positions on the horizon where sun and moon rose and set that people orientated themselves, and attempted to achieve a harmonious relationship with a divine cosmos. In Ireland, that task was primarily organized from Uisnech. Particular attention was paid to the solstices, equinoxes, and the mid-points between them – the quarter days, which served as the thresholds of the farming year.

What was done at Uisnech did not, of course, obviate the need to carry out comparable rites at the local level. So, nineteenth-century farmers in Co. Kilkenny, accompanied by servants and domestics, walked the boundaries of their land after Beltaine sunset, carrying the implements of husbandry and seed corn, stopping at intervals to address the four quarters from east, sunwise, to north.[40]

At Uisnech all these parochial efforts, and the achievements of major sacred sites in each of the four surrounding provinces, were integrated into one grand design. Seen from Uisnech, the gods did their rounds

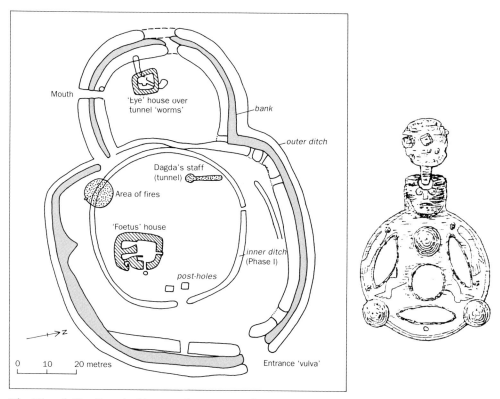

The Uisnech Fire Temple, 'the most important enclosure upon the summit of Uisnech.' Neolithic ring ditch and fire area are overlain by an Iron Age temple. The whole may forms an architectural Ériu image, an incarnate squatting goddess, incorporating 'eye' and 'womb' chambers

(Right) Squatting goddess, Iron Age, 4 cm wide, tinned bronze with green glass eyes, from Feltrim, Co. Dublin

of the country in a fair distribution of divine favours. This unceasing display of attention must now be explored.

The Uisnech view of Ireland as the living divinity, Ériu-Fódla-Banba, depended partly on seeing the surrounding array of hills and mountains in combination with sun and moon risings and settings on critical days in the annual cycle. These 'coincidences' showed that the sacred intelligence and metabolism was working properly, and in a state of continuous flux, to sustain the processes of the island world.

For it to work properly, the act of seeing had to be a two-way process, involving the human worshipper. Similarly, Indian darśan[41] – 'seeing the divine image', remains the most common and significant element in Hindu worship. Through the eyes, one gains the blessing of the icons. As in Ireland, this favour is obtained as much through the darśan of place as from sculpted effigies. Thus Hindu pilgrimage still involves climbing hilltops to receive the darśan of local goddesses.

Hills, suns, and bonfires combined with the worshipping community to make seeing a divine contact – a way of beholding and being observed by the godhead, in shared regard.

Uisnech-centred Ireland continues to offer a means of finding the holy in the visible, an art sometimes believed lost to the Western world. A Mide walk undermines the enthronement of dualism.

For millennia the life of the Uisnech-centred divinity remained identifiably the same. Her bones – the array of hills and mountains – continued to articulate around Uisnech as they had for thousands of years, while rhythms of light and dark fed energy to and from her earthy flesh. Encouraged further by the music of rainfall and rivulet, from Uisnech Ériu renewed her annual promise to bear pasture and corn-child, cow and pig, in an immense play of activity.

Far from being an exception to archaic norms, this Irish pattern is orthodox for the ancient world. As Markey points out, 'In the so-called primitive stages of many societies, webs of associations, highly symbolic in nature, are frequently woven between periods of the day, cardinal points, seasons, colours, and social-spiritual values.'[42]

Nor is it true to say that Ériu's Uisnech-centred web has been destroyed, since today we may continue to observe the same natural forces at play over the same topography as was viewed in antiquity.

To that extent at least, we can enjoy and become part of the old drama, as it unfolds again around Aill na Mireann.

Twelfth-century chancel window at Rahan, Co. Offaly. The solar chevrons familiar from prehistoric Irish gold discs here face east, towards the sunrise, around a four-plus-one central pattern

Ériu's Eye
National Observations

The Island Array

The plan on p. 214 shows how quarterday and solsticial sunrises and sunsets, as seen from Uisnech, relate to an array of mountain peaks, hill tops, and striking water features.

An Uisnech-based sunwise rotation through these correlations will now be attempted, encompassing the whole island.

Alignments of the sites from Uisnech are stated in degrees from true North. Their distance from Uisnech as the crow flies is given in kilometres. An asterisk is used to indicate intervisibility between neighbouring sites on the same alignment. A double asterisk denotes intervisibility with Uisnech.

2°E: Granard, Co. Longford, Grianan Ailigh (or Ailech) and Malin Head, Co. Donegal

(i)   Granard, and the Ash of Uisnech [32 km]★★

Craeb Usnig, the mythic Ash Tree of Uisnech, was the central tree of all Ireland. It crashed northwards in the time of the sons of Aed Slane, c. AD 600. The date corresponds with the destruction of the pagan cosmic scheme by St Patrick and his followers. In falling, the tip of the tree reached Granard (another Grian-derived name), in Co. Longford. 'The Ash of populous Usnech... due northward [it] fell, as far as Granard,'[43] showing that Craeb Usnig was no ordinary tree, but a national *axis mundi*, acting as a cosmic spindle or centre pole. Then it swung like a compass needle into northern darkness, when seen by the light of a Christian god's agent.

The pedigree of the tree is given by Fintan. He claimed to have planted it as a berry, and set four other berries at distances of scores of miles around it, in a reiteration of the one-plus-four pattern,[44] echoed by the Roman augur.

(ii)   Grianan Ailigh [170 km]

Beyond Granard, on the same alignment stands the major sacred hilltop site of North Ulster. Three concentric ring banks enclose a massive stone 'cashel', whose wall is five paces thick at the base, and can be entered only through one east-facing door, barely a metre wide.

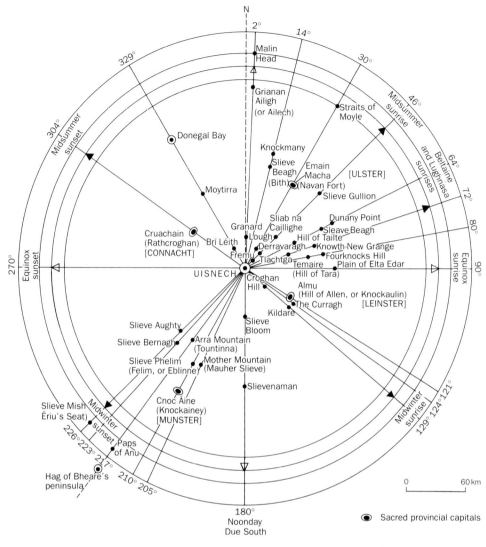

Labels on the diagram (clockwise from North):

N
2°
14°
Malin Head
Grianan Ailigh (or Ailech)
30°
Straits of Moyle
329°
Midsummer sunrise
46°
Donegal Bay
Knockmany
Slieve Beagh (Bith)
Emain Macha
Navan Fort
[ULSTER]
Slieve Gullion
304° Midsummer sunset
Beltaine and Lughnasa sunrises
64°
Moytirra
72°
Dunany Point
Sleave Beagh
80°
Cruachain (Rathcroghan) [CONNACHT]
Granard
Sliab na Caillighe
Lough
Brí Léith
Derravaragh
Hill of Tailte
Knowth·New Grange
Fourknocks Hill
Fremu
Tlachtga
Temaire
Plain of Elta Edar
(Hill of Tara)
270° Equinox sunset
Equinox sunrise 90°
UISNECH
Croghan Hill
Almu
(Hill of Allen, or Knockaulin)
[LEINSTER]
The Curragh
Kildare
Slieve Aughty
Slieve Bloom
Slieve Bernagh
Arra Mountain (Tountinna)
Slieve Phelim (Felim, or Eblinne)
Mother Mountain (Mauher Slieve)
Slievenaman
Midwinter sunrise 121°
124°
129°
Slieve Mish Ériu's Seat)
Midwinter sunset
Cnoc Áine (Knockainey) [MUNSTER]
226° 223° 217°
Paps of Anu
210° 205°
Hag of Bheare's peninsula
180°
Noonday
Due South

0   60 km

◉ Sacred provincial capitals

Ériu's Eye: a year of regard. Ériu's eyes were like flashing sunbeams, says the medieval Cóir Anmann. Significant solar sunrise and sunset alignments link sacred sites in the four provinces to the fifth, Uisnech

(Left) Ash-tree growing on Uisnech, 1990

214

The hill is cited in *Lebor Gabála* as the northern marker of Partholón's four-fold division of Ireland. The Dagda is said to have lived there, along with the solar husbands of Ériu, Fódla, and Banba. The word *grianan*, 'sunhouse', derives from *grian*, 'sun', and Grian, the sun goddess. Grianan Ailech may be regarded as her midnight and midwinter hiding-place.

The theme of incarceration is developed further in the *Dindshenchas* stories of Aed ('fire'), son of the Dagda, who was buried there, and Ailech-the-white, a divine maiden who had a house built around her on the same site. Made of 'red yew' (a síd wood), it was overlaid with pure unwrought silver, gold and bronze, and decked inside with bright gems, so that 'alike were day and night in the midst of it'.[45]

The Grianan thus stood for a state of equilibrium, prior to seasonal and diurnal fluctuation, and may therefore be regarded as equivalent to the Indian condition of *ātman*, where the undifferentiated world-soul is revealed at the deepest level of individual awareness. Ailech knew, lived by, and perhaps *was* that universal design. Like Tennyson's Lady of Shallot, her existence is an expression of the whole. Parted from it, she would soon die, so she stays imprisoned in totality.

But Grianan Ailigh was also the home of that most active god, the Dagda, who was 'good at everything', and the master of crafts, including agriculture and warfare. His feats emanated from a Uisnech-Grianan Ailigh base-line. Having a house at both places, he was Ruad Rofhessa, Lord of Perfect Knowledge, and Eochaid Ollathair, Father of All. This comprehensiveness (cf. Indian Śiva) was the hidden foundation of his energetic performance in the world. As the rising sun shooting into the Grianan entrance demonstrates, the Absolute (Indian *Brahman*) includes the flash of particular acts.

Grianan Ailigh, or Ailech, Co. Donegal. This mighty cashel with one small east-facing door was home to the Dagda. It was also the grianan, *or house of hibernation, for Gráine, the sun goddess, and the supernatural maiden Ailech*

(iii)   Malin Head [211 km]

'The development of the mythical feeling for space always starts from the opposition of day and night, light and darkness', writes Cassirer,[46] and from Uisnech the search for darkness runs on towards Malin Head, Ireland's most northerly point, lying on the same northern line.

The headland is still referred to on local roadsigns as Banba's Crown; Banba was the version of Ériu most closely associated with the underworld. Malin Head is a toothy crown of dark rock, licked white in places by far-flung ocean spray. Gales frequently rage here. Folk custom made the Head the scene of an annual pilgrimage, described by McParlan in 1802.[47]

14°E: Slieve Beagh, Co. Fermanagh. Knockmany, Co. Tyrone

(i)   Slieve Beagh [97 km]★★

Slieve Beagh is the burial place of the mythic founding father, Bith or Cosmos. Viewed from Uisnech, Bith's mountain-grave aligns with the famous Neolithic chambered cairn at Knockmany, 11 kilometres further north.

(ii)   Knockmany [108 km]★

This ruined monument stands on top of a steep-sided conical hill, and its megaliths are incised in the passage grave style of *c.* 3000 BC. One face shows Áine-the-hag, cloaked, and bent with age, yet busily generating the phenomenal world. While Bith, as ultimate God-Head, dreams up the reality of all-inclusiveness, on the same Uisnech axis Áine, goddess of specific actions, stirs the re-creation mound, to empower the eruption of separate forms. He inhales everything, and holds a long pause.

30°E: Lough Derravaragh. Emain Macha. Straits of Moyle

(i)   Lough Derravaragh [23 km]

From Uisnech this line clips the wings of the swan-shaped Lough Derravaragh. The lake, 10 kilometres from tail to open beak, was regarded as sacred in oral tradition, and illustrates the opportunistic nature of the Irish mythic process. Because the lough was swan-shaped, it attracted swan stories. The route to imagining often starts in physical coincidence, as Neolithic cultures throughout the world demonstrate.

At Lough Derravaragh, the four children of Lir (father of the sea god, Manannán) were turned into white swans by his jealous second wife, and condemned to spend three hundred years there, and three hundred on the Straits of Moyle between Ireland and Scotland. After that, 'when the woman of the South is mated with a man of the North, the enchantment is to have an end'.[48] Since three of the swan children were boys, there is a suggestion of male swan gods, migrating from the far north (as swans in fact do, every year) to a point close to the umbilicus and the Eiscir Riada in order to wed with the southern

Malin Head, called Banba's Crown, Co. Donegal, the northern tip of Ireland. There Manannán mac Lir, sea god, lay with the land goddess. At nearby Main Well Fair, men and women 'frisked and played in the water all stark naked'

half of the country. The line of this narrative combines accurate bird-watching with a desire for a north-south sacred marriage, at a swan-shaped inland water.

(ii) Emain Macha [110 km]

According to *The Fate of The Children of Lir*, it was 'to the Hill of the White Field in Armagh' that the swans flew at the end of their sufferings, to visit their father Lir, who lived there. This 'White Field' may possibly be Emain Macha, the ancient capital and chief sacred site of Ulster. Measured along the same $30°$ line, Emain Macha is exactly midway between Lough Derravaragh and Garron Point, the Irish shore of the Straits of Moyle, or North Channel, separating Ireland from Scotland, where the *same* swans were forced to spend another three hundred years.

Here symmetries in the story are also expressed as equal distances in the landscape, which may even have influenced the choice of the

217

Emain Macha site. Waterman's excavations prove that Emain Macha was in use prior to 3000 BC, and was progressively elaborated till its abandonment in the fourth or fifth century AD.[49]

Throughout the accumulating Uisnech web, there was a strong inclination to regard sacred places as 'Place-Events', and as the living embodiment of the founding act. So, for example, Emain Macha was drawn on the ground by the goddess of Ess Ruaid, using the golden pin of the brooch, *eo*, that was at her neck, *muin*; hence 'Eomain', or 'Emain', says the *Dindshenchas*.[50] Then she made five captive princes dig the ramparts and ditches of the enclosure she had described. From *muin*, 'neck', to *mide* 'neck', an identical meaning cast in different words, unites Mide to her most troublesome province, Ulster, at its sacred heart.

Another tale says that *emuin* means 'twins', and that the goddess Macha, though heavily pregnant, was forced to race against the King of Ulster's chariot team, across the arena named after her. She won, but the effort caused her to give birth to a son and daughter 'at the end of the field'.[51]

This may reflect the Neolithic goddess delivered in bondage to warlike newcomers. Brought back under duress to a royal enclosure once sacred to her, she nevertheless outclassed them in fecundity and speed. Then she transferred her labour pains on to the assembled warriors, and so reaffirmed the priority of natural processes over an addiction to warfare, viewed in isolation. Their periodic paralysis may be compared to the suspension of military operations during Demeter's festival at Eleusis in ancient Greece. Emain Macha is now often called Navan Fort, and Macha eventually took a keen interest in warfare. It came to represent an additional aspect of her destructive Winter Hag role. She made Ulster the supreme province of winter *and* battle.

Yet a visit to Emain Macha is enough to confirm that her birth-giving aspect was retained. The swelling natural hill, enclosed by the banks, and culminating in the large earthen mound, 6 metres high and 45 metres across, continues to evoke the theme of pregnancy. The North could not survive without it.

Emain Macha and Cnoc Áine

All the provinces, including Ulster and Munster, were believed to join at Aill na Mireann. Now it should be added that if the line from North Strait via Emain Macha to the Uisnech omphalos is projected southwards into Munster (210° E of N), it passes over Fódla's seat on Slieve Phelim, and then bisects the summit of Cnoc Áine, which, with the nearby Lough Gur, forms the principal sacred metropolis of Munster. This straight line joins the capitals of Áine and Macha, and locks their respective provinces across the Uisnech centrestone. Straight as a sunbeam, or a shaft of moonlight, the axis depicts the inescapable rivalry between dark and light, sacrifice and birth.

By their incorporation into the line, Fódla and Ériu (representing island-wide interests) ensured that the lively tension between North

Emain Macha (Navan Fort), Co. Armagh, the sacred and political capital of pre-Christian Ulster. In myth, the enclosure was drawn by the horse goddess, Macha, with her brooch pin. Inset: silver-gilt brooch from Drogheda, Co. Meath, eighth century AD

and South was kept within manageable bounds, for the good of the parts and the preservation of the whole. This mythic achievement formed the basis of a political unity, surviving hundreds of wars. The Ériu-Fódla balance was maintained until the mass settlement of Ulster by the British caused the myth to be rejected in the northern province, with well-known consequences.

The fact that Uisnech lay both physically and mythologically on the Navan-Cnoc Áine line is confirmed by the presence at Cnoc Áine of two gods from Uisnech, Uainide ('Green'), and Eogabal (*eo*, tree, plus *gabal*, a fork, a gable). Ireland's green cloak came originally from its Uisnech centre, the myth implies.

Other northeast-southwest relations are expressed at Slieve Phelim, seat of Fódla, which got its name from Eblend, daughter of a 'bright' north-eastern king from the magic Brug of New Grange on the southern border of Old Ulster. Her name means 'a skip, a spring, a leap'. She eloped with her young lover to Slieve Phelim, in Munster, as part of a parallel interprovincial solar myth.

Kenney makes the point that early Irish literature *typically* retains an island-wide perception, addressing the widest issues in a common language, without regional dialectical distinctions.[52] The early texts may be said to perpetuate the unifying spirit of the Uisnech web.

48°E: Sliab na Caillighe, Co. Meath [40 km].** Slieve Gullion,* Co. Armagh [101 km]

By undertaking a slow rotation at Uisnech, the hold of the central hill on the surrounding country seems gradually to accumulate, and the sharp outline of Sliab na Caillighe (the Mountain of the Hag) comes into view. This ridge of three summits, known locally in 1828 as 'The Witches Hops',[53] is the site of the famous Loughcrew 'Cemetery'. In every sense this is an outstanding group of fourth-millennium passage graves, profusely decorated with engraved designs of the same era. The central summit is crowned with the biggest 'tomb', Cairn T. Cairn T was known in the locality (and in archaeological literature) as the tomb of Ollamh Fódla. The Book of Four Masters says that he was 'the first law-giver of Ireland', and arbitrarily assigns his death to 1277 BC. *Ollamh* means the highest rank of poet, and Fódla is none other than Ériu's sister, the goddess of divisions, here seen applying her power to the division of time as well as space, within nature's law. Seen from Uisnech, Cairn T aligns with midsummer sunrise. If this line is extended a further 65 kilometres it runs straight into the hollow body of the Cailleach at the hag-shaped chambers of the south cairn on Slieve Gullion, Co. Armagh, where Finn was swallowed up and turned into an old man (see p. 56).

Pondering on the folk beliefs current around Loughcrew and Slieve Gullion in the 1830s, O'Donovan concluded that the Co. Meath hag '*is* the [same] very old lady whose shade still haunts the lake and carn of Slieve Gullion', adding that at Sliab na Caillighe she was called Evlin by the people, 'for whom she was and is still a living presence.... [This] famous hag of antiquity, Cailleagh Bheartha (Vera), came from the north to perform a magical feat in this neighbourhood, by which she would obtain great power if she succeeded. She dropped her apronful of stones on Sliab na Caillighe.' (The apron is the divine womb, translated into the language of dress.) O'Donovan noted the belief that the same Cailleagh had turned Finn (the youthful sungod) into an old man on Slieve Gullion.[54] After midsummer, old age was his fate.

From Uisnech the paired monumental hags of Leinster and Ulster burst into flames together on Midsummer morning. Though Slieve Gullion is not visible from the national centre-stone, the message and the spectacle could be passed on from Sliab na Caillighe which *is* intervisible with the Co. Armagh mountain. Here is another instance of sacred communication along the Uisnech radial spokes, suggested by Macalister. A mighty throne-shaped limestone boulder, set into the periphery of Cairn T as part of its original furnishings and known as The Hag's Chair, offers the necessary two-way view to Uisnech and Slieve Gullion.

The critical sunrise was probably encouraged by the lighting of Midsummer Eve bonfires at all three locations – a seasonal ceremony which persists to this day in some districts.[55]

The white quartz pebbles which originally surrounded and perhaps

Around her sunray skirt, the solar goddess plays the game of the year with golden orbs, keenly regarded. Engraved slab from Patrickstown, Loughcrew

Plan of Cairn 'T' at Sliab na Caillighe (Loughcrew), Co. Meath (left), constructed 3200 BC. The head chamber of this hag-shaped tomb displays a megalith carved with sun symbols (above). The monument bestrides the midsummer sunrise axis from Uisnech

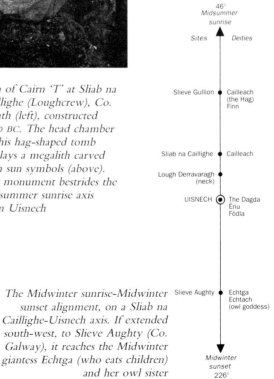

The Midwinter sunrise-Midwinter sunset alignment, on a Sliab na Caillighe-Uisnech axis. If extended south-west, to Slieve Aughty (Co. Galway), it reaches the Midwinter giantess Echtga (who eats children) and her owl sister

221

covered Cairn T suggest a concern with light, which is borne out by the many solar-eye designs, engraved within the goddess-shaped interior of the monument. Ollamh, the chief poet of Fódla, lived and died inside the goddess whom he served, for the 'tomb' described her living essence. Her legs are the entrance passage, the central chamber her body, off which lead two arms and a head. The 'head' chamber displays a fine array of 'sun-eyes'. Fieldwork by Mullen and his team has proved that the rising sun at the March and September equinoxes also featured in the original range of concerns, being the average of the midwinter and midsummer extremes.

Equinoctial sunrises still illuminate and bring to life the two most elaborately engraved 'eyes' in the Cairn T 'head'.[56]

In 1863 Conwell was struck by the remarkable east-west view of Ireland, from sea to sea, obtainable from Loughcrew. To the east lay Dundalk Bay at a distance of 55 kilometres. To the west, Ballysadart Bay was also faintly discernible. Long before the age of mapmaking, Ériu-the-island could be *seen* to have a 'neck', given the right weather conditions.

On the hill of Patrickstown, the eastern summit, Conwell found a Neolithic engraving consisting of a 15 cm diameter solar eye, set beneath a suggestion of a brow and nose (p. 221). The eye rises over a strong horizontal neck line, beneath which deeply incised rays fan out in a skirt shape. Here perhaps we may see the Hag viewing all her territories. Because it is engraved on the north-west face of an upright stone, the design comes to fullest life at midsummer sunrise and midwinter sunset.

From Sliab na Caillighe a reversed view across Uisnech aligns with *midwinter sunset* (with flanking moonsets swinging to either side of the 226° line, as they do through their nineteen-year cycle). The fact that midsummer sunrise occurs on the horizon opposite to, and 180° *from* midwinter sunset, gave a balanced logic to Uisnech-centred wheelings and dealings. Quarterday risings and settings, in November and May, are coupled in a similarly complementary manner.

Seen *from* Slieve Gullion, the reverse of the 46° midsummer sunrise alignment devours Sliab na Caillighe *and* Uisnech in the fire of a south-west midwinter sun*set*, at 226°.

The same 226° line passes over Uisnech and down the Shannon valley to the head of Lough Derg, where the bloody sun-king Dergderc lost his eye to the cruel poet from Ulster, Ferchertne, who can be seen as the agent of the Slieve Gullion hag, and engaged in her work.[57]

Beyond that, the midwinter sunset axis terminates in a view of the Slieve Aughty Mountains, Co. Galway. Their name comes from Echtga, 'an awful daughter and horrible goddess', who fed there on children's flesh. (Sliab Echtga translates as Aughty Mountains). Her sister was Echtach, the owl goddess, whose shrieks ripped through the winter sky after sunset.

Echtga-the-Awful, as the Rennes *Dindshenchas* calls her, was wooed successfully by one Fergus, who had reared a worm in his guts since

The owl deity,
Kings Mountain
megalith, Co. Meath

birth – another sign of the chthonic hag at work in her underworld,[58] and perhaps of her midwinter influence projected down the line from Co. Armagh.

64°E: Hill of Tailte, Sleave Beagh, Co. Meath. Dunany Point, Co. Louth

(i) Hill of Tailte [56 km]★
From Uisnech this is the line of sunrise at the May (Beltaine) and August (Lughnasa) quarterdays. Down this line Ériu could look to the place of her death at Tailte, or Teltown, its Anglicized form. Teltown was renowned as the greatest start-of-harvest *oenach*. There the goddess of the corn, Tailtiu, symbolically gave her life under the sickle, having first cleared the forest to create the fields.[59]

About the Calends of August she died, on a Monday, on the Lugnasad of Lug; round her grave from that Monday forth is held the chief fair of noble Erin. White-sided Tailtiu uttered in her land a true prophecy, that so long as every prince should accept her, Erin should not be without perfect song. A fair, with gold, with silver, with games, with music of chariots, with adornment of body and soul, by means of knowledge and eloquence. A fair without wounding or robbing of any man, without trouble, without dispute.

After her death, St Patrick said, 'Victorious was the proud law of nature; though it was not made in obedience to God, the Lord was magnifying it.'[60]
 Of the earthworks, the most prominent is the circular raised platform, 112 metres diameter, and 5 metres high, formerly surrounded by an outer ring.

(ii) Sleave Beagh [71 km]★
The same axis incorporates Sleave Beagh – another hill named after Bith. Prehistoric ring banks and tumuli decorate the 227-metre summit of this ridge. From there the sightline runs on, across Mount Oriel, to Dunany Point, on the coast.

(iii) Dunany Point [95 km]
By name and folk belief, Dunany brings the goddess Áine into this harvest line. The people of Dunany village regarded her with awe on the three days following Lammas, and would not put to sea during that time, fearing her wrath.[61] The juxtaposition of Áine and Bith sites, seen also on the Knockmany alignment, may be only coincidental, or the alignment could be a deliberate attempt to re-emphasize the contrast, well known to Indian religions, between transcendental

eternity and the active power of the world process. In Ireland, Bith is the first, an Absolute, and a profound repose, equivalent to Indian Śiva or Consciousness, while Áine epitomizes Śakti, or word-play, in *maya*. Bith and Áine are complementary, and interdependent.[62] Gathered together on Ireland's primary harvest line, they even become 'the same' (cf. Indian *Brahman*).

72°E: Tlachtga (Hill of Ward), Knowth-New Grange, Co. Meath

(i)   Tlachtga [46 km]★★

This prominent hill near Athboy, Co. Meath, rises to 116 metres. Its importance was emphasized by a massive prehistoric ring fort, consisting of four concentric banks and ditches, surrounding a platform 8 metres wide, which crowns the hill-top. This format seems to echo the Uisnech design of centre-stone and four provinces.

It is worth noting that the $72°–252°$ axis, joining the two sites, points to a late November sunset, and to the Samain moon at the southern standstill of its nineteen-year cycle. At Tlachtga, sky-earth relations were observed and maintained by monumental and bonfire responses, which divided the year into winter and summer halves.

Linkage across this vital threshold also involved a north-south dialogue. Thus although Tlachtga stands in the northern Half of Conn, the king of Munster, representing the souther Half of Mug, by tradition had a claim to the site.

'All November fires in Ireland were called *Tine tlach'd-gha*, after that place in Co. Meath where the arch-druid of the realm had his fire on said eve,' wrote Toland in 1740.[63] A century earlier, Keating stated:

the ritual Fire of Tlachtga was lit on the eve of Samhain, when the druids of the four provinces of Ireland gathered there to offer sacrifice to all the gods. It was at that time that they used to burn their victims, and it was an obligation, under penalty of fine, to quench the fires of Ireland on that night. The men of Ireland were forbidden to kindle fires except from that fire, and for each fire that was kindled from it the King of Munster received a tax of a screaball, or three-pence.[64]

(If extended beyond Uisnech to the sea, the Tlachtga-Uisnech line meets the Munster ford at Áth Cliath Medraige, at the west end of Eiscir Riada, and so brings the equinoctial division of the country into the pattern again, and simultaneously touches the border of Munster.)

The ringfort at Tlachtga represents an Iron Age warrior superimposition on a Neolithic site, and it was from here that the fire of the Uisnech cycle was 'stolen' by the new capital, set up 20 kilometres to the east at Tara. Samain, the perilous gap between years, represented a point of weakness in the Uisnech design. Here the incoming hierarchy struck. By simultaneously honouring and bending the Uisnech web, they used its ancient authority to suit their rival purposes, in an adroit manipulation of the mythic order.

Keating attributes this change to King Tuathal, who was the first to burn victims at Tlachtga as a signal that the Tara *Feis* or Festival might start. Tara and Tlachtga are intervisible.

Law-making and, in time, the writing of annals, were aspects of the Tara event, where each new King 'married' the goddess of the land, yet where women were debarred from entering the banqueting hall. (The new masters maintained an ambivalent relationship to the feminine.)

(ii)   Knowth-New Grange [73 km]

Extending the Medraige-Uisnech-Tlachtga line by 27 kilometres to the north-east, into old Ulster, we come to the great bend of the river Boyne, where stands the fourth millennium monument called Knowth. Damaged in the Iron Age, the twin passages under its Neolithic mound open due east and west, to receive equinoctial sunrises and sunsets.[65]

80°E: Temair (Hill of Tara). Fourknocks Hill

(i)   Tara [63 km]★★

'Like two kidneys in a beast' was how Fintan described the relationship between Uisnech and Tara. Intervisibility between the two sites may just be possible across the northern shoulder of the intervening hill at Killuoan. As the seat of the High King of Ireland in the first millennium AD, Tara's power was superimposed over the old egalitarian union that had been focussed on Uisnech since the Stone Age. Nevertheless, the claim of every Tara King to rule over the provincial kings depended entirely on his marriage to the goddess of the island, Medb, at a place named after the goddess Tea, who had died at Tara and imbued the hill with its original sanctity.[66] Thanks to Tlachtga and Tea (*te*, 'hot, lustful, wanton'), Tara remains within the compass of the Uisnech design.

The megalith called Lia Fáil stands close to the centre of the Tara monuments. *Fal* or *Fáil* was another term for Ireland. As a language word *fál* means 'arm-bracelet'. When this stone arm was combined with the gold ring made by the moving sun, the kingdom was re-established by divine right. Hence the Lia Fáil is the Stone of Destiny, which roared when Kings stood on it. Perhaps the sound combined the orgasm and labour pains of Tea with those of another recurring Tara 'queen' – Medb. The Tara Medb, central to kingship rites, is probably an eastern version of Medb, goddess of Connacht, whose sanctuary lies at Rathcroghan in Connacht, and almost the same distance as Tara from Uisnech.

(ii)   Fourknocks [79 km]★

Tara aligns between Uisnech in the west, and the notable Neolithic tomb at Fourknocks Hill, 17 kilometres further east. There, in the large central chamber of the main temple, stands an image of the goddess, engraved with eyes, a nose composed of the lozenge motifs,

Temaire (Tara), Co. Meath, from the air.
In Ireland the eyes of the past open on to
the future. From Tea's House to St
Patrick's Statue, every phase of Irish
myth-making is represented in the Tara
monuments

Lia Fáil, the Stone of Destiny, Tara (above). When
kings stood on the pillar, it roared in recognition

At Fourknocks tomb, Co. Meath (right), a carved
megalithic deity smiles in the face of death. The
underworld mother greets her returning children

226

familiar in many parts of the Neolithic world, and with a smile as broad as a cow's horns. The stone was instantly recognized by the workmen who excavated the site as anthropomorphic,[67] and later accepted as such by the archaeologist.

90° (due East, equinox sunrise): The Plain of Elta Edar, Co. Dublin [90 km]

According to the *Dindshenchas*, this coastal plain was the first to be settled in all Ireland. To it, Partholón returned to die. From the Uisnech navel stone, the founding act of agriculture aligns with sunrise at the equinoxes, and the average of all sunrises throughout the year. Howth Head (Benn Étair) is associated with the sun goddess Étar (wife of the divine ploughman-king, Eochaid Airem). She overlooks the plain and the eastern end of the Eiscir Riada.

Eastern sunrise and the first arable land were thus aligned by the national Uisnech eye, so that Étar and her ploughman could complete the necessary task.

121°E: Almu (The Hill of Allen or Knockaulin), Co. Kildare [55 km]★★

This 202-metre-high hill is completely surrounded by bog, to a degree that in nineteenth-century maps it is called The Isle of Allen.

Long after it was abandoned as the sacred seat of the Leinster kings in the eighth century AD, 'it continued to symbolize the ancient glories of the Leinsterman, taking its place in the national scene alongside Emain Macha and Rathcroghan',[68] the sacred capitals of Ulster and Connacht.

'Far-famed Alenn! delightful knowledge,' sang the Old Irish *Hail Brigit* poet. What knowledge? Smyth insists that 'the importance of the symbolism and ancient associations of these sites, as preserved in the *senchus*, or traditions, cannot be overestimated', and points out that eulogies to Almu continued to be written into the seventeenth century, despite the Norman and Tudor conquests.[69]

Rising from water, Almu served as a creation mound, a world mountain – a new hope in the flood, close to the midwinter sunrise line from Uisnech.

As so often in the Uisnech pattern, Almu was a goddess, who continued to be acknowledged (having by then been reduced to the rank of a human female) into the Middle Ages. 'Almu, beautiful was the woman...one of no common line...Almu the all white...she was fair of foot, the daughter of Beccán the bright-robed.'[70] 'All white is the fort...as if it had received the lime of all Ériu...Almu the all-white.' Here the white maiden, the white goddess of dawn, paints the walls of her home – a colour complementary to the blood red hue of Rathcroghan in Connacht, the midsummer sunset house. This stood at 180° to the Almu-Kildare complex at the reversed end of an axis

Almu (Dún Ailinne, Hill of Allen or Knockaulin), Co. Kildare. Reconstruction of the Iron Age enclosure [B. Wailes, 1990] showing the tiers of wooden seats. The 'head and body' plan of the monument repeats the Uisnech temple plan (page 211). From the 'body' of Almu's parade ring horses may have cantered out to nearby Curragh racecourse

drawn through Uisnech to Rathcroghan, which was the western home of the goddess Medb.

The see-saw operated by a white and a red goddess around the Uisnech pivot is referred to in what Meyer calls 'a very ancient poem', coupling the two sites: 'Round Alenn, Cruachu fairest...'[71] In a seventh-century poem 'Round Alenn, [and] Cruachu' are again put together.[72]

Thus Leinster and Connacht are united through Uisnech via their sacred centres, as firmly as Ulster and Munster were held by Emain and Cnoc Áine, across the same Uisnech stone. Whoever 'ruled' Almu in the political sense, tapped into this mythic resource. For example, Finn MacCool, born at Almu (with or without historical reality), was bound to assume the status of a rising sun god, since that role was a function of the site. Keating says that 'the hill came to belong to him in the right of his mother.'[73] His 'chair' is a small mount on the summit, on which a battlemented tower was erected in 1859.

Recent excavation, 1969–75, has proved that, as with Emain Macha, the Neolithic community was established on the summit of Almu, where they dug a circular trench, more than 20 metres diameter, and left pottery, stone arrowheads, and a disc bead in the ground.[74] Continuing occupation through the Bronze Age led eventually to successive circular timber structures being built in the Iron Age over the Neolithic circle, implying continuity. The grandest was a double arena, with tiered seating, and a fenced approach, fanning open towards the east. This building has been interpreted as a ritual corral for animals. The 'head and body' arenas, joined at the neck, also suggest the 'fat lady' shape of the Mother Goddess-as-Architecture, known from Neolithic Irish passage graves, and later prehistoric sanctuaries both in Britain and Ireland. (In a mythic age, buildings modelled on the shapes of gods were thought to be the most effective.)

On Almu, the architectural openings of her eye and womb face east. Traces of a similarly shaped timber figure, 39 metres long, were found under the mount at Navan (p. 218). There the earliest version was

The White Mare, or láir bhan, was paraded at midwinter in many districts in Ireland, evoking Brigit as solsticial fire-horse. A boy hidden beneath the frame worked the jaws. These solar horses rode through the shortest day, in harmony with December sunrises, witnessed over Co. Kildare from Uisnech

built *c.* 700 BC, and recreated several times, generation after generation, on the same ground, as the footings show.[75] Sited at one end of Macha's horse race arena, the structure takes on the significance of a divine stable, and in the shape of the mother goddess. At Almu and Navan, the combined evidence suggests that the wellbeing of the provinces depended upon horse deities, racing from their provincial stables to inspire the cosmos into movement. For Almu's Leinster steeds, the sacred course lay nearby at The Curragh. Racing at The Curragh continues to this day, as Ireland's premier – one might say *sacred* – horse-racing venue. The Old Irish poet wrote: 'The Curragh with its glitter remains.'[76] At certain times of the year, as in antiquity, it holds the nation in a thundering spell.

124°E: The Curragh, Co. Kildare [61 km]

As a language word, *curragh* or *currac* means 'a racecourse, a plain', and a 'journeying or flowing, as of a horses mane, or human hair'.

Comparable to the chariot track around Lough Gur, and Macha's course at Navan, The Curragh was where the Kildare goddess of the midwinter fire, and the Almu kings of Leinster came together with one of the fastest of earth's creatures, the horse. (Horse racing on the ground was an important ritual means of urging the solar chariot across the sky, for the two zones were inter-dependent.)

The Lives of Irish Saints sometimes describe Brigit in a chariot, coming from Heaven to Kildare, and her pre-Christian equine form perhaps lived on as the White Mare, or *láir bhan*, until recently paraded at Midwinter, in the form of a hobby horse.[77]

Since Labraid, Leinster's founder, was also a horse-god, a meeting with Brigit as solar mare on the race-course stretching between their Co. Kildare strongholds seems at least possible.

Kildare-The Curragh-Almu is perhaps to be understood as a triple site, and another instance of a sacred landscape ensemble whose sports were concerned with the play of elemental unity.

129°E: Midwinter sunrise: Croghan Hill, Co. Offaly. Kildare (Cill Dara), Co. Kildare

(i)   Croghan Hill [25 km]★★

Seen from Uisnech, the midwinter sun rises over Croghan Hill, a cone-shaped peak, 232 metres high, 25 kilometres from Aill na Mireann. Tradition says that St Brigit, the chief female saint of Ireland, was born close to Croghan, and took the veil on the hill.[78] This conjunction of the midwinter sunrise, seen from Uisnech, and St Brigit at Croghan Hill, replicates in the landscape what the New Grange entrance-box framed architecturally.

At midwinter all Uisnech eyes were turned in anxious hope towards Croghan Hill, and the magic underworld beneath it, known as Brí Ele. In early literature, Ele is represented as a maiden and a goddess of awe-inspiring beauty. Every year one of Finn's young men went out from the Hill of Alenn (Almu), his stronghold in Co. Kildare, to meet her, and was lost for ever, in her síd beneath Croghan Hill. *Ele* means 'prayer, praise, incantation and salve'. In this spirit the youth gave his life in worship.

The repeated tribute paid by Finn to Ele amounts to his acknowledgement that as a solar demi-god, he derived his power from the hidden sun goddess in her winter basement. In return, his provincial power in Leinster was linked to a national grid.

'Ele' was probably a twelfth-century pseudonym for Brigit in her underworld guise, and designed to allay Christian disquiet over the continuing worship of the pagan fire goddess, whose name is derived from 'Brig', 'the Great One'.[79]

(ii)   Uisnech, Croghan, Cill Dara, and the triple Brigit

The well-known tendency for the prehistoric goddess to manifest as a trinity has been explored in the Ériu-Fódla-Banba trio, and it can be shown that Brigit also spread herself in three equal parts down the Uisnech-Croghan-Kildare axis, following the line of the first midwinter sunbeam. She is the 'fiery arrow' who joins her sanctuaries together.

Cormac explained her triple nature as that of three sisters, the first of whom was goddess of poetry, and daughter of the Dagda. Since *he* often lived at Uisnech, so did she.

She was the spark of thought, and the flaming word, when poet and listener cry out: 'I see!' 'Therefore this Brigit is a goddess whom poets worshipped for very great and famous was her superintendence.'[80] Viewed from Uisnech, the second being of the trinity, Brigit-as-Begoibne, or 'woman of the smithery', was inferred to underlie the distant Croghan Hill, whose pointed summit coincided with the midwinter sunrise.

Croccan means 'vessel, pot or cauldron', and at Crochan Hill the smith-goddess made pots, including the sacred cauldrons from which the future was poured. 'The future' included the river Shannon as known to humanity. The *Dindshenchas*, in one version, states that its source lay under Brí Ele on the Eiscir Riada, at a well called Linn

Bronze bowl, c. 1000 BC, from Adabrock, Lewis, 28 cm diameter, with solar chevrons engraved round the rim. Beneath Croghan Hill, Brigit-the-Smith made vessels of every kind

Bronze cauldron from Donaghadee, Co. Down, 43 cm diameter. The vessel with 'eyes' incorporates, and portrays, the divine presence

Mna Feile, 'the Pool of the Modest Woman'.[81] Thus the chief north-south *and* east-west natural co-ordinates of Ireland were believed to flow from the same supernatural bowl at the start of each solar cycle, when the land was recreated by dawning sunlight.

As Knox observed, Crúachan Brí Ele 'was not merely the name *of* the hill, but of something from which the hill took its name'[82] – a magic vessel. Its supernatural crafting was considered to be the fundamental event, underlying, and in a sense *causing* the natural hill to arise. Brigit's pagan cauldron lived on as the Christian 'grail', and St Brigit is credited with 'mending a wonderful vessel, one of the rare treasures of the King', which had been smashed.

A bronze bowl, *c.* 1000 BC, from Adabrock, Lewis, shows the solar wheel, engraved in chevrons around the rim, while four figures of Brigit-as-Smith-goddess offer the 'eyes' of their heads as handle-loop sockets, so visibly conducting the dance of the year, within the Irish sphere of influence.[83] Another Bronze Age cauldron found at Donaghadee, Co. Down, may show the eyes of the goddess in two pairs set in the fretted supports of the handles.

(iii)   Cill Dara (Kildare), The Church of the Oak Grove [58 km]
Visible from Uisnech down the midwinter sunrise axis, across the level Bog of Allen stand the Dunmurry Hills, and beyond them on the same line is St Brigit's Cathedral of Kildare. There her cult took its Christian form on a prehistoric foundation. Outside the North Wall of the cathedral, the substantial footings of her cell, a Christian fire church, are preserved, where the 'eternal flame', which survived until 1530, opens towards Uisnech.

If the Uisnech midwinter sunrise axis, 129°, is extended from Kildare a further 37 kilometres, it cuts into the southern flank of the tallest mountain in Leinster, Lugnaquillia, named after the young sun god Lugh. Beyond lie the prehistoric gold mines of the Wicklow Mountains, Ireland's chief source of gold, in use by 2000 BC. Gold was the uncorruptible deity in the rock.

180°: **Slieve Bloom,** Co. Laois. **Slievenaman,** Co. Tipperary

(i)   Slieve Bloom [45 km]★★

The next important stations on the national sun cycle lie due south from Uisnech. Down the line of the noonday sun stand the Slieve Bloom Mountains. They, and the highest point of the range, Árd Éireann (the Height of Ireland, 526 metres), had great mythic importance.[84]

Uisnech and Slieve Bloom enjoyed a seasonal and topographic partnership. Uisnech's chief festival was at Beltaine (the low hill of May Day), while Slieve Bloom was the World Mountain of the next quarterday festival, Lughnasa, when the pregnant goddess gave birth.

Standing north and south of the Eiscir Riada at comparable distances from that equinoctial line, Uisnech and Árd Éireann, as a pair, jointly achieve a dynamic equilibrium within the annual process.

The grassy summit of Árd Éireann is called Crúachan, and there the national harvest bowl, fashioned in midwinter at Croghan Hill, was at last filled to the brim. Slieve Bloom remained an important place of Lughnasa pilgrimage till 1940.

The ceremonies had more than local significance. As the name Árd Éireann implies, the mountain was *the* Height of Ireland, and stood symbolically for the whole country. It was the culmination of a birth process drawn from sea to sea, and raised under the noonday sun, as seen from Uisnech.

The *Dindshenchas* infers that the raising from infancy to adulthood of Ériu the island-goddess was synonymous with the uprearing of her central mountain: 'growing as grew the woman . . . so gloriously grew the hill above earth's bright surface'. Moreover, it was Ériu herself who checked the process, in the interests of moderation, thereby giving Ireland its varied landscape of mountain, hill, and plain, for at an early stage she had cried out: 'I am heaved up on high so that the sun scorches me' . . . – 'unless she had said *that*, the peak would have grown until Ireland was full thereof', states one version of the myth.[85]

Its cosmogonic role is further underlined by the rivers Nore, Suir, and Barrow, the Three Sisters at whose mouth Cesair, the founding goddess of Ireland, landed. All three rivers rise in the neighbourhood of Slieve Bloom, so associating the mountain with a primary birth act, the bringing of Ireland into existence.

Stone figure, 55 cm tall,
squatting in the birth
position, from Knockarley,
near Árd Éireann

Slievenaman, Co. Tipperary, standing against the horizon due south of Árd Éireann and Uisnech. To this síd flew the god Midir and his wife Étaín, as two swans, after he had freed her from Tara

It was in the woods of Slieve Bloom that the eastern sungod Finn grew up, safe from his father's enemies, until the time came for him to make himself known and to embark on his Slighe Mhór campaign against Connacht.

(ii)   Slievenaman [112 km]★

Slievenaman's conical form (719 metres) overlooks the most southerly of the three sisters, the river Suir, and carries the eye from Leinster into Munster.

One might expect beliefs to have accrued at this mountain, since it marks the climax of the daily solar arc viewed from Aill na Mireann. And, indeed, the divine events of Slievenaman represent a peak in the daily and annual drama.

The stories often revolve around Étaín, a sun goddess, whose beauty gave rise to the phrase 'as fair as Étaín'. Caught in a triangle of love, she was torn between Midir, the 'elf-king' of the north-west, her husband, who lived under Ardagh Hill, Co. Longford, in the síd of Brí Léith, and her *second* husband, Eochaid, the eastern horse-king of Tara. This conflict, described in *Tochmarc Étaín* (The Wooing of Étaín),[86] expresses her solar movements around and under the horizon. (A straight line between Brí Léith and Slievenaman passes directly over Árd Eireann, the highest point of Slieve Bloom.)

Étaín's arrival at Slievenaman (which means 'mountain of the cunning feet'), followed her seizure by Midir from Eochaid's court at Tara. Although surrounded by his rival's armed retainers, Midir

233

escaped from there with her. Holding his sunspears in his left hand, Midir threw his right arm around her, and the couple rose lightly into the air, and disappeared through a roof-window in the palace. The last that the king and his warriors saw of them was as two white swans circling once, before they pointed their necks towards Slievenaman, and vanished in the southern sky.

'The top of the morning to you' remains an enthusiastic Irish greeting, and in the great Uisnech array, Slievenaman denotes the top of every morning, and the start of afternoon.

At Slievenaman the 'solar wife' theme is revealed in alternative names for the mountain – 'radiant Sliab Femen' (*femen*, 'wife, woman'), and Sliabh ma n'Ban (*ban*, 'white, fair, bright').[87] As a member of the Áine-Grian trinity of sun goddesses, Étaín was accustomed to circling Ireland. In the form of a butterfly she had been whirled all over the country. Her name probably derives from *étan*, 'front or brow', and from *etan*, 'poetry'. Hers is the poetry of connections. She had lived in each of the four quarters and in the surrounding seas. In Ulster, she had been a mere fly; falling thus into a woman's cup, she had been accidentally swallowed and was then reborn in human form. She *is* the poetry of metamorphosis, one energy in a thousand forms, a compendium of Being, where every creature under the sun enjoys a fundamental identity with all others.

Étaín was the embodiment of One World, where space and time met in Event. She was affirmation's golden ball, topping the steeple of Ireland's noonday axis. Étaín, like the poetry of her name, though now largely unsaid and unread, will not be finally over till the human sense of harmony fades beyond the range of hope.

From the union of Midir and Étaín, their son Donn was born. Finn saw Donn under the mountain, presiding over a magic mansion, where 28 warriors were entertained by as many beautiful blonde virgins, one of whom sat on a crystal throne, and played the harp. It was as if the peak of the sun's path had cast dark Donn's bright antithesis deep into the rock. Taking after his father Midir, whose name means 'Rays of Sun', Donn fills the underworld with a confident display of buried light – a fire unseen on the mortal plane. As a sungod, Finn had a seat (Seefin), on top of the mountain, which proves, says the historian Keating, that he *really* existed. Until recently, young local women would race each other up the mountain, for the privilege of 'marrying' him there.

Ériu appeared as Banba's sow, at Slievenaman. In one legend, Finn kills the guardian of the síd as he enters, carrying the animal. The god Bodb is said to have kept a herd of swine on the same mountain which reappeared as soon as they had been cooked and eaten.[88] The regular roasting of Banba's divine beast at the feast of the noonday sun was her self-sacrifice and eternal replenishment, echoed in a different form by the Scandinavian element in Irish mythology, where the sky pig with golden bristles is the boar who overlays and mates with the great land sow.

Furiously chasing after Étaín, his abducted wife, Eochaid arrived at the mountain, and dug up the elfmound, but someone came out and told him that she was no longer there. Midir had taken her towards his stronghold at Brí Léith, Co. Longford. Eochaid was advised 'to set out thither till you come to it', so he and the flower of Ireland's manhood headed northwestwards in pursuit.[89]

205°E: Mother Mountain (Mauher Slieve), Co. Tipperary [102 km]★★

This is one of twelve mountains in a compact area called The Twelve Mountains of Éblenn, named after a goddess of that name from Brug na Bóinne, who eloped with a young lover, after deserting her husband, the King of Cashel. 'That there was originally a Lughnasa assembly on Mother Mountain can hardly be doubted,' says MacNeill.

Being the tallest of the group, it may be regarded as the maternal aspect of the libidinous Éblenn, and is visible from Uisnech by bonfire light.

210°E: Slieve Phelim, Cnoc Áine, Co. Limerick

(i)   Slieve Phelim [114 km]★
It was on nearby Slieve Phelim, alias Eblinne (480 metres), that Fódla and Ériu, representing the parts and the whole of Ireland, took turns to keep watch (see p. 203).

O'Rahilly says that Eblinne was both a mountain and goddess name. She and it were synonymous. 'The idea underlying the word *éblenn* is the radiation of heat and light, and the resultant feeling of pleasure and well-being, or of energy and passion.'[90]

Such energy has affinities with Indian *sákti* or power (usually identified as feminine). Éblenn suggests the Irish version of a common Indo-European heritage, tapped by Ériu and Fódla, in their visits to the mountain.

(ii)   Cnoc Áine [139 km]
Cnoc Áine, and the associated Lough Gur monuments, have a secure place in the Uisnech design.

215°–217°E: Arra, Co. Tipperary. Paps of Anu, Co. Kerry. Bheare Peninsula, Co. Cork

(i)   Arra Mountain (Tountinna) [90 km]★★
This mountain (460 metres) was the home of Fintan the White, restorer of Uisnech, who arrived in the first boat with Cesair. Arra, where he survived the Flood, is Ireland's Ararat. It rises at the meeting of Leinster and Munster, with a fine view across Lough Dergderc and the Shannon into South Connacht. The remains of megalithic tombs, now called the Graves of the Leinstermen, stand below the summit.

(ii)   Paps of Anu [214 km]
Across the east flank of the Arra Mountain and 124 kilometres distant, an Uisnech-to-Paps-of-Anu alignment carries a beam of national intelligence from the centre to the most remarkable topographic symbols of maternity. Fintan's flood mountain therefore enjoyed the remote protection of these combined influences, and may have been selected on that basis.

(iii)   Bheare Peninsula [261 km]
Extended to the coast, the same alignment ends on the Bheare Peninsula. There Áine-as-Hag, the Caillighe Bheare, reputedly had her home. On the surface of Ireland there is, after all, no escape from the cycle of life and death, nor from the sea that both nourishes and inundates.

223°E: Slieve Bernagh, Co. Clare [97 km]★★

Aibhinn, the fairy queen of West Munster, sister of Áine, lived on this mountain (590 metres) on the west of Lough Dergderc, and she is still spoken of in the district. Her síd was at a crag called Craganeevul, near a well called Tobereevul, which gushes from under a low rock among the ferns. Aibhill, alias Aibhinn, meaning 'the lovely one', was said to be the queen of twenty-five County Clare banshees. She featured prominently in eighteenth- and nineteenth-century Irish verse of the region, and was seen washing clothes in a stream prior to a disaster. She foretold the death of the king-hero, Brian Boru. She is ultimately an appellation of the sun goddess, and, as a language word, describes 'cattle on heat'.

A dairy farmer, working in his vest one hot summer's evening in 1989, regretted that since its afforestation, he could not say precisely where on the mountain she had lived. A woman babysitting at a nearby bungalow called Craig Lea said that her *brother* knew where Craganeevul was, but that he had emigrated to America twenty years before.

Journeying up and down the tracks between the almost impenetrable blocks of conifers failed to settle the matter. However, at a point where one trackway had recently been blasted through a spur, the vertical face so exposed offered its own kind of revelation. Immediately below the two metres of peat accumulated since the original Neolithic deforestation was a greyish layer, only 10 cm deep, directly blanketing the bedrock. This represented the natural forest floor developed between the end of the Ice Age and the start of human interference. On its upper surface Aibhill may have sat in a sacred grove to watch the sunlight filter through deciduous tree-trunks. Deities like her are a cultural deposit – as much part of the structure of Ireland as any other geological formation. The contemporary surface is sustained by Aibhills, even in their total neglect.

226°E: Slieve Aughty Mountains, Co. Galway [82 km]★★

This range is 358 metres high and is the line of midwinter sunset, seen from Uisnech. As with Ériu in her flesh-tearing guise (p. 222–3), so here, the owl goddess tears into the remains of the year with beak and claw. On the same midwinter sunset line, 124 kilometres beyond the summit of Slieve Aughty, lies Slieve Mish, Co. Kerry, which, *Lebor Gabála* says, was Ériu's seat in the far south west. There, with Banba, she presided over the death and rebirth of the year.

304°E: Crúachain (Rathcroghan), Co. Roscommon [61 km]

Just as the midwinter sunrise, seen from Uisnech, led to a special sanctity being ascribed to the Almu-Curragh-Kildare landscape in the south-east, so sacred value was attributed to the midsummer sunset in the north-west. The Uisnech balance was maintained by recognizing such complementary opposites.

By following the sunwise story of Midir and Étaín, via Slievenaman, we are eventually led to the spot where, in the Uisnech design, they touched ground on the evening of the summer solstice. Étaín and her retinue embodied this annual event – the most northerly sunset of the year, when they entered a síd, called Síd Sinche, in Co. Roscommon, identified with a souterrain also called the Cave of the Cats.

This cave, which aligns with midsummer sunset on the Uisnech web, became the supernatural focus around which the sacred capital of Connacht developed. No fewer than sixty-eight pre-Norman monuments 'which appear to be mainly ritual in character',[91] are bunched together around the síd. These are from every period, including the fourth millenium BC.

Étaín is said to have travelled to Crúachain from Slievenaman (the apex of the sun's course), in the company of her maid, Crochen Croderg.[92]

Crochen was the setting sun personified. Her first name is based on *croch*, 'saffron or cream', and her second, Croderg, means 'blood red'. Given in full, her name describes how the sun changes from yellow to red as it sets – the very transformation that she embodies. The Bodleian account states that her eyebrows, eyelashes, and entire head were red. Keating calls her 'Redskin'.

Crochen admired the radiant síd to which Étaín and Midir had led her. 'Then said strong Crochen, "What fine house is this where we have halted? O Midir of the splendid feasts, is this thy spacious dwelling?"'[93] Midir explained that his own home lay 'nearer to the sunrise', but as a reward for her journey, he gave Crochen the sunset síd, and renamed it Crúachain after her. Then Midir and Étaín, concerned to start the next solar cycle, passed northwards, leaving Crochen behind at Crúachain. In due course, she gave birth there to Medb, goddess-queen of Connacht.

Cats pursue a solar bowl of cream, Book of Kells. Into the Cave of the Cats at Rathcroghan the midsummer sun-maid, Crochen Croderg, descended at dusk

Oweynagat, The Cave of the Cats, is Crochen's síd, 700 metres south-south-west of the great mound of Rath Crúachan. The cave is a modified natural limestone fissure, 130 metres long, and probably refers to the cats, who, in north-west European myth, drew the solar chariot across the sky. Cats' eyes, blazing in the dark, naturally confirm their daytime mythic duties. The involvement of cats in solar orbitings may also help to explain Aill na Mireann's other name, The Cat Stone, since folk names are rarely arbitrary.

In 1779, the Oweynagat Cave was known as 'The Hellmouth Door of Ireland', challenging St Patrick's Purgatory for the title, except that here, instead of Christian associations there was a belief that a woman, clinging to the tail of an unruly calf, had been led through the cave, down an underground tunnel, and had re-emerged, 29 kilometres to the north at the Caves of Keshcorran, the haunt of the Winter hags.[94] Beranger teased his guides about this, and with their help searched the Cat's Cave for a possible lower exit, 'but the solid rock was everywhere; and there was neither door nor window nor crevice where the woman and her calf could pass'. Not to be denied, 'the country people said that the Devil had stopped up the tunnel'. And it could be argued that a devil-ridden Christianity had indeed blocked the worship of the great cycle which spun between midsummer eve and Keshcorran.

Rathcroghan's síd also played an important part in quarter day rites. It was from here that the giant Olca Ái arose to drive the young people of Connacht into a Samain frenzy, and here Queen Medb or Maeve initiated the Bull of Cualgne expedition.

The events pouring to and from the síd of Crúachain remind us that there were eight important festivals in the ancient solar year, yet the cave's primary purpose was nonetheless linked to the midsummer solstice. The *Dindshenchas* says that Midir's intention, in visiting the site, was to see his relative, Sinech, who lived in there: 'because of his affection for her'.[95] *Sinech* means 'having large paps'.

Above ground, as if to echo the opulence of the midsummer síd, the prehistoric human community created a monument in the shape of a vast 'land breast', which is now called Rath Crúachain, or Rathcroghan.

Rath Crúachain, the principal monument in the complex, consists of a natural mound, artificially scarped in antiquity into a near-circular shape, 90 metres diameter, with a domed surface, and a crowning 'nipple'. The 'nipple' was a 2-metre-high mound on the summit, surrounded by a circular 'aureole', in the form of a bank and ditch,

10 metres across. This summit feature was clearly visible in a nineteenth-century survey, and in Beranger's drawing of 1779, though only faint traces of it now remain. Here the kings of Connacht were inaugurated, by marriage to Crochen's daughter, Medb. The word *Medb* is cognate with English, *mead*, the intoxicating drink fermented from the honey of flowers, including elder flowers, and associated with the English fairy queen, Mab.

In Irish, Medb's name means 'The Intoxicating One', and Connacht was called 'The Fifth of the Intoxicating One'.[96] Her liquor gave access to a hidden maternal domain, symbolized in her own mother's *crochen* or drinking cup.

Medb of Connacht was regarded as sister to, or 'the same as' Queen Medb of Tara, whom the High King of all Ireland had to marry before he could assume the title. Tara and Rathcroghan lie 64 and 61 kilometres respectively from Aill na Mireann. Joining east and west together, Medb appeared in both places, to offer her cup to the King, just as Étaín had served wine at Tara to her eastern husband, Eochaid, prior to arriving at Rathcroghan with Midir.

For the island vessel to ring true, it had to be rotated throughout the year from season to season, and from síd to síd, on either side of Croghan Hill, Co. Offaly, where Brigit-the-Smith worked on it so hard. Then it could be filled to the brim with the potent spirits of divine biographies, annually distilled from all quarters in story-telling and ritual, and offered for human consumption.

329°E: Brí Léith (Ardagh Hill), Co. Longford [22 km]★★

Seen from Uisnech, Brí Léith (198 metres), the síd of Midir and Étaín, is only 31° from true North, where, at Irish latitudes, no setting sun has ever reached. Yet what was invisible as a surface phenomenon shone brightly in the imagination. In mythic consciousness, withdrawal from one plane of reality implied re-emergence on another. Consequently the sun goddess Étaín, alter ego of Áine, is described 'on the fair green of Brí Léith' as a 'woman with a bright comb of silver adorned with gold, washing in a silver basin, wherein were four golden birds, and little bright gems of purple carbuncle in the rim of the basin'. She wore a cloak with 'silvery fringes and a brooch of fairest gold . . . On her head were two golden-yellow tresses, in each of which was a plait of four locks, with a bead at the tip of each lock. That hair seemed to them like the flower of the iris in summer, or like red gold after burnishing.'[97]

Étaín was the epitome of inaccessible glory and was coveted by the mythic horse-king of the east, Eochaid, after he had seen her standing naked before Brí Léith.

A reversed version of *east-west* affairs is revealed in the place name Brí Léith, which, according to the *Dindshenchas*, combines the name of Midir's daughter, Brí Bruach-Brecc ('of the varied borders', 'famous for her excellencies') who was loved by Liath, a god of the east coast.

The Ardagh Chalice, found in Co. Limerick. Its silver, gilt and red stones echo the description of the sun goddess Étaín at Brí Léith (Ardagh, Co. Longford)

She wanted to return his affection, but Midir was against the match and would not allow Liath near his house. So she 'journeyed for Liath's sake and met him at Temair [Tara] eastwards'.[98]

Liath means 'grey'. He waited in the grey before dawn for the daughter of the hidden sun to re-emerge from her northwestern hiding place. They had agreed to meet at the Grave of the Girls at Tara, but in the event were kept apart by Midir's slingers. Brí then returns to Midir's home, and dies there, heartbroken, after re-naming it Brí Léith. Brí Léith brings together the names of the frustrated lovers from East and West. This name defines Midir's síd as a place constructed from the attraction of opposites – a principle inherent in the entire Uisnech pattern.

46°E: Fremu (Frewin Hill), Co. Westmeath [13 km]

Radio masts point skywards from Frewin Hill's 171-metre-high twin summits, whose flanks are subdivided into small fields by hedgerows running wild. Some of the pastures are being invaded by bracken. Ireland has hundreds of hills in a similar state. What makes Frewin Hill special is its weight of myth. Here Eochaid Airem, horse king of the east, dared to settle close to the east-west frontier, and only 22 kilometres from Brí Léith, Midir's stronghold. Frewin Hill has been identified as Dun Fremu, the fort of Eochaid-as-Culture Hero and innovator. It was 'his mansion and ancestral home' towards the end of his life.[99]

His first name derives from the plural of horse, '*eocu, eocho*'. His second, '*Airem*', means 'ploughman', or 'tiller of the soil'. Joining the two parts together creates a horse-drawn plough-team and the god of agriculture, who possessed the combination of human ingenuity and equine strength to introduce farming.

Eochaid's mythic function was appreciated in the seventeenth century, when Keating wrote: 'Eochaid Airiomh, it was he who first dug a cave in Ireland. Airiomh is the same as *ar uaimhe*, 'ploughing', or 'digging of a cave'.[100] This 'first digging' is implanted in the place-name. Present-day Frewin Hill is identical with Fremu of the medieval accounts, and derived from the word *frem* – literally 'a root', and 'to implant'. Figuratively it means 'a source, origin, or rootstock', and is related to *Fremamail* – 'radical, primary'. In Irish myth Fremu Hill, or Dun Fremu, marks a departure from the wilderness in favour of farming. Considering the effect of ploughing as a form of cutting, it comes as no surprise to learn that Fremu was considered 'a judgment seat of Fótla'.[101] The island-wide goddess of divisions and furrows appeared to give her approval to the new work.

The five-thousand-year-old Uisnech design, as a cultural product, was crafted into shape at a time when no one imagined that the dialogue with Nature could be broken off. Rather, the Uisnech fire-eye sees nature mainly from the inside, for it was constructed by people for whom culture was primarily a means of gaining access to nature via worship of her deities. It was not seen as an alternative, far less a *rival* to Nature.

Yet it appears that from the outset the Uisnech Eye contained something of the tension between Nature and Culture so familiar to our own times. This is especially evident in the zone around the north side of Uisnech Hill. In that quarter, Midir and Eochaid came to their final battle, where Midir stood for the repository of elemental powers, and Eochaid was the innovative god, deviser of machinery and agricultural techniques.

With hindsight, one can see this was the start of the long struggle between forest-dwellers and hamburger economies, now reaching its climax around the world.

Support for Eochaid, the ploughman of Fremu came from the Fir Bolg, whose task in Irish agrarian myth was to help prepare the soil. Normally associated with Connacht, the *Dindshenchas* described how, having first visited Tara, Eochaid's palace in the east, two Fir Bolg brothers arrived in Co. Westmeath and gave their names to Loughs Owel and Ennell, which lie close to Fremu. Then they began to marl the land, 'hauling clay over slabs of stone, to make ploughlands and pastures . . . it was a rough service'.[102]

They were 'giants'. The first, *Ainind*, means 'mighty', while Uair his brother was described as 'a boy of huge stature'. At Lough Owel, named after him, he was permitted to break a taboo which said he should drink only cold water from the sea, which suggests that the lough might be regarded as an interior ocean – the amniotic sea. As a language word *uair* means 'coldness' and 'an hour', the twenty-fourth part of a day. So, the subdivision of space, by ploughing and marling, had an effect on time, changing it from an undifferentiated continuum into a succession of task-laden periods – a definite cultural advance, for better or worse.

His first furrow also opened up Ireland to a whole field of sexual connotations, already established in the Neolithic cultures of mainland Europe, and of Asia, where the furrow is the land goddess's vulva.[103]

Keating's statement that Eochaid dug the first cave in Ireland is possibly related either to sexualized agriculture or to mining. (Eochaid undermined Slievenaman, looking for the golden Étaín, who was gold-adorned buried sunlight, a sexual partner, *and* the first gold ore personified; mining was a mythic enterprise begun before 2000 BC.)

Eochaid's subsequent attack on Brí Léith, still in pursuit of Étaín, alludes to his use of siege engines, which Midir, representing raw nature, spent nine years trying to sabotage before his defences were overwhelmed by Eochaid's ingenuity. In defeat, Midir nevertheless outwitted his adversary by demonstrating the subversive truth that to nature, all gods and goddesses are ultimately the same. He assembled fifty women and invited Eochaid to pick out Étaín. Eochaid failed to distinguish between her and his own daughter, and inadvertently selected the latter.[104] It was after this debâcle that Eochaid settled at Fremu, 'and his mind was troubled'.[105]

On midsummer morning, who should rise at Fremu, which stands on the Uisnech-Sliab Caillighe alignment, but Midir, Étaín and her handmaiden Croghen Croderg, according to the *Dindshenchas, and* to watchers of that annual dawn. They are on their way to Rathcroghan, making the longest sky-ride of the year. In rising thus at Fremu, Midir, the god of unqualified Nature, can be seen to have already infiltrated Eochaid's stronghold of culture, implying that nature and culture cannot be kept apart.

To confirm as much, Midir admits that the idea of yoking two oxen together to drag a plough originated in his own hot-bed of elemental nature, Brí Léith, from where, he says, Eochaid obtained the secret.[106]

Thanks to Midir, King Eochaid was spared the indignity of having to pull as well as steer his own plough. The anecdote enables us to regard our own technology as a special kind of natural phenomenon, which, like any other species in nature, grows towards extinction at a speed proportional to its degree of over-specialization.

Both Fremu and Brí Léith lay in the ancient district of Tethba, which, considering its location around the north side of Uisnech, is derived from surprisingly hot ingredients: *teth*, meaning 'warm, hot, scalding, ardent, sultry', and *tethin*, 'of the sun', and 'like a fiery blaze'. Tethba was also the secret name of Étaín's daughter, fathered by Eochaid;[107] Tethba the girl, and Tethba the district resolve the enmity between Midir and Eochaid. Her name may derive from *tet*, 'a rope or cord'. She ties one midsummer sunrise alignment to the next, and her birth-string leads straight to the omphalos on Uisnech hill.

There is no gap, and no rest between the annual cycles, but Tethba's young legs are there to take up the running.

Mide, All and One

Uisnech and Consciousness

After completing the Grand Circuit, to return to the starting point at
Aill na Mireann is to visit again the eye of a ceaseless event-storm.
The Ireland of the five provinces was an immensely busy place.

One of the functions of the centre stone was to anchor all this
activity into a sense and a point of repose, without denying the need
for action. This paradox was resolved through the god, Mide, who
was synonymous with the centre stone, and the central province which
bore his name.

Mide, the master of ceremonies at Uisnech, combined in his ancestry
the complementary qualities of wakefulness and somnolence. He was
son of Brath, and *brath* means 'act of reconnoitering, of revealing, a
revelation, a sign'. Yet this Brath was in turn son of Deaith, and *deaith*
is 'idleness, inactivity and indolence'.

In Indian terms one may say that Mide absorbed *maya*, the play of
events, into the Absolute, or *Brahman*. He is the words of creation
and the silences between the words; the waking and the sleeping.

Inherited opposites come together in Mide, and in this respect the
ancient myths are confirmed by studies of consciousness conducted by
modern psychology. Uisnech may be deserted, but it is no more 'out
of date' than is Freud's classic statement of 1927:

The division of mental life into what is conscious and what is unconscious is
the fundamental premise on which psycho-analysis is based. Psychoanalysis
cannot accept the view that consciousness is the essence of mental life, but is
obliged to regard consciousness as one property of mental life, which may
co-exist along with its other properties, or may be absent. The mental
phenomena of hypnosis and dreams necessitate this conclusion.[108]

Similarly, the Beltaine bonfires were lit only once a year, but may
burn on, as buried memories, long after their flames falter, and
conscious thought of them has died away. Freud writes of 'the
importance of *optical memory* [by which] it is possible for thought-
processes to become conscious, through a reversion to visual residues,
and in many people this seems to be a favourite method. Thinking in
pictures [he adds] is unquestionably older than thinking in words.'[109]

It follows that the Uisnech myth may originally have been seen
before it was heard. Equally, another ring of bonfires might be the

best means to recall lost Uisnech words, glowing like peat, with the energy of completed summer songs.

Freud continues: 'A mental element, for instance an idea, is not as a rule permanently conscious. On the contrary, a state of consciousness is characteristically very transitory and often lies latent, or unconscious.'[110] He then distinguishes between the *latent* capacity for recall, which he calls a task of the *pre*conscious, and the churnings of chaos and raw appetites in the *un*conscious, or *id*.

In terms of Irish myth, the id might be characterized as the realm of the Fomorians.

Irish myth shows that the boundaries between psychic realms are neither impermeable, nor static. Over thousands of years, much transference has taken place between what, in prehistoric times, was known at a conscious or preconscious level, to the level of the modern id, and there, if nowhere else, the Uisnech eye lives on.

In the id, which is capable of being inherited, are stored up vestiges of the existences of countless former egos [including those which looked out from Uisnech in antiquity]. The experiences undergone by the ego seem at first to be lost to posterity, but when they have been repeated often enough and with sufficient intensity in the successive individuals of many generations, they transform themselves, so to say, into experiences of the id, the impress of which is preserved by inheritance, and when the ego forms its super-ego out of the id, it may perhaps only 'be reviving images of egos that have passed away, and be securing for them a resurrection.'[111]

In this way, the fire of prehistoric Uisnech rekindles in the depths of our being, and the lure of the archaic takes on a strength verging on the irrational; for that is where, in our make-up, it is usually lodged, till permitted to rise from the depths.

Conle at Uisnech

As omphalos, Uisnech was the route to the id *par excellence* for every adult generation. It stood at the gate, forever closed, forever the focus of longing, leading to the state of prenatal bliss. (In Babylon the omphalos was believed to rest on the Gate of Apsū. *Apsū* means 'the water of Chaos before the Creation'. Similarly the Rock of Jerusalem was said to go down into the subterranean waters of *tehõm*.)

Therefore the story of Conle at Uisnech is the tale of Everyone. He was the son of Conn of the Hundred Battles, High King of Ireland in the second century AD, and Conle's Adventures are known from eighth-century manuscripts.

One day Conle the Red was beside his father on the hill of Uisnech. He saw a woman in wonderful attire approach him. Conle said: 'Where do you come from, woman?' 'I come', said the woman, 'from the Land of the Living, a place where there is neither death, nor sin, nor transgression. We enjoy lasting feasts without preparing them and pleasant company without strife. We live in great peace. From that we are known as the People of Peace.'

'With whom do you speak, boy?' said Conn to his son, for none saw the woman save Conle alone. The woman answered:

'He speaks to a beautiful young woman of noble race whom neither death threatens nor old age. I love Conle the Red, I call him to the Plain of Delight, where reigns a king victorious and immortal, a king without weeping or sorrow in his land since he became king.

'Come with me, Conle the Red of the jewelled neck, red as flame, your hair is yellow over the bright noble face of your royal form. If you come with me, your beauty will not lose its youth or its fairness forever.'

Conn consulted with his druid Corán, who

sang against the woman's voice so that Conle did not see the woman after that, . . . [but] she threw an apple to Conle. Conle was for a month without food, without drink. He cared not to eat any food but his apple, and his apple did not diminish for what he used to eat of it, but was still whole. A longing then came on Conle for the woman he had seen.

A month from that day Conle was beside his father in the plain of Archommin and he saw the same woman approach him, and she said to him: 'There above sits Conle among lifeless mortals waiting for a gloomy death. Living immortals invite you. You are a hero for the people of Tethra.' Then Conle says, 'It is not easy for me, for I love my people, but a longing for the woman has come upon me.' The woman answered then and said this: 'You have a longing greater than all other desires to go from them over the sea, so that we may come in my ship of glass to the dwelling of Boadach [boadach, 'pre-eminent'] . . . though it is far away, we shall reach it before night. It is the country which delights the mind of anyone who goes there. There are no people there save only women and girls.' When the maiden had finished speaking Conle sprang away from them so that he was in the ship of glass, or crystal coracle. The pair rowed then over the sea away from Ireland and they were not seen since, and it is not known where they went.[112]

Perhaps they travelled to that submarine well of wisdom called Connle, the mythic source of the Shannon, in the western ocean. Connle may have been named after Conle of Mide, in a conscious attempt to re-establish the link between Ireland's longest river, the flood of prenatal waters, and Ériu's principal omphalos, Aill na Mireann.

The voyage involves no split between spirit and matter, and no division into good and evil. Instead, as so often in Irish tradition, the mysterious female offers a fusion of materiality with the ineffable.

Beyond the sunset and beyond the visible, her ship carries this achievement into the realm of pure and timeless bliss.

But who *was* she? MacCana argues that 'she can hardly be dissociated from those goddesses such as Áine and Aoibheall, whose fairy dwellings constituted familiar landmarks in the Irish landscape.'[113] The apple-woman's journey extended the rings of Ériu's bonfires, in the Uisnech array, till they merged with an ocean of stars, visible and invisible, securing in that union the prospect of eternity.

That is how far the Uisnech eye can see.

'The Churn' or Harvest Home, Toome, Co. Antrim, c. 1910. The grandmother
seen eating in the harvest field on page 57 joins the family at Harvest Supper. The
Churn or corn-dolly, now rafter-hung, presides over the event

Conclusion
Home

The Gods come Home

The gods whom poets celebrated, priests worshipped, and kings obeyed, depended for their popularity on frequent entry into the homes of the people. In the ordinary house, divine adventures were rediscovered in the corresponding domestic and farmyard events of birth, marriage, and death. The real-life dramas of human existence, when considered in their vivid contrasts and reiterated patterns, were absorbed into the doings of the heroes and gods, as told and retold around the domestic hearth.

This conjunction of supernatural and natural affairs was further reinforced by family ceremonies, repeated in an annual cycle. Domestic rites ensured that humanity's share in the divine drama was not left to chance or to poet-priests, but belonged to all. By house rites, the quality of eternity was touched at regular intervals and formalized into a reliable framework. A collective inner tranquillity thus survived the impact of physical hardship and remorseless change.

It is no coincidence that Brigit, the deity most obviously identified with the sacred flame, has lasted the longest in popular esteem. No god has leapt the pale between pagan and Christian worlds more successfully than she. For millennia she linked the human hearth to the Uisnech wheel, bringing its grandeur into the home, and Brigit-on-the-hearth remained the focus of worship long after the Uisnech design had been lost. Her fire was the central feature of every house, and constituted one end of a flaming axis reaching to the chamber of pure imagination. She put the family in direct touch with ultimate mysteries. 'Brigit, excellent woman, a flame, golden, delightful. May she, the sun-dazzling, splendid, guide us to the eternal Kingdom,' sang St Broccan in the seventh century.[1]

Christian history tells that St Brigit was a woman born in a druid's house at Tocharmaine in AD 453. Yet she invested her humanity with divine qualities, for her name continued to mean 'the Great or Sublime One', from the root *brig*, 'power, strength, vigour, force, efficiency, substance, essence and meaning'.

At sunrise on the first day of spring, her birthday, February 1st the quarter day, a column of fire rose from her infant head, and neighbours saw the house aflame from earth to heaven; but when they entered to rescue her there was no fire.[2] This brief supernatural flame joined cradle to sun and night to day.

It was told how a druid watching the stars in the middle of the night saw a fiery column arising out of the house where she was residing, at Loch Mask.[3] She reached up to the unfathomable heights of space from smoke-filled ordinariness; she was a great traveller.

Her head-fires also served to associate Home with Temple. For example in Ardagh 'a fiery column flamed out of her head up to the ridge of the church',[4] while her own religious house at Kildare revolved around a fire, which was kept alight continuously. Equally she enabled people to see flames coursing through their farm tools, so bringing those worn sticks into the sacred realm:

Brigid went into a house and brought out a harrow [a wooden rake]. She held it up over her head and every one of the pins gave out a flame like a candle. All the people turned back to look at the shining harrow that was such a great wonder.[5]

Human clothing was created under the comprehensive circle of her cloak, for she had laid it, 'wet on the rays of the sun, and they held it up the same as hooks'.[6] The human family's garments could share the virtue of her cloak, providing the right rituals were observed.

Dozens of stories concerning Brigit's miraculous doings point towards the numinous opportunities playing around the home, and to the need for householders to offer hospitality to the goddess-saint, so that her benefits might accrue. The well-known Irish instinct for hospitality may be traced to the expectation of entertaining the divine.

The Celts inherited a series of morning devotions centred on the hearth, called Blessing of the Kindling. 'The Kindling of the fire is a work full of interest to the housewife, and when 'lifting' the fire in the morning the woman prays in an undertone that the fire may be blessed to her and to her household. The people look upon fire as a miracle of the Divine Power provided for their good,' wrote Carmichael of Hebridean attitudes c, 1850,[7] which originated in Ireland.

Before retiring for the night, the fire would be 'smoored' with loving care. With the hearthstone normally in the middle of the floor, the embers were evenly spread in a circle, which was then divided into three equal sections, with a small boss being left in the middle. A sod of peat was laid between each section, with each sod touching the central boss. Then the whole circle was covered over with some ashes, and the central heap referred to as The Hearth of the Three. The woman then closed her eyes, stretched her hands, and slowly intoned 'a formula'. In Ireland this ran:

> I cover this fire
> As noble Christ did.
> Mary on top of the house,
> And St Brigid in its centre.

Hearth of a County Antrim kitchen, early twentieth century. Oatcakes or farls, seen baking here, were cut as one 'seasonal' quarter of an 'annual' disc. Household and farmyard tools, like the wooden spade on the right, were originally viewed as images of working gods and goddesses

The subdivision of the fire into three around a central boss may well refer to Brigit as a trinity within the outer ring of her unity.

As a working icon her image in the hearth was also a nightly resurrection of the great fire-eye seen engraved in Neolithic tombs, such as Dowth, and was a small-scale version of the Uisnech-centred fire-eye. All three placed the believer under the protection of the ash-hidden fire goddess during the hours of darkness. Aalen points out that in Ireland a central hearth was once fundamental, 'though now it can be found only in West Galway, having long since been moved to the gable end[8] in other districts'. (Possibly the last people to sit around a central open hearth were a Mr and Mrs Lawless of Menlough, Co. Galway, *c.* 1966.) As recently as the seventeenth century, both round and rectangular Irish dwellings were focussed on a central fire, 'and round it they sleep on the ground, lying all in a circle about the fire, with their feet towards it'.[9] This fire, essential to survival in winter, and to cooking throughout the year, was regarded as a spiritual gift, blessing the entire house. The Irish word *tellach*, 'hearth, fireplace', also means 'household' and 'family'. So the central domestic light united habitation and inhabitants in a single word.

In Ulster it was unlucky to be the first house to show smoke on May morning.[10] On this, the first day of the 'summer half' of the year, there was a tendency for every domestic fire to fly from the house to rejoin its parental blaze in the síd, or in the supernaturally arising sun itself.

The Pot

By speaking of the underworld síd, fire ran *below* the domestic hearth into the territory of Begoibne, Brigit's 'sister', the woman of the smithy and pot-maker.[11] Her workshop beneath Croghan Hill offered a divine prototype to householders, who likewise buried a pot in front of their hearthstone. Examples of small 'pot-oven' burials include one found under a kitchen floor at Mahoonaghbed, Co. Limerick, hung from two thin iron rods laid crosswise over the hole. Clare, Kerry and Tipperary have provided similar evidence of a 'síd-in-miniature' beneath the cottage floor.[12]

The buried pot represented the abyss, lower hemisphere, and fundament of Brigit. Therefore when St Columcille was trapped in Breccán's Cauldron, the notorious whirlpool near Rathlin Island, it was to her that he prayed. 'He besought Brigit that a calm might come to him.'[13] She obliged, and he reached Scotland safely.

The issue here is the elasticity of the domestic *coire* or cauldron, which reaches through the topographic scale towards infinity, a range reflected in language. *Coire* means 'cauldron, large pot, gulf *and* whirlpool'. The word *aigen* means 'a large metal vessel used for washing hands', and the ninth Rule of Tallagcht states that after it had been returned to the smith to be tapped all round, three times, it could be employed to brew liquor, fleshment, or porridge.[14] This tapping was a ritual appeal to the triple goddess of the waters, clean and foul. *Aigean* also means 'the ocean, the deep, and abyss'. Similarly, the pot buried beneath the house floor was overflowing with meanings, connected by symbol and mythic word.

The Hanging-Bowl Light

Until recent centuries, most Irish houses had no windows. Domestic life was lived largely in the dark, pierced by Brigit's fiery arrow, the shaft of sunlight coming through the south door, as Synge discovered among the Aran islanders, where the angle of the shadow still told the time of day. After sunset, illumination came almost entirely from the hearth-fire, but was sometimes supplemented by the oil light of a hanging bowl. These vessels were suspended from the roof by three cords or chains, passing through three lugs around the rim. Whether made of bronze, wood, or stones, they are generally regarded as having more than utilitarian ambitions, for they evoke the sun boat at night,

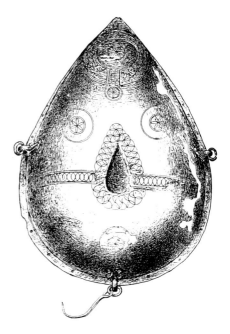

*St Brigit at St Brigit's Well,
Liscannor, Co. Clare, in her
virginal glass house. Brigit-as-nun
holds* Ecclesia, The Church

*Wooden cauldron, Altartate, Clones, Co. Monaghan,
late Iron Age, 49 cm diameter, incised with a solar
rocking pattern around the rim*

*Bronze hanging-bowl lamp from Ballinderry, Co.
Westmeath, Iron Age, 24 cm long, incised with vulva
and belt symbols*

transporting the wavering glimmer through oceans of darkness. With that in mind, the passage of the submarine sun was engraved in a rocking pattern around the rim of the wooden Altartate vessel, found at Clones, Co. Monaghan (currently dated 500 BC–AD 450).[15]

A bronze lamp fom Ballinderry Crannog, on the Eiscir Riada, four kilometres from Croghan Hill, displays the kind of vulva symbol depicted in continental Europe since Palaeolithic times. The same shape is also embossed into the base of the vessel.[16] Seen from below (as it *would* have been seen), this magic pudendum is surrounded by the rotating pattern of incised sun circles, attached to and bordered by a belt of running solar symbols. Perhaps it evoked the east-west Eiscir Riada as the national 'Belt of Brigit', complementing her straw belt, which, as we shall see, played a big part in the 1st February ritual.

The rosette at the tip of this vessel is surrounded by an applied collar, neck (or mide?). Over it the wick would have floated and shone. The loops are formed by cast animals who bite the rim.

Other bowls suggest a journey to the sacred interior by showing Brigit's vulva in their overall form, as with the Kilgulbin East vessel, or by the shape of and engraving on the lugs, as at Ballynacourt.[17]

St Brigit's Eve

The greatest occasion in the traditional domestic year was, arguably, the festival of Brigit's birth, on February 1st, the Imbolc or Oimelg quarterday, and start of spring.

On St Brigit's Eve it was customary to limewash the house inside. 'A good big fire was put down and the animals were bedded on clean straw. The whole interior had an air of cosiness and comfort ready to receive Brigit into the house.'[18] In Co. Mayo the man of the house procured a garment to use as a mantle, or *Brat Bride* (the clothing of the infant goddess). The article chosen was the one which would be in greatest use by the member of the house whose occupation was the most dangerous, such as the muffler of a fisherman. The man took it to the yard, drew a good long sheaf of straw from the stack, and wrapped the garment around the straw to give it a rough outline of a human body. Then, carrying it as if it were a child, he set it down outside the back door, and went into the house.

So placed, this straw child also evokes the birth of St Brigit. Her *Life* states that she was born neither within the house nor without. Her pregnant mother, visiting a queen, had 'put one of her two footsteps over the threshold of the house, the other foot [still] being outside . . . *Then* she brought forth her daughter, even St Brigid.'[19]

The door is implicitly equated with the vulva of the saint-goddess's mother.

In Co. Mayo folk ritual, the straw child who was refused entry at the back door represented Brigit of the completed winter quarter. Consequently that door (which usually faced north) remained shut at Imbolc, the start of spring. Instead, when the preparations for supper were complete, the man rose to say that he must fetch Brigit through the front or south door to share the feast. Going outside again, he knelt, and cried to the family: 'Go on your knees, open your eyes, and let Brigit in!' Inside, they responded: 'She is welcome.'

The formula was repeated twice more, and while the people within continued to chant 'she is welcome', the man brought 'Brigit' around to the front door and entered with her, whereupon all cried: '*Mush! Se beatha agus a slainte*' – 'How wonderful! She is welcome, and seeing that, a toast.' The straw baby Brigit was then laid respectfully against a table leg, or, if need be, placed on a sick cow's back to effect a cure.[20]

Brigit brought the wheelings of the cosmos into the cabin. By her entry she took over the house, which was accordingly born (in both senses) from the dark travail of the winter environment, towards the growing light. The occupants acted as midwives to the double event, which re-sacralized the entire structure in the way that a Hebridean chant suggests:

> May Brigit give blessing
> To the house that is here...
> Brigit, the fair and tender,
> Her hue like the cotton grass.
> Rich-tressed maiden,
> Of ringlets of gold;
> Both crest and frame,
> Both stone and beam;
> Both clay and wattle;
> Both summit and foundation;
> Both window and timber;
> Both foot and head;
> Both man and woman;
> Both wife and children;
> Both young and old;
> Both maiden and youth.[21]

At the Imbolc festival, to ensure that every member of the family came into direct contact with Brigit's power, a three-metre ring of plaited straw rope was made, to which three or four straw crosses were attached. It was called *Cris, Crois Bride*, or St Brigit's Belt. The

St Brigit's Cross (right), a pre-Christian sun-wheel traditionally hung in Irish kitchens.
Far right: Crios Bride, *St Brigit's Belt, Co. Galway*

'belt' was carried from house to house, and all the occupants drew it over their heads and down their bodies before stepping from the golden ring.[22] In performing this ritual they literally *wore* the track of the sun-goddess' annual circuit. (Irish *Cris* is cognate with Welsh *gwregis*, which takes on solar connections in the phrase *gwregys Iau*, 'the belt of Jupiter', and dives into the ocean in *gwregys'r mor*, the 'sweet sea weeds, or sea belts'.[23])

Some idea of the range of Irish *crois* comes from Keating, *c.* 1650, who measured the breadth of Ireland as 'four and a half degrees of the solar *crois*, which is called the zodiac'. The word was also applied to the 'zones of heaven and earth' of earlier cosmological speculation.[24]

As a human belt it was the equivalent of Ireland's medial road between equinoctial sunrise and sunset, the Eiscir Riada. Woven in straw, it was prophetic of a successful corn-harvest to come, reaching from sea to sea. The Christian tradition says that St Brigit had herself worn the belt, before giving it to a beggar girl, who in turn loaned it to the sick, for cures and general circulation.[25] All subsequent belts were descended from the sacred prototype, the one worn by the saint-goddess.

To complement the *Cris*, a silk head-ribband called *Ribin*, or *Ribe Bride* was left outside the house on Bride's Eve, and was believed to lengthen during that night; afterwards it was used as a cure for headaches. (In Bride, the health of mind and body were of equal importance.) Her head ribbon can perhaps also be seen wound around Uisnech, in the word *ribeann*, which O'Donovan defines as 'a royal hill on which royal parleys were held'.[26] The *Ribin* is the linear form of her energy, and ultimately relates it to the monster serpent who accompanied her in the boat from Scandinavia. It surfaces again as Caoranach at Lough Derg, Co. Donegal, facing St Brigit's well.

Roof Tree and Wall

Together, Ribbin and Crois helped to complete the Cosmos-House-Human amalgam known to many religions, and still the subject of speculation in India, especially in Jainism, where a hatha yoga text speaks of the human body as 'a house with one column [the spine] and nine doors'.[27] Through the apertures of human anatomy, the architecture of the cosmos enters its sentient home.

In old Irish, the human spine, the roof tree of a house, and the world axis came together in the word *Cli*, meaning 'an oaken pillar or support, the mighty balk, great and good under roofs of fortune, and a radiant body', as in *gorm a chli*, meaning 'bosom or heart'.

The goddess Brigit inhabited both the Uisnech ash (the national *axis mundi*) and (as sunrise goddess) the sacred oak of Leinster, at Cill Dara, now known as Kildare. As a saint, her religious house continued the traditions centred on the self-same oak.

Another name for the domestic centre-pole was *cleithe*, which means 'dwelling, top, the crown of the head, the heavens, firmament, and

Lighting the 'Needfire'. When building a new house, the first hearth-fire was sometimes generated from the friction of timbers arranged in a Brigit's cross design

sky, culmination and perfection'. In the case of homes of rectangular shape, the word *cleithe* was also used to describe the ridge-pole, the highest horizontal member. Thus, one word encompassed both principal axes, together with the human brow, and (naturally) the universe. (On an intermediate scale, *benn*, 'gable, or spire', also meant mountain, or peak, as in Benn Étair, Howth.)

Cleithe lent grandeur to the latitude and longitude of everyday life, while simultaneously touching the remotest regions of space with everyday routine. A sense of unshakeable 'belonging' was the outcome. With such an outlook, what could the inhabitants know of real poverty? By observing the leaky thatch, black with peat smoke, they enjoyed a world-view far beyond the dreams of twentieth-century comfort, since every hut was potentially 'the mystic hut of poetic inspiration', the play-house of the gods. Consequently the word *tuige*, 'thatch', was close to *tuigen*, 'a mantle worn by poets'.

The Old Irish word *fraig*, 'a panel of mud and wattle, usually the inside of a house wall', also meant 'to the utmost extent, entirely', and included 'the borders of a country with the sea'. Ireland's outermost 'wall' is composed of cliff and shingle, and so turns the entire island into the earthen floor of one home. Land then becomes homeland. Seen from the outside, the sea-bounding wall, *fraig*, was echoed in mariners' phrases such as 'the wave my thatch and beach my wall'.[28]

Because a sailor had to make his home on the sea, he called the horizon, edging the furthest ocean, *fraig*, a 'sky-wall'. These were not esoteric ideas, confined to the language of a poetic élite. Rather, *fraig* and *cleithe* spoke of the majestic quality of popular experience.

The twin human needs are for a home, and for horizons of reach beyond it. As Buttimer says, together they make 'the lived reciprocity of rest and movement, territory and range, security and adventure, house-keeping and husbandry, shelter and expedition'.[29] Thus every home (it may be said) repeats in its own fashion the centrifugal and centripetal pulsing of Uisnech-the-omphalos.

255

Fraig and *cleithe* stood for the merging of physical, emotional and intellectual bonds joining together far and near, subject and object, thought and action, individual and environment.

At a personal level the word *fraig* meant 'the rim of a shield', and the shield defines the navel of the human trunk which it protects. *Fraig* is also 'a bush of hair' (encircling birthplace and mind); 'human clothing' (weaving between skin and air), and 'part of a sheep's fleece'.

In Ireland, as in other parts of Europe, the domestic dwelling was normally shared with sheep and cows. This intimacy is reflected in Brigit's title as the golden-haired Bride of the Kine. She may originally have had the power to *become* a cow, and she was often portrayed in a cow's company. Through her worship, the unity of life (self-evident when every house was a Noah's Ark at anchor) found a means of acknowledgment.

The Four Quarters

Devotion to St Brigit has survived recent transformations of house interiors. The cross of Bride, as old as the Neolithic,[30] still hangs in many a modern Irish kitchen, at least 'for luck'. Made either of rush or wheat straw, these crosses combine harvest gold with Brigit's yellow flame. Whether in lozenge shape, quartered wheel or free-legged, the dynamic of the solar year is conveyed, showing the original god-given plan for the Island and its attached Otherworlds.

Equally, the qualities of the quarters typically determined the orientation of a rectangular house. The main door should face east, or south. Only with great reluctance would a house be extended towards the west, the zone of misfortune. These issues were matters of spiritual (and therefore physical) life and death, because, in Eliade's words, every house is 'the choice of a universe that one is prepared to assume by creating it'.[31]

This act of alignment with the cosmos (reiterated in the layout of the Classical city) explains why in Ireland an English silver florin coin, having a quartered design on the back, was much favoured as an offering to be placed under the threshold of the door. Its pattern repeated that shown on quartered gold discs made in late Neolithic Ireland. In Co. Limerick housebuilding, a florin was tossed at the outset, and work would only go ahead if the coin landed with the quartered design uppermost. This 'superstition' was concerned with the correct fixing of a centre and projection of horizons, in what Eliade calls the 'cosmosizition' of a territory and its transformation into a replica of the exemplary universe, created and inhabited by the gods.[32] The simplest dwelling repeats the pattern by declaring a World Centre.

When considering the site for a new house in nineteenth-century Ireland, 'Very few people were content with preparations of a material kind'.[33] Out of respect for them, sites of ancient occupation, or activity, such as prehistoric earthworks or megaliths, were avoided. By consulting with the oldest living inhabitants the builders also hoped to avoid accidentally blocking routes taken by local divinities, or by spirits of the mortal dead on their funeral path to the grave. Throughout Ireland a strong belief persisted that if a new house was constructed across a fairy path, the inhabitants would suffer broken furniture, plates smashed in the night, destruction of crops, sickness among the animals and human fatalities. To avoid these calamities, four piles of stones were left as markers at the corners of the chosen site. If the gods left them undisturbed during the following night, work might safely start thereafter. The importance attributed to the four quarters of the Irish house reiterates Asiatic conviction, where they were held to incorporate the four winds in heaven, the four rivers of Paradise, and other zones beyond the earth.

Among Irish householders, it was the fire goddess, Brigit, queen of the sun's cardinal movements, at once so powerful, yet so measured, the bringer of fire, yet the protectress from conflagration, who carried her far-flung riches back into the house, like a harvest home, and distributed them among the family.

With the help of Ulster midwives, these gifts included the 'Moon of the Four Quarters', as their chant was called. It was addressed to the woman-in-labour. The midwife marked the four house corners with Brigit's crosses, and on the threshold she sang:

> Four corners to her bed.
> Four angels at her head.
> Mark, Matthew, Luke and John;
> God bless the bed that she lies on.
> New moon, new moon, God bless me.
> God bless this house and family.[34]

To this sound, the newborn child entered the world.

Home again

Brigit's work is nearly done. Creeping secularism is making her visits unnecessary, so she stays away.

The mythless shell, a house without gods, was described by Samuel Beckett some decades ago. His *Endgame* (1957) is set in a chamber where high upon the rear wall are two small windows, like the Sandymount Martello tower, curtains closed, which 'suggests that the room may represent the inside of the skull of a man who has his eyes on the external world'.[35] The scene both inside and out denotes a dying world, a Machine Age where there is 'no more nature'. When Clov (French *clou*, 'nail') looks out of the window, he says all is 'corpsed'. The waves are 'lead', the sun is 'zero', the light is an even grey, 'light black from pole to pole'. The master of the house, Hamm (hammer) is dying, and the curtain falls as Clov teeters on the threshold of the room, neither in nor out, gazing at walls blackened by nihilistic power, and wondering if an alternative form of habitation is possible.

'No symbols where none intended,' Beckett wrote at the end of his novel *Watt*, realizing that his house of non-meaning was essentially a denial of the entire mythic tradition. Only chop down the roof tree, *Cleithe*, and the Home-on-earth, as a system of poetic interconnections, is bound to collapse. Technology will then have freedom to do what it likes with the debris. In a post-symbolic age, the tree which stands at the centre of Beckett's *Waiting for Godot*[36] is a shadow, a meaningless *anti*-symbol, at once mocking and describing a deprived state.

Into this lassitude now breaks the sudden thunder of an ecological endgame, rumbling beyond the living-room windows like Eogabal-the-tree-god's last laugh. He is trying to say that if we do *not* belong in Nature we belong nowhere, and so must face final eviction and perpetual homelessness.

The same truth may underlie a *Litany of Creation*, written by an Irish cleric in 1575. As he peered from his chapel window at what he was supposed to regard as a cursed, sin-laden, soulless wilderness, an apparently irresistible gust of affirmation swept over him. He suddenly loved what he saw out there. In a passionate appeal, he called up the despised glories of physical reality, so that the universal soul and the house of individual consciousness might re-unite.

'I entreat Thee by water, and the cruel air. I entreat Thee by fire. I entreat Thee by earth. I entreat Thee by land and sea unresting...I entreat Thee by the triad, wind, and sun, and moon. I entreat Thee by the compass of the tuneful firmament; I entreat every stately-branching order, the host of the bright stars. I entreat Thee by every living creature that ever tasted death and life. I entreat Thee by every inanimate creature because of thy fair beauteous mystery. I entreat Thee by time with its clear divisions, I entreat Thee by the darkness, I entreat Thee by the light. I entreat all the elements in heaven and earth. That the eternal sweetness may be granted to my soul...this, in brief, is the wise 'besom of devotion'.'[37]

For us, as for him, the besom or broom belongs to Nature, and sweetness in the soul depends on inviting her back into the house of human culture, there to break into her old song once more:

Icham of Irlaunde	I am from Ireland
ant of the holy londe	And from the holy land
of irlaunde,	Of Ireland,
gode sire pray ich thee	Good sir, I beg of you,
for of saynte charite	For Holy charity,
come ant daunce wyt me	Come dance with me
in irlaunde.	In Ireland...[38]

Acknowledgments

I am much indebted to generations of scholars for bringing so many aspects of Irish mythology to light. These workers are not responsible for my errors. I wish to thank the Irish Folklore Commission; also many helpful public and university libraries, and Mrs T. Astbury, who cheerfully typed several versions of the manuscript. Finally I recall with pleasure the heartwarming friendliness of the Irish people whom I encountered on my travels.

Source of illustrations

Archaeologia: 144. Author's collection 11, 23, 27 top, 27 bottom left, 27 bottom right, 34, 65 above left, 75, 79, 89 above, 89 below right (M. Dames, *The Silbury Treasure*, Thames and Hudson, 1978), 99 above, 102 above right, 103, 107 right, 111 above, 116 above, 116 below, 142, 148 above, 148 below, 153 below left, 153 below right, 156 right, 169 below, 179, 189, 195, 207 below left, 214 above, 214 below, 217, 221 below right, 253 left. After the Book of Kells: 175, 238 (L. Bieler, *Ireland*, 1963). G. Coffey: 65 below right, 121 far right. Commissioners of Public Works in Ireland: 127 below right, 149, 183 below left, 205 below, 221 above left, 226 below right. *Connacht Tribune*: 165 inset. T. Crofton-Croker: 81 above, 89 below left. K. Danaher: 102 above left, 229, 253 right (*The Year in Ireland*, Mercier Press, Cork, 1972). G. Eogan: 16 right. Dr J. Feehan: 232. C. Fox: 87 bottom left. P. Gelling: 83, 121 above right, 123 bottom (*The Chariot of the Sun*, 1969). M. Gimbutas: 81 below right, 88 (Belgrade University Collection), 99 below right (Naturhistorisches Museum, Vienna). J. Gooders: 111 below right, 161 (*Field Guide to Birds of Britain*, Kingfisher Books). W.A. Green, Ulster Folk Museum: 57 below left, 57 below right, 205 above, 246, 249 above. HSC: 65 below left. Hunt Museum (University of Thomond, Limerick): 99 below left. Irish Tourist Board: 38 left, 127 top, 153 above, 163. *JRSAI*: 38 right: 41, 177 above left, 177 far right, 211 right, 212, 221 top right, 223, 251 below right. *JKAHS*: 107 left, 183 above. H.E. Kilbride-Jones: (after) 146. Shane Leslie: 54. R.A.S. Macalister: 199 above, 199 centre left, 199 centre right, 207 above, 211 left. M. MacNeill: 163. From Olaus Magnus: 123 above. Collection Ajit Mookerjee (photo Thames and Hudson): 45 below right. National Museum of Ireland: 47, 63, 97 (Chute Hall, Co. Kerry, and Dromabest, Co. Antrim), 118–19, 127 below right, 177 centre, 183 above, 219 inset, 240, 249 below right. After S.P. Ó'Ríordáin: 77, 81 below left. PRIA: 45 top right. After A. and B. Rees: 16 left and 16

centre. Photo Rex Roberts ABIPP: 2, 60–1, 150–1, 169 above, 226 top. J. Rykwert: 133. Edwin Smith: 121, 251 above. R.A. Smith: 87 top, 87 centre left, 87 centre right. University Collection of Air Photographs, Cambridge: 219, 233. B. Stone Collection, Birmingham Reference Library: 18 top, 115 centre. E.S. Twohig: 207 below right, 221 below left. Ulster Museum: 192–3, 231 right. *UJA*: 56 left. B. Wailes: 228. W.F. Wakeman: 45 top, 59, 184, 255. Photo Warburg Institute: 20–21, 187. Photograph R. J. Welch, Ulster Museum: 57 top, 156 right, 165, 173, 183 below right, 215, 226 below left. T.J. Westropp: 65 above right, 115 top, 115 bottom. J. Windle: 102 below.

Maps and diagrams appearing on the following pages are drawn by Annick Petersen: 8, 11, 16 (after Rees and Rees), 18 (after Rees and Rees), 27, 65 (after Ordnance Survey, Phoenix Park, Dublin), 77 (after Ó'Ríordáin), 102 below (after J. Windle), 107 right, 127 below left, 156 left (after Rees and Rees), 199 above (after R.A.S. Macalister), 207 above (after R.A.S. Macalister), 211 (after R.A.S. Macalister), 214 above, 221 below right.

Text quotations

The pamphlet of St Patrick's Purgatory is quoted by courtesy of The Most Reverend Joseph Duffy, Bishop of Clogher. All material from the manuscript collections of the Department of Irish Folklore, University College, Dublin, is quoted by kind permission of the Head of the Department. Miles Dillon's translation of *Echtrae Conle* is quoted from *Early Irish Literature*, 1948, with permission of University of Chicago Press; Elizabeth Gray's translation of *Cath Maige Tuired* with the permission of the Irish Texts Society.

Notes on the Text

Introduction: Setting Out *(pages 9–19)*

1 *Táin Bó Cualgne*, 146.
2 Woodman, P.C., 'Problems in the colonisation of Ireland', *UJA*, 49, 1986, 16.
3 Gimbutas, M., *Gods and Goddesses of Old Europe*, 1978.
4 Popper, K., *The Rationality of Scientific Revolutions*, in Hacking, I. (ed.), *Scientific Revolutions*, 1981.
5 Gimbutas, M., *JIES*, 17, 1989, 195.
6 MacCana, P., in O'Cuiv, B. (ed.), *A View of the Irish Language*, Dublin, 1969.
7 MacCana, op.cit., 61.
8 Beckett, S., 'Dante-Bruno-Vico-Joyce', in *Transition*, Paris, 1929, 248.
9 ibid. 248.
10 Gwynn, E., Todd Lecture Series, MD, I–IV. Dublin, 1903–1935, and Stokes, W., in *R C*, IV, 1895, 272.
11 See *Prose Edda of Snorri Sturluson*, trans. Faulkes, A., London, 1987, 18.
12 MacCana, P., op.cit., 67. See also: MacCana, P., 'Early Irish Ideology and the Concept of Unity', in Kearney, R., *The Irish Mind*, 1988.
13 Connolly, C., *Life and Letters*, 1929.

PART ONE: ULSTER

1 St Patrick's Purgatory *(pages 22–42)*
1 Attributed to Jesus Christ, in Matt. VI, 9–13, and Luke, II, 1–4.
2 Also called 'The Angelic Salutation', from the words of Gabriel to Mary, in Luke I, 28, and of Elizabeth; Luke I, 42. The prayer was not in general use till the sixteenth century.
3 The Apostles' Creed; introduced into the Liturgy in the fifth century.
4 Giraldus Cambrensis, *Topography of Ireland*, 1186, v, 63.
5 Roger of Wendover, *Flores Historiarum*, trans. Giles, G.A., 1849, I, 511. Written at St Albans and revised by M. Paris. The MS exists in two copies, of AD 1300 and AD 1350. Roger may have used an earlier compilation, see Vaughan, R., *Matthew Paris*, 1958, pp. 21–3.
6 Giraldus, op.cit., v, 63.
7 NCE, 11, 1967, 1034.
8 Roger of Wendover, op.cit., 511.
9 Lithgow, William, *The Rare Adventures and Perigrinations of*, 1619. London, 1928.
10 The Narration of Henry of Saltrey concerning St Patrick in 1153; BM, MS Arundel, 292. Saltry, op.cit.
11 Roger of Wendover, op.cit., 515–22.
12 NCE, 11, 1034–6.
13 Whitley Stokes, ed., *R C*, 12, 1891, 420.
14 AU, AD 820.
15 *Ériu*, I, 1904, 187.

16 Murphy, G. (ed.), in *EIL*, poem 42, 107.
17 Bieler, L., The Irish Penitentials, 1963, quoting Penance of Finnian, sixth century AD. 46.
18 ibid., 115, Pennance of Cummean. See also McNeill, J. and Gamer, H., Mediaeval Handbooks of Penance, 1938, p. 104.
19 Joyce, J., *F W*, 1939, 204, 15.
20 OSL, Donegal, 1835, 25.
21 *Vision of Tundale*, trans. Stevenson, T.G., 1843, 215.
22 *Fis Adamnan*, trans. Boswell, C.S., 1908, 21–3.
23 Murphy, G., ITS, XLIII, 1954, 398, and vol. VII, poem L.
24 Stokes, W., and Meyer, K., *Archiv für Celtische Lexicographie*, III, 216, q. 2.
25 Translated Meyer, K., *Stories and songs from Irish Mss*, 1899, The Vision of Laisren, Bodl, Code Rawl. B. 512 f. 44 aI – 44b2.
26 Annals of Leinster, lxiv, 28–9.
27 Quoted in Leslie, S., *St Patrick's Purgatory*, 1932, 64.
28 In Tieck's play, *Fortunatus*, of 1815, based on Fortunatus' travels in Ireland, printed in Augsburg in 1509.
29 Trans. Duff, J.W.; Virgil died in 19 BC.
30 Plato, *Phaedo*, 65, c-d, 66b, 67d.
31 BM, MS Royal 10, B.9., trans. Yonge, J., in *New Ireland Review*, April 1909.
32 Acta Sanctorium, VIII, 588, of Pope Benedict XIII. See also AU, 1497.
33 Richardson, J., *The Great Folly, Superstition, and Idolatry of Pilgrimages in Ireland*, Dublin, 1727.
34 Bishop Spottiswoode; letter to Archbishop of Armagh, 31 October 1632, quoted in Bishop Henry Jones, *St Patrick's Purgatory*, 1647.
35 Hewson, bound with Richardson, op. cit., 1727.
36 Dixon, P., *The Holy Wells of Ireland*, 1836, 27–9.
37 Bishop D. Rothe, *Distinction of Purgatories*, 1624; quoted in Messingham, T., *Florilegium Insulae Sanctorium*, 1624.
38 Kelly, M., *Cambrensis Everus*, 1848.
39 Baring-Gould, S., *Lives of the Saints*, IV, 1914, 54–8.
40 Dante Alighieri, *Purgatorio*, c. 1300.

2 The Water Monster *(pages 43–54)*
41 Leslie, op. cit., xiv.
42 Richardson, op. cit., 115.
43 Frazer, W., *JRSAI*, 26, 1896, 158.
44 Crozier, I.R., *UJA*, 3, 1940, 105.
45 Wakeman, W.F., *JRHAAI*, 1875, 458.
46 Otway, C., *A Tour of Connaught*, 1839, 311–15.
47 IFC, MS 163, 106–114. Recorded 1935, at Cornamona, Co. Galway.
48 Otway, C., *Description of Lough*

Derg, 1829, 311–15.
49 IFC, MS 104, pp. 373–5. Recorded 1935.
50 Richardson, J., op. cit., 2–4.
51 Quoted in Evans-Wentz, W.Y., *Fairy-Faith in Celtic Countries*, 1909, 139.
52 O'Donovan, J., OSL, Ballshanny, 1 November 1835.
53 O'Kelly, J.J., ed., *Leabhar na Laoitheadh*. Dublin, 1913.
54 OSL, Donegal.
55 Hyde, D., *Legends of Saints and Sinners*, 1915, 287–9.
56 Schärer, H., *Ngaju Religion*, 1963; quoted in Kuiper, F.B., *Cosmogony and Conception*; HR, 10, 1970, 72.
57 *Rig Veda*, X. 82–5.
58 Fodor, N., *The Search for the Beloved.* New York 1949.
59 Stricker, B., *De Geboorte van Hoorus*, I, Leiden, 1963–8.
60 ibid; quoting the 4th Hymn of Tiruvakanam.
61 Rank, O., *The Trauma of Birth*, 1929, 106–7.
62 Fodor, op.cit., 219, and 383.
63 Eliade, M., *Birth and Rebirth*, 1961.
64 Fodor, op.cit., 391.
65 Rank, O., *The Trauma of Birth*, 1929, reprinted 1973, 136. See also Rank, O., *The Myth of the Birth of the Hero*, 1952.
66 OSL, Donegal, 1835.
67 Burdy, S. *Life of Philip Skelton*, London, 1824.

3 The Cailleach and Bith *(pages 55–9)*
68 Brooke, C. *Reliques of Irish Poetry*, 1789, 70–1.
69 Patterson, T.G.F., 'Folk Tales from Creggan Parish', *UJA*, 1, 1938, 36. See also *UJA*, 26, 1963, for excavation report.
70 Patterson, T.J.F., 'Harvest Customs', *UJA*, 7, 1944, 114–15.
71 ITS, 1939, from fifteenth-century *Book of Lecan*. Macalister argues that this divine brother-sister union only later developed into a triad; ibid, 248, and text xxiv, verse 7.
72 Canon O'Connor, D., *JRSAI*, 24, 285–6. See also Chart, A., *Preliminary Survey of Ancient Monuments of Northern Ireland*, 1940, 175, 221.
73 Lévy-Bruhl, L., *Les Functions Mentales dans les Sociétés Inferieures*, trans. Clare, L.A., *How Natives Think*, London, 1926.
74 See Wheeler, J.A., *Foundational Problems in the Special Sciences*, ed. Butts, R.E. and Hintikka, J., Reidel, Dordrecht, 1977; and Wheeler, J.A., in *The Nature of Scientific Discovery*, ed., O. Gingerich, 1975, 261–96, and 575–87; and Wheeler, J.A., 'Some Strangeness in the Proportion', in Woolf, H., *Centenary Symposium in honour of Albert Einstein*.

260

75 Macalister, *L.G.*, II, 173.

PART TWO: MUNSTER

1 Inherited Words *(pages 62–72)*
1 CG, 4.
2 Stokes, W., in *Ériu*, III, 1907, 11–12.
3 IFC, MS 1799, 1972.
4 *JRSAI*, 54, 1924, 128.
5 Fitzgerald, D., in *RC*, IV, 1879–80, 189.
6 Manannán mac Lir', in *JCHAS*, II, 1896, 366–9.
7 Fitzgerald, op.cit., 189.
8 ibid., 188–9.
9 IFC, MS 1799; 115–119.
10 Fitzgerald, op.cit., 190.
11 Westropp, T.J., *PRIA*, 34c, 1917, 138.
12 'Áine's History. Tell it to Me': a poem by Ua Chiarmaic (AD 1080–1120) in Egerton MS, 92f, 376, and in S G App., Vol. II, 575.
13 IFC 1971, MS 1799, 116.
14 Prayer recorded by Carmichael, A., Carm. Gad., Edin. 1928 and 1941, III, no. 317, 311. Late nineteenth century.
15 Danaher, K., *Irish Folk Tradition*, 224; in O'Driscoll, R., *The Celtic Consciousness*.
16 MacCana, P., 'Irish Literary Tradition', 35, in O'Cuiv, op.cit., 1969.
17 Westropp, T.J., in *PRIA*, 34c, 1917–19, 15.

2 Lough Gur *(pages 73–112)*
18 Fitzgerald, op.cit., 189.
19 IFC, MS 1799, 1972, 2, 32.
20 ibid., 26.
21 Fitzgerald, op.cit., 187.
22 IFC, op.cit., 14.
23 ibid., 14–18.
24 Fitzgerald, op.cit., 189.
25 ibid., 186–7.
26 RD, in *RC*, XVI, 278.
27 *PRIA*, 54c, 1951, 39.
28 IFC, op.cit., 59.
29 ibid., 62.
30 IFC, Schools' Collection, MS 516, 1938, 5c, 216, and Lynch, *JCHAS*, 1911, 11.
31 DF, ITS, IV and VII.
32 *EIHM*, 290.
33 Joyce, P., *Irish Names of Places*, II, 242–4.
34 Wood-Martin, W.G., Vol. I, 1902, 348–9.
35 MacCana, P., in *ER*, 3, 148–66.
36 Lehmann, R.P.M., op.cit., 1982.
37 *JRSAI*, IV, 1856–7, 134.
38 IFC, op.cit., 23–4, 53, 97.
39 *PRIA*, Liv. c, 1951, 39.
40 *JCHAS*, 1897, 182.
41 *DF*, I, 28 and 127; III, 24–27, and 345.
42 Windle, B.C.A., 'On Certain Megalithic Remains at Lough Gur', *PRIA*, 30c, 1912, 69.
43 Dumézil, G., *L'ideologie tripartie des Indo-Européens*. 1958, I–III. See also Littleton, C. Scott, *The New Comparative Mythology*, 1982.
44 Fox, C., *Ant J*, 30, 1950, 192–4.

45 *Man*, XX, 1920, no. 45, fig. 67.
46 Lynch, *JCHAS*, 1911, 11, and Fitzgerald, Rev. P., *History of Limerick*, quoted *Gentleman's Magazine*, 103, I, 1833, 111.
47 Foder, N., op.cit., 391. See also Roberts, J., *Exploring West Cork*, 1988, 53.
48 Written accounts date from the seventh to eighth centuries, e.g. *Voyage of Bran* and *The Adventures of Conle*.
49 Leagh's description of the palace in Magh Mell, trans. Hull, E., *The Poem Book of the Gael, 151*.
50 IFC Schools' collection, MS 516, 3B, 212.
51 Lynch, op.cit., 209, and IFC, MS 1977, 96–7.
52 Harkness, R., *Quarterly Journal of Science*, IV, 1869, 395–6.
53 O'Kelly, M.J., *NMAJ*, IV, 1942.
54 *DF*, I., ITS, XII, twelfth century; poem XIII, ed. Murphy, 24–29; and pages xiii, xxix.
55 Lynch, *JCHAS*, XIX, 1913, 10.
56 *DF*, VII, 1908, pp. 128–30.
57 *DF*, VII, lines 165–9.
58 *RC*, VII, op.cit., 1886, lines 187–94.
59 ibid., lines 209–11
60 IFC, op.cit., 60.
61 CG, 5.
62 'Colloquy of the Two Sages', quoted *SG*, 181.
63 IFC, MS 1799, 60.
64 Coles, J., *P P S*, 1962, 156, and 1964, 311; and *Ant*, 1965, 217–19.
65 Lynch, op.cit., 12 and IFC, Schools, op.cit., 215.
66 ibid., 216.
67 ibid., 217.
68 Related to Croker by J. Punch, who lived close to the South causeway, and IFC, MS 1799, 66.
69 Campbell, J.F., *Popular Tales of the West Highlands, orally collected*, 1890, I, lxx–lxxi.
70 O'Kelly, *NMAJ*, IV, 1944, 39. See also *PPS* 30, 1964, Plate XIX.
71 MacNeill, M., *The Festival of Lughnasa*, 1962, 28.
72 *JNMAS*, I, 4., 1911, 214.
73 O'Kearney, N., *JRSAI*, II, 1852, 35.
74 MacNeill, op.cit., 416; ibid., 401, and IFC, MS 489, 54–9.
75 Windle, op.cit.
76 Westropp, T.J., *JRSAI*, 49, 1919, 16.
77 O'Danachair, C., *NMAJ*, X, 1966, 47–49, and Hall, Rev.J., recorded in Limerick City. *Tour Through Ireland*, 1813. See also: O'Dwyer, M., *Three County Limerick Fairs*, in Rynne, E. (ed.), North Munster Studies, 1967, 483–5.
78 Ó'Ríordáin, op.cit., plate I, and pp. 44–5.
79 CMT, 47–9.
80 ibid.
81 *Tidings of Conchobar Son of Ness*, trans. Stokes, W., in *Ériu*, IV, 26–7.
82 Béal, XVIII, 1948, 142–199, and O'Rahilly, *EIHM*, 481–4.
83 *Carm Gad*, III, 1940, 279.
84 Lithgow, W., *The Rare Adventures*

and Peregrinations of . . . 1632, ed. Phelps, G., 1974, 25.
85 Harkness, op.cit., 396.
86 A Cl, AD 1398, 320.
87 Carney, J., *Literature in Irish*, 1169–1543, 697–8; in A New History of Ireland, II, 1987.
88 Duanaire Ghearoid Iarla, *Studia Hibernica*, III, 1963, 7–59.
89 O'h'Ogain, op.cit., *The Dawn*, I, 9.
90 IFC, MS 1799, 59.
91 Fitzgerald, op.cit., 191.
92 IFC, MS 1799, 2–3.
93 Fitzgerald, op.cit., 191.
94 Dawn, op.cit., 12.
95 Ó'Ríordáin, S., *PRIA*, 56c, 1953–4, 321. Site B.
96 IFC, MS 1799, 22–4.
97 Yeats, W.B., 'High Talk', 1938.

3 From Lough to Province *(pages 113–17)*
98 O'Rahilly, T.F., *EIHM*, 126–7; and *Ériu*, I, 1904, 187–8.
99 *RC*, III, 347, and MD, 225; and Westropp, T.J., *PRIA*, 35c, 382.

PART THREE: LEINSTER

1 Leinster Approaches *(pages 120–4)*
1 Rose, H.J., in *Journal of Roman Studies*, XIII, 1923, 90.
2 MD, II, Lagin, I, 50–51; and Keating, I, 120–3; and BD, *Folk-lore*, 3, 1892, 472.
3 O'Rahilly, T.F., *Ériu*, 13, 1892, 471.
4 Ó'hUiginn, R., 'The Literature of the Laigin', in *Emania*, 7, 1990, 5–9.
5 Wittgenstein, L., *Philosophical Grammar*, I, 1974, trans. Kenny, A., prop. 3.
6 Poem in Praise of Labraid Loingsech, trans. Meyer, K., 1914.
7 Meyer, op.cit., quoted in Dillon, M., in *EIL*.
8 *JRSAI*, 69, 1939, 190–225.
9 MD II, 50. Dind Rig is Leighlin Bridge, on the river Barrow, south Leinster.
10 RD, in *RC*, XVI, 1895, 145.
11 CG, 41.
12 ibid., quoting Bod., Rawl., B., 514, f. 50b2.
13 MD, IV, 31–3. Magnus Olaus, *Historia*, 1565.
14 LG, V, ITS, XLIV, 1956, poem LXXII, 115–17.
15 Gelling and Davidson, op.cit., 53–67.
16 See also Coffey, G., *New Grange*.
17 Almost gone are the days of book censorship, which drove James Joyce away. Explosive literature is now nothing to declare, though the embargo on books 'calculated to arouse sexual passion' (the Irish Censorship Board's definition of obscenity) still officially stands. (See Carlson, J., *Banned in Ireland*, 1990). Since 1980, the arts in the Irish Republic have been officially encouraged.

2 Dublin, The Real Dream *(pages 125–44)*
18 Davenport, G., *The Geography of the Imagination*, 22.

19 Gluck, B.R., *Beckett and Joyce*, 1979, 190.
20 ibid., 97.
21 Arp, H., et. al., 'Poetry is Vertical', in *Transition*, June 1927, and March 1932, Paris.
22 Davenport, op.cit., 22.
23 *FW*, 3.
24 *FW*, 628.
25 Yeats, W.B., *Essays; Ideas of Good and Evil*, 1924, 217.
26 Hart, C., *Structure and Motif in Finnegans Wake*, 1962, 45.
27 Dillon, M., in *EIL*, 165, trans. Meyer, K.
28 MD, III, 105.
29 *RC*, XV, 1894, 331.
30 MD III, 105, and MD III, Bend Etair II, 113–17.
31 *RC*, XV, 1894, 331.
32 See ER, 4 534–5; Ovid, *Metamorphoses*, 4, 347–388; and Brisson, L., *Le Mythe de Tiresias*, Leiden, 1976.
33 LG, III, 1940, 220 and 21.
34 Heidegger, M., *Basic Writings*, trans. Krell, F., 1978; 'The Question Concerning Technology', 284–5 and 316.
35 DDH, in *RC*, XXII, 1902, 24.
36 Ptolemaeus, C., *Geography*; trans. Stevenson, E.L., 1932. See also *JRSAI*, 1894, 115–128, and *Archaeologia*, XIVIII, (2), 680.
37 Somerville-Large, P., Dublin, 1979, 23.
38 Buick, G.R., 'Irish Flint Arrowheads', in *JRSAI*, 1895, 41.
39 Gilbert, J.T., *A History of the City of Dublin*, 1854–9, III, 73–4.
40 *The Europa World Year Book*, 1990, 1380; projection from 1986 figure of 920, 956.
41 Rykwert, J., *The Idea of a Town*, 1976, 45–65.
42 Varro, *On the Latin Language*. VII, 7–9; trans. and ed. Warmington, E.H.
43 Rose, H.J., in *Journal of Roman Studies*, XIII, 1923, 82.
44 Varro, *De re rustica*, 2, 5, 16, trans. Hooper, W.D., 1934.
45 Pike, B., *The City as Cultural Hieroglyph*, 1986, 126. See also Gromaticus, H., *Constitutio Limitum*, Codex Arcerianus, sixth century, 41.
46 Varro, op.cit., 7, 8.
47 NLEM, 1968, 213.
48 Lydus, J., *On the Months*, ed. Bekker, 1837, 85–6.
49 Script of BBC Radio talk, 8 September, 1931.
50 Yeats, W.B., *A Vision*, 1937, 279–80, and *Sailing to Byzantium*, 1926.
51 See Hawkins, P.S. (ed.), *Civitas*, 130–2.
52 Howard, E., *Garden Cities of Tomorrow*; see also Le Corbusier, *La Ville Radieuse, The City of Tomorrow and its Planning*; trans. Etchells, F., 8th ed., 1931.
53 Buchanan, Colin, *Traffic in Towns*, 1963, Introduction, 19–24.
54 Buchanan, op.cit., 23–4.
55 O'Shea, T., and Toibin, C., *Dubliners*, 1990.

56 Gluck, B.R., *Beckett and Joyce*, 1979, 97.
57 Clarke, H.B., 'Topographical Development of Early Medieval Dublin', *JRSAI*, 107, 1977, 29–50.
58 Clarke, op.cit., 36–7.
59 RD, in *RC*, 15, 1894, 329.
60 Siege of Howth, *RC*, VIII, 1887, 47–9.
61 ibid., 51–3.
62 Lucas, A.T., 'Furze in Custom and Belief', *Béal*, 1960, 1–18.
63 *RC*, 1887, op.cit., 55.
64 Douglas, M., *Purity and Danger*, 1966, 207.
65 DDH, trans. Stokes, W., *RC*, XXII, 1901, 9–61, and 165–215, and 282–329, 390–435.
66 ibid., 313.
67 ibid., 42.
68 ibid., 54.
69 Quoted Sayers, W., *Ériu*, 37, 1986, 99.
70 DDH, 400, appendix, MS Egerton. 123a 1–123a2.
71 ibid., 401.
72 Campbell, J., and Robinson, H.M., *A Skeleton Key to Finnegans Wake*, 1947, 296–7.
73 ibid., 297.

3 Original Landings *(pages 145–9)*

74 Kilbride-Jones, H.E., *JRSAI*, 69, 1939, 190–220.
75 BD, op.cit., 472; see also MD, II, 50.
76 LG, III, 1939, 170–7, and 194.
77 ibid., 193–4 and 248.
78 Baring-Gould, S., op.cit., January, 408.
79 Plummer, C., *Lives of Irish Saints*, II, 1922, 177–215.
80 LG, II, 213–15; and LG, III, 173 and 248.
81 MacNeill, M., op.cit., 221–5.
82 Green, S.W. and Zvelebil, M., in *PPS* 56, 1990, 57–88.
83 Thomas, J., 'Neolithic Explanations Re-visited' in *PPS*, 54, 1988, 59–66; see also Cooney, G., in *Ant*, 64, 1990, 741–53.

PART FOUR: CONNACHT

1 Battle of East and West *(pages 152–70)*

1 Simms, J.G., 'Connacht in the Eighteenth Century'; in *IHS*, 11, 1959, 116.
2 Gilbert, J.T., op.cit., I, 295.
3 Middle Irish travellers' prayer, trans. Meyer, K., *Ériu*, VI, 112.
4 MD, I, 55.
5 See also *RC*, XV, 10, 301.
6 Whittow, J., *Geology and Scenery in Ireland*, 1974, 128. See also Synge, F.M., 'The Glacial Deposits around Trim', in *PRIA*, 53, 1950, 108.
7 Lochlainn, C.O., in *Essays to Eoin MacNeil*, 1938, 465–71.
8 LL, 107, AD 1160.
9 MD III, 285.
10 *JRSAI*, 31, 1901, 230–1.
11 BD, *Folk-lore*, 3, 1892, 492.
12 *Ériu*, VI, 1912, 123.

13 *Ériu*, I, 17–19, trans. Gwynn.
14 *Ériu*, VI, 1912, 123–4.
15 *PRIA*, II, 1844, 314–15 and 595; and *RC*, XV, 1894, 140.
16 A Cl, 162, 110, 116; ed. Murphy, D., 1896.
17 *DF*, ITS, VII, 1908, 102–5.
18 *DF*, 104.
19 ibid., xxxvii.
20 Fraser, J., ed., '1st Battle of Moytura', *Ériu*, VIII, 1916, 1–63.
21 *EIHM*, 278.
22 ibid., 278.
23 Dumézil, G., *The Destiny of the Warrior*, trans. Hiltebeitel, A., 1970, 3.
24 Hennessy, W.M., *PRIA*, 10, 1869, 421–7.
25 *Bruiden Da Choca*, ed. Stokes, W., *RC*, XXI, 1900.
26 *Battle of Magh-Rath*, ed. O'Donovan, J., 198.
27 *DF*, ITS, VII, xliii–xliv.
28 ibid., poem XXI, 163.
29 ibid., 207.
30 O'hInnse, S. (ed.), *Miscellaneous Annals*, 1144–1437, 1947.
31 16 February 1990. Report by Farragher, F.
32 *DF*, X, 123.
33 *DF*, XXXV, 206.
34 *DF*, X, 122.
35 See Westropp, T.J., 'The Legendary Islands of the North Atlantic', *PRIA*, 30c, 1912–13, 223–256; and Westropp, T.J., 'Early Italian Maps of Ireland', *PRIA*, 30c, 1912, 400–420.
36 R. Dudley Edwards, 'Anglo-Norman Relations with Connacht, 1169–1124' in *IHS*, I, 1938–9, 135.
37 Westropp, *PRIA*, 30c, 1912–13, 415.
38 Page, J.R., *Ireland: Its Evils Traced to their Source*, 1836, 33.
39 Dixon, P., *Holy Wells of Ireland*, 1836, 31.
40 MacNeill, op.cit., 83.
41 Thackeray, W.M., *The Irish Sketch-book of 1843*, 103–4.
42 Whittow, op.cit., 140.
43 MD, Sinann I, lines 49–52.
44 Bergin, O., *Irish Bardic Poetry*, 60.
45 *TH*, 24.
46 Information volunteered by people around Cuilcagh Mountain in 1989.

2 Erne Weddings *(pages 171–84)*

47 Wright, J.K., *Geographic Lore at the time of the Crusaders*, 1925, 339.
48 O'Clery, M., *The Book of Conquests of Ireland*, quoted *PRIA*, 10, 1869, 444.
49 *JRSAI*, 26, 295–6.
50 Stokes, W., *Tripartite Life of St Patrick*, Rolls Series, 1887, 147–51.
51 Caithrem Ceallachain Caisil, twelfth to thirteenth century, MS, 89.
52 RD, in *RC*, XVI, 1895, 32, 281.
53 MD, IV, 3 and 7–9.
54 *RC*, XVI, 1896, 32–3.
55 *EIHM*, 278.
56 *RC*, XVI, 1894, 417.
57 Macalister, R. A. S. (ed.), ITS, xxxv, 1939, 265–6.

58 *Anecdota*, I, 27., and DIL.
59 MD, IV, Ess Ruaid I, 5.
60 *RC*, XVI, 1895, 32.
61 MD, IV, 5, and *RC*, 16, 32; BD, in *Folklore*, 3, 1892, 505.
62 Edited Bergin, O., in *Medieval Studies for G.S. Loomis*, 1927, 399–403.
63 *DF*, II, 'The Magic Pig', poem LIV, and ITS, XLVIII, 1967, 89; *The Pursuit of Diarmaid and Grainne*, ed. Nessa Ni Sheaghdha.
64 *DF*, poem LIV.
65 *JRSAI*, 55, 1925.
66 Ellis Davidson, H.R., 'The Sword at the Wedding', in *Folk-lore*, 71, 1960, 1–10.
67 Baring-Gould, S., op.cit., August, 254.
68 *LG*, II, 1939, 266–7, and footnote 266. On the coalescence of Bith-Partholón, see *LG*, III, 91 and 111.
69 *LG*, III, 1940, 232.
70 ibid., §233, p. 39.
71 ibid., verse 75, p. 71.
72 *LG*, II, 266.
73 Keating, I, 161–7.
74 *LG*, III, 1940, 234, p. 41.
75 *LG*, III, 207, and p.88.
76 ibid., §206, and p. 87, and 210, 90.
77 Béal, 3, 1932, 285; recorded O'Fionusa, P., from his great aunt who lived 1845–1932.
78 *LG*, III, 87.
79 MacNeill, M., op.cit., 86.
80 MD, III, 461–7.
81 ED, in *Folk-lore*, 4, 1893, 476–7.
82 MD, III, 465–468, and *RC*, XV, 1894, 484.
83 Lowry-Corry, D., *PRIA*, xli, c. 1932–4, 200–3.
84 *JRSAI*, xli, 1911.
85 ED, 476.
86 Chart, D.A., *Ancient Monuments of Northern Ireland*, 1940, 146, and Burl, A., *Stone Circles of the British Isles*, 1976, 250. The recumbent stone between the horns is 1.1 metres long.
87 *UJA*, 3rd Series, III, 1940, 103.
88 Dubhtaigh, N.O., born 1874, recounting her mother's adolescent experiences. trans. Danachair, C.O., in *Folklife*, 22, 1983, 'Summer Pasture in Donegal', 49.

3 Flood, Fish, Word *(pages 185–91)*
89 CMT, 49, and note 135. *Indech* – woof and weft, and interweaving. Indech is son of De Domnann, perhaps from *domnann*, 'the transitory world', DIL.
90 ED, op.cit., 476.
91 Lehmann, R.P.H., *EIV*, Winter, 15–19.
92 Lithgow, W., op.cit., 153.
93 MD, IV, Oin Aub, 303.
94 MD, IV, 295, Mag Muirthemne (Plain of Louth).
95 MD, IV, 165.
96 Rank, O., *The Myth of the Birth of the Hero*, quoting Lessman, H., *Die Kyrossage in Europa*, 1906, 265.
97 CMT, 132.
98 Keating, I, 181.
99 MD, III, 429.

100 BD, *Folk-lore*, 3, 192, 506–8.
101 *LG*, IV, 1941, 3–4.
102 Keating, I, 185, and Keating quoted in *JRSAI*, 57, 1921, 50.
103 Eochy O'Flann, c. AD 960, quoted Rolleston, op.cit., 110.
104 CMT, 1.
105 CMT, 80–1, p. 45. See also Éigse, 18, 1981, 1–24.
106 ibid., 23.
107 *LG*, III, 1940, 236, p. 43 and note 102.
108 Winter, W., in *JIES*, 10, 1982, 168–79.
109 Muus, B.J., and Dahlstrom, P., *Freshwater Fish of Britain and Europe*, 1971.

PART FIVE: MIDE

1 The Centre Stone *(pages 194–212)*
1 Rees and Rees, op.cit., 121, and 146–172.
2 Cassirer, E., *The Philosophy of Symbolic Forms*, II, 1955, 85.
3 Dumézil, G., *The Destiny of a King*, trans. Hiltebeitel, A., 1983, 9–10.
4 'The Settling of the Manor of Tara', in *Ériu*, IV, 1910, 23–32. trans. Best, R.
5 *FW*, 474.20.
6 O'Donovan, J., OSL, West Meath, 1837.
7 O'Donovan, J., OSL, West Meath, 12.9.1837; and Borlase, op.cit., II, 372–3.
8 *TH*, IV, 117–18.
9 Quoted in Eliade, M., *Patterns in Comparative Religion*, 297.
10 Macalister, R.A.S., *PRIA*, 39c, 1929–31, Plate viii, and 54–85.
11 Book of Armagh, 21a, *Tripartite Life of St Patrick*, ed. Stokes, W., 310 and 80.
12 Geoffrey of Monmouth's British history, twelfth century, Book VIII, Ch. 12; in Giles, J.A., *Six Old English Chronicles*, 1848, 215–17.
13 See also Tatlock, J.S.P., *The Legendary History of Britain*, 1950, 40–3.
14 Leslie, J., 'Anthropic Principle, World Ensemble and Design'; in *American Philosophical Quarterly*, 19, 1982, 144.
15 *LG*, V, 1956, 35–7 and 392.
16 *Ériu*, 14, 1946, 21.
17 *LG*, V, 392, p. 37.
18 Gernon, Luke, *A discourse of Ireland*, 1620. Quoted in *Illlustrations of Irish History*, p. 348–50.
19 *EIHM*, 297.
20 *LG*, V, 414, 55, 439, p. 79.
21 Gimbutas, M., *Gods and Goddesses of Old Europe*, 1974, 211–14.
22 MD, II, Mide, 43.
23 *RC*, 15, 1894, 297.
24 Keating, op.cit., I, 112.
25 MD, II, op.cit., 43 and BD, Mide, in *Folk-lore*, 3, 1892, 476.
26 MD, 45, BD, 476, and MD, II, 45.
27 Macalister, *PRIA*, 38c, 69–70.
28 Eliade, M., *Images and Symbols*, 1961, 40.
29 Macalister, op.cit., 70.
30 Crawford, O.G.S., *The Eye Goddess*, 1957.
31 Gould, P. and White, R., *Mental Maps*, 1974, 190.

32 Toland, J., *A Critical History of the Celtic Religion and Learning, containing an Account of the Druids*, 1740, 101–4.
33 Keating, op.cit., II, 247.
34 Ledwich, E., *The Antiquities of Ireland*, 2nd ed., 1804, quoted Wood-Martin, I, 28.
35 Macalister, R.A.S., *Ancient Ireland*, 102.
36 *PRIA*, 38c, 126–7.
37 CG, 33.
38 Murphy, G., op.cit., 1954, LXVIII.
39 Whitley Stokes, Preface to CG, Codex A, 1862, xxxv.
40 O'Kearney, quoted in *UFL*, 8, 1962, 374–5.
41 Eck, D., HR, 1981, 1–14.
42 Markey, T.L., *Morning, Evening and Twilight*, 1987, 303.

2 Ériu's Eye: National Observations *(pages 213–42)*
43 *RC*, 16, 1895, 278.
44 *Ériu*, 4, 1910, 29.
45 MD, IV, 93 and MD, IV, Ailech II, 107, and *RC*, 16, 1895, 41–2.
46 Cassirer, E., *The Philosophy of Symbolic Forms*, III, 96.
47 McParlan, J., *A Statistical Survey of Donegal*, 1802, 117.
48 Rolleston, op.cit., 139–42.
49 Waterman, D., excavations 1963–71, unpublished; see Mallory, J.P., *Navan Fort*, 1988.
50 MD, IV, 309, and *RC*, 16, 1895, 281–83.
51 MD, IV, 311; See also Gantz, J. (trans.), *The Labour Pains of the Ulaid, and the Twins of Macha*, 1981, 129.
52 Kenney, James F., *The Sources for the Early History of Ireland*, I, 1929, 6.
53 Beaufort, L.C., *Trans. Royal Irish Acad.*, 6, 1828, 129. See also: Coffey, op.cit., 97–8, and Conwell, E.A., in *PRIA*, IX, 1864–66, 355–79.
54 O'Donovan, J., OSL, 30 July, 1836.
55 Conwell, op.cit., 372.
56 Mullen, M., *The Stars and the Stones*, 1983, 94 and Shee, E., *JRSAI*, 102, 1972, 207.
57 MD, *RC*, 15, 1894, 462.
58 *RC*, 15, 1894, 458–9.
59 MacNeill, M., op.cit., 311–38.
60 MD, IV, 149–153.
61 MacNeill, op.cit., 311–38.
62 Stutley, M. and J., *Hinduism, A Dictionary of*, 1977, 120.
63 Toland, op.cit., 104.
64 Keating, II., 247 and 251–3.
65 Brennan, op.cit., 102. See also Thomas, N.L., *Irish Symbols of 3,500 BC*, Dublin, 1988, 34.
66 MD, I, 4–6.
67 Ó'Ríordáin, S., *Antiquities of the Irish Countryside*, 1965, 68–70.
68 Smyth, A.P., *Celtic Leinster*, 1982, 49.
69 ibid., 49.
70 MD, II, Almu I, 17–18, and Almu II, 1–5.
71 Rawl, B., 502, 116c. See also Meyer, K. (ed. and trans.), *Hail Brigit*, Dublin, 1912, 6–7.

72 Ascribed to Senchán Torpéist, 7th century.

73 Keating, II, 331.

74 Johnston, S.A., in *Emania*, 7, 1990, 26–32.

75 Mallory, J.P., op.cit., 10.

76 *Hail Brigit*, trans. Meyer, op.cit., verse 4.

77 Plummer, C., *Lives of Irish Saints*, II, 183 and 266–7.

78 O'Brien, M.A., *The Old Irish Life of St Brigit*, IHS, I, 1938, 122, 125.

79 *Ériu*, 26, 1975, 19.

80 CG, 23.

81 *RC*, 15, 1894, 457.

82 Knox, H.T., *JRSAI*, XLI, 1911, 93–9.

83 *PSAS*, XCIII, 1959, fig. 5 and p. 49.

84 MacNeill, M., op.cit., 233.

85 MD, IV, 184 and 268. See also *RC* 16, 1895, 60.

86 trans. Bergin, O. and Best, R.I., in *Ériu*, XII, 1938, 137–193.

87 Smyth and Kennedy, op.cit., 1989, 45.

88 ibid.

89 *Ériu*, XII, 185.

90 O'Rahilly, T.F., *Ériu*, XIV, 1946, 4.

91 Herity, M., *JRSAI*, 113, 1983, 121.

92 Keating, II, 187.

93 MD, III, 351, and *RC*, 15, 463.

94 Beranger, H., quoted in Wilde, W.R., *JRSAI*, II, 1871, 247–9.

95 *RC*, 15, 463.

96 O'Maille, T., ZCP, XVIII, 1928, 144.

97 Tochmarc, Étaín, in *Ériu*, XII.

98 MD, IV, 228, and Note 437.

99 Tochmarc, Étaín, 22.

100 Keating, II, 120.

101 MD, I, 73, 355.

102 MD, IV, 233.

103 See Dames, M., *The Avebury Cycle*, 1977, 103.

104 *Ériu*, XII, 21.

105 MD, II, 3.

106 *LU*, 131, and MD, II, Note 90.

107 MD, IV 230–1.

3 Mide: All and One *(pages 243–5)*

108 Freud, S. *The Ego and the Id*, 1927, trans. Rivière, J., 1935, 9–10.

109 ibid., 23.

110 ibid., 10–12.

111 ibid., 52.

112 *Echtrae Conle*, trans. Dillon, M., in *EIL*, 102–4.

113 MacCana, P., 'The Sinless Otherworld', in *Ériu*, xxviii, 1976, 95.

CONCLUSION: HOME *(pages 247–58)*

1 Stokes, W. (trans.), *Lives of the Saints, from the fifteenth-century Book of Lismore*, 1890, 1738. See also Bowen, E.G., *The Cult of St Brigit*, in *Studia Celtica*, 8, 1973.

2 Book of Lismore, 184.

3 O'Brien, M.A., in *IHS*, I, 1938–9, 122.

4 *Tertia Vita*, c. 28, and Stokes, op.cit., 322–3.

5 St Broccan's hymn, op.cit., p. 20.

6 A hymn made for Brigit by Brennan.

7 Carmichael, A., CG, I, 231–4. See also O'Sullivan, S., *The Folklore of Ireland*. London, 1974.

8 Aalen, F.H.A., in *JRSAI*, 96, 47–50.

9 Itinerary, 1617, Vol. IV, 202.

10 Buchanan, R.H., *UFL*, 8, 1962, 29–30.

11 See *Ériu*, 26, 1975, 19.

12 O'Danahair, op.cit., 22.

13 *JCAHS*, 1955, 128.

14 Lucas, A.T., *JRSAI*, 95, 1965, 82.

15 *JRSAI*, 42, 1935, 14–16.

16 *PRIA*, 43c, 1936, 194–206.

17 *JRSAI*, 96, 1966, 32–34.

18 *Folklife*, 11, 1973, 64.

19 Stokes, W., op.cit., 184.

20 *Folk life*, op.cit., 70.

21 Carmichael, A., *The Sun Dances. Prayers and Blessings from the Gaelic*, Edinburgh, 1954, 49–51.

22 Danaher, K., *The Year in Ireland*, 34.

23 Pughe, W.O., *A National Dictionary of the Welsh Language*, 2 vols., 3rd ed., 1866.

24 Keating, op.cit., I, 130–9.

25 Book of Lismore, ed. Stokes, 192.

26 Baring-Gould, S., op.cit., 273.

27 *Graksa Cataka*, 14.

28 *LU*, 297a, and DIL.

29 Buttimer, A., *The Human Experience of Space and Place*, 1980, 170.

30 Folklife, II, 1964, 58–9.

31 Eliade, M., *Symbolism, the Sacred and the Arts*, 1986, 119.

32 ibid., 119.

33 O'Danachair, C., *The Luck of the House*, UFL, 15, 1970, 20–22.

34 Black, W.G., *Folk Medicine*, Belfast, 1883.

35 Webb, E., *The Plays of Samuel Beckett*, 1972.

36 *Irish Litanies*, ed. Plummer, C., in BS, 62, 1924, 103–7 and xxiv.

37 Anon., early fourteenth century, MS Bodl. Rawlinson, D 913. 'A genuinely popular minstrels' song, of lightness and gaiety, as shown by its realistic content, simple form, and casual manner of preservation'; see Sisam, K., *XIVth Century Verse and Prose*, 166. R.T. Davies called it 'a fascinating chance relic, left stranded on the shore by a tide that has long since receded.' *Medieval English Lyrics*, 1963, 30–1.

Pronunciation of vowels in Irish

a short, as in English 'man'.	**á** long, as in English 'awe'.
e short, as in English 'err'.	**é** long, as in English 'there'.
i short, as in English 'ill'.	**í** long, as in English 'eel'.
o short, as in English 'other'.	**ó** long, as in English 'old'.
u short, as in English 'up'.	**ú** long, as in English 'rule'.

Bibliography

Abbreviations

AC	Annals of Connacht	JIES	Journal of Indo-European Studies
ACl	Annals of Clonmacnoise	JNMAS	Journal of the North Munster Archaeological Society
Ant	Antiquity	JRHAAI	Journal of Royal Historical and Archaeological
Ant J	Antiquaries Journal		Association of Ireland
AU	Annals of Ulster	JRSAI	Journal of Royal Society of Antiquaries, Ireland
BD	Bodleian Dindshenchas	LG	Lebor Gabála Érenn
Béal	Béaloidias, Journal of Folklore Society of Ireland	LL	Book of Leinster
Carm Gad	Carmina Gadelica	LU	Lebor na hUidre
CG	Cormac's Glossary	MD	Metrical Dindshenchas
CMT	Second Battle of Mag Tuired	NCE	New Catholic Encyclopedia
DDH	Da Derga's Hostel	NLEM	New Larousse Encyclopedia of Mythology
DF	Duanaire Finn	NMAJ	North Munster Archaeological Journal
DIL	Dictionary of the Irish Language	NMD	National Museum of Ireland, Dublin
ED	Edinburgh Dindshenchas	OED	Oxford English Dictionary
EIHM	Early Irish History and Mythology	OSL	Ordnance Survey Letters
EIL	Early Irish Lyrics	PPS	Proceedings of Prehistoric Society
EIV	Early Irish Verse	PRIA	Proceedings of the Royal Irish Academy
ER	Encyclopedia of Religion	PSAS	Proceedings of Scottish Antiquarian Society
FL	Folk-lore	RC	Revue Celtique
FW	Finnegans Wake	RD	Rennes Dindshenchas
HBS	Henry Bradshaw Society	SG	Silva Gadelica
HR	History of Religion	TH	Topographia Hibernia
IFC	Irish Folklore Commission	UJA	Ulster Journal of Archaeology
IHS	Irish Historical Studies	UFL	Ulster Folk Life
ITS	Irish Texts Society	VSH	Vitae Sanctorum Hiberniae
JCHAS	Journal Cork Historical and Archaeological Society		

ANNÁLA CONNACHT, ed. Freeman, A.M., Dublin, 1944.

ANNALS OF CLONMACNOISE, trans. Mageoghagan, C., 1627, ed. Murphy, D., Dublin, 1896.

BARING-GOULD, S., Lives of the Saints, Edinburgh, 1914.

BARROW, J.D., The Anthropic Cosmological Principle, London, 1988.

BECKETT, SAMUEL, Endgame, London, 1958.

—, Waiting For Godot, London, 1954.

BERGIN, O., 'White-eared Cows', in Ériu, xiv, 1946.

BEST, R.I., (ed. and trans.), 'The Settling of the Manor of Tara', in Ériu, 4, 1910.

BIELER, L., The Irish Penitentials, Dublin, 1963.

BOLLE, K.W., 'Myth: an overview', in ER, 10, New York, 1987.

BORLASE, W.C., The Dolmens of Ireland, London, 1897.

BOWEN, E.G., 'The Cult of St Brigit' in Studia Celtica, 8, 1973/4.

Bruiden Da Choca, ed. Stokes, W., RC, xxi, 1990.

BUCK, C.D., A Dictionary of Selected Synonyms in the Principle Indo-European Languages, Chicago, 1949.

BUCHANAN, C., Traffic in Towns, London, 1963.

BUCHANAN, R.H., 'Calendar Customs', in UF, viii, 1962, and ix, 1963.

BUTTIMER, A., The Human Experience of Space and Place, London, 1980.

CAMPBELL, J. and ROBINSON, H.M., A Skeleton Key to Finnegans Wake, London, 1947.

CARMICHAEL, A., Carmina Gadelica, 5 vols, Edinburgh, 1928–1941.

CASSIRER, E., The Philosophy of Symbolic Forms, London, 1955.

Cath Maige Tuired (The Second Battle of Mag Tuired), ed. Gray, E.A., Naas, 1982.

CHART, D.A., Preliminary Survey of Ancient Monuments of Northern Ireland, Belfast, 1940.

CLARKE, H.B., 'Topographical Development of Early Medieval Dublin', in JRSAI, 107, 1977.

COFFEY, G., New Grange and other incised tumuli in Ireland, Dublin, 1912.

CRAWFORD, O.G.S., The Eye Goddess, London, 1957.

CROKER, T. CROFTON, Researches in the South of Ireland, London, 1824; reprinted Shannon, 1969.

—, 'Antiquities of Lough Gur' in The Gentleman's Magazine, 103, pt I, 1833.

CROSS, T.P., Motif-Index of Early Irish Literature, New York, 1969.

DAMES, M., The Silbury Treasure, London, New York, 1976.

—, The Avebury Cycle, London, New York, 1977.

DANAHER, K., The Year in Ireland: Irish Calendar Customs, Cork, 1972.

DANTE ALIGHIERI, The Purgatory, ed. and trans. Butler, A. J., London, 1892.

DAVIES, P.C.W., Other Worlds, London, 1980.

DAVENPORT, G., The Geography of the Imagination, London, 1984.

DE PAOR, L., 'The Viking Towns of Ireland', in Almquist, B. (ed.), Proceedings of the Seventh Viking Congress, Dublin, 1976.

DE PAOR, M. and L., Early Christian Ireland, London, 1958.

DICTIONARY OF THE IRISH LANGUAGE, ed. Quin, E.G., et al., Dublin, 1913–1976.

DILLON, M. and CHADWICK, W., The Celtic Realms, New York, 1967.

Dindshenchas, Metrical (MD), ed. Gwynn, E., Dublin, 1903–35.

265

Dindshenchas, Rennes (RD), ed. Stokes, W., in *RC*, 15–16, 1894–5.

Dindshenchas, Bodleian (BD), ed. Stokes, W., in FL, 3, 1893.

Dindshenchas, Edinburgh (ED), ed. Stokes, W., in FL, 4, 1893.

DINNEEN, P.S., *An Irish–English Dictionary*, Dublin, 1904.

Duanaire Finn ('The Poem Book of Finn'), ed. MacNeill, E., Dublin, I, 1908; II, 1933; III (ed. Murphy, G.), 1954.

'Duanaire Ghearoid Iarla' in *Studia Hibernica*, III, 1963.

DUMÉZIL, G., *The Destiny of the Warrior*, trans. Hiltebeitel, A., New York, 1970.

—, *L' idéologie tripartie des Indo-Européens*, Paris, 1958.

DWELLY, E., *The Illustrated Gaelic–English Dictionary*, Glasgow, 1949.

Echtrae Conle ('The Adventures of Conle'); trans. Dillon, M., in *EIL*.

ELIADE, M., *Birth and Rebirth: the religious meanings of initiation in human culture*, trans. Trask, W.R., New York, 1958.

—, *Myth and Reality*, trans. Trask, W.R., New York, 1963.

—, *Symbolism, the Sacred, and the Arts*, New York, 1986.

—, *The Sacred and the Profane*, New York, 1959.

ELLIS DAVIDSON, H.R., *The Sword at the Wedding*, FL, 71, 1960.

EOGAN, G., *Knowth and the Passage Tombs of Ireland*, London, 1986.

—, *The Hoards of the Later Irish Bronze Age*, Dublin, 1983.

FITZGERALD, D., *Popular Tales of Ireland*, in *RC*, IV, 1879.

FITZGERALD, REV. P., and M'GREGOR, J.T., *The History, Topography, and Antiquities of Limerick*, Dublin, 1826–7.

FODOR, N., *The Search for the Beloved*, New York, 1949.

FOUR MASTERS, THE, Annals of the Kingdom of Ireland, ed. O'Donovan, J., Dublin, 1848–51.

FOX, C., 'Chariot fittings from Lough Gur', in *Ant J*, 30, 1950.

FRASER, J. (ed.), 'The First Battle of Moytura' in *Ériu*, 8, 1916.

FREUD, S., *New Introductory Lectures on Psychoanalysis*, trans. Sprott, W.J.H., London, 1933, 78–107.

GANTZ, G. (trans. and ed.), *Early Irish Myths and Sagas*, Harmondsworth, 1981.

GARVIN, J., *James Joyce's Disunited Kingdom*, Dublin, 1976.

GELLING, P. and ELLIS DAVIDSON, H.R., *Chariot of the Sun*, London, 1969.

GEOFFREY OF MONMOUTH, *Historia regum Britanniae*, in Giles, J.A., *Six Old English Chronicles*, London, 1848.

GILBERT, J.T., *A History of the City of Dublin*, Dublin, 1854–9.

GIMBUTAS, M., *Gods and Goddesses of Old Europe*, London, 1978.

—, 'The Social Structure of Old Europe' in *JIES*, 17, 1989.

GIRALDUS CAMBRENSIS, *Topographia Hiberniae*, trans. Wright, T., London, 1905.

GLUCK, B.R., *Beckett and Joyce*, New York, 1979.

GOULD, P. and WHITE, R., *Mental Maps*, London, 1974.

Hail Brigit!, ed. and trans. Meyer, K., Dublin, 1912.

HALL, REV. JAMES, *A Tour Through Ireland*, London, 1813.

HALL, MR and MRS S.C., *Ireland, Its Scenery and Character*, London, 1841–3.

HARBISON, P., *The Archaeology of Ireland*, London, 1976.

HART, C., *Structure and Motif in Finnegans Wake*, London, 1962.

HAWKINS, P.S. (ed.), *Civitas*, London, 1986.

HEIDEGGER, M., *The question concerning technology*, trans. Lovitt, W., London, 1977.

—, *Poetry, Language, Thought*, trans. Hofstadter, A., London, 1975.

HENRY OF SALTREY, *De Purgatorio S. Patricii*, in *Patrologie Cureus Completus*, Scriptores Latini, II, Tom. 180, Paris, 1855.

HERITY, M. and EOGAN, G., *Ireland in Prehistory*, London, 1977.

HUGHES, K., *Early Christian Ireland: Introduction to the Sources*, London, 1972.

HULL, E., *Folklore of the British Isles*, London, 1928.

—, 'Legends and Traditions of Cailleach Bheara' in FL, 38, 1927.

IFC, Schools Collection, MS 516, 1938.

IFC, MS 1799. Lough Gur and Knockainey.

JAMES, G. and JONES, T. (trans.), *The Mabinogion*, London, 1974.

JOYCE, JAMES, *Dubliners*, London, 1926.

—, *Ulysses*, London, 1937.

—, *Finnegans Wake*, London, 1939.

JOYCE, P.W., *Irish Names of Places*, 2 vols, Dublin, 1901.

KEARNEY, R., *Poetics of Imagining*, London, 1991.

—, *The Wake of Imagination*, London, 1988.

KEATING, G., *Foras Feasa Ar Eirinn* (The History of Ireland.), 4 vols, ITS, Dublin, 1901–13.

KENNEY, J.F., *The Sources for the Early History of Ireland*, Dublin, 1929.

KILBRIDE-JONES, H.E., 'Excavations at Drimnagh, Co. Dublin' in *JRSAI*, 69, 1939.

KUIPER, F.B., *Cosmology and Conception*, in HR, 10, 1970.

LEASK, H.G., *Irish Churches and Monastic Buildings*, vol. I, Dublin, 1955.

LE CORBUSIER, *La Ville Radieuse. The City of Tomorrow and its Planning*, trans. Etchells, F., 8th edition, 1931.

LEDWICH, E., *The Antiquities of Ireland*, 2nd edition, Dublin, 1804.

LEHMANN, R.P.M. (trans.), *Early Irish Verse*, Austin, 1982.

LESLIE, J., 'Anthropic Principle, World Ensemble and Design', in *American Philosophical Quarterly*, 19, 1982.

LESLIE, S., *Saint Patrick's Purgatory*, London, 1932.

LIETAERT PEERBOLTE, M., *Prenatal Dynamics*, Leiden, 1954.

LITHGOW, W., *The Rare Adventures and Peregrinations of . . .*, ed. Phelps, G., London, 1974.

LOOMIS, R.S., *Celtic Myth and Arthurian Romance*, New York, 1927.

LUCAS, A.T., 'Furze in Custom and Belief' in *Béal*, 1960.

MACALISTER, R.A.S., *Ireland in Pre-Celtic Times*, Dublin, 1935.

—, (ed. and trans.), *Lebor Gabála Erenn*, 5 vols, ITS, 1938–41.

—, *Tara, a pagan sanctuary of ancient Ireland*, London, 1931.

—, *The Archaeology of Ireland*, London, 1928.

MACALISTER, R.A.S. and PRAEGER, R.L., 'Report on the Excavations at Uisneach', *PRIA*, 38c, 1928–9.

—, 'Excavations at Togherstown, Westmeath', *PRIA*, 39c, 1929–31.

MACCANA, P., *Celtic Mythology*, London, 1970.

—, 'Early Irish Ideology and the Concept of Unity' in Kearney, R., *The Irish Mind*, Dublin, 1988.

MACNEILL, M., *The Festival of Lughnasa*, Oxford, 1962.

MALLORY, J.P., *In Search of the Indo-Europeans*, London, 1989.

'MANANAAN MAC LIR', 'Folklore of the Months' in *JCHAS*, vols. I–III, 1895–97.

MASON, T.H., 'St Brigid's Crosses' in *JRSAI*, lxxv, 1945.

MAXWELL, C., *Irish History from Contemporary Sources, 1509–1610*, London, 1923.

MEYER, K. (trans.), *The Voyage of Bran*, 1903.

—, 'The March Roll of the Men of Leinster' in *Ériu*, VI, 1912.

—, 'Middle Irish Travellers' Prayers' in *Ériu*, VI, 1912.

MINK, O., *A Finnegans Wake Gazeteer*, New York, 1978.

MITCHELL, F., *The Irish Landscape*, London, 1976.

MULLEN, M., *The Stars and the Stones*, London, 1983.

MURPHY, G., *Early Irish Metrics*, Dublin, 1961.

—, (ed. and trans.), *Early Irish Lyrics, 8th to 12th Centuries*, Oxford, 1956.

O'BRIEN, M.A., 'The Old Irish Life of St Brigit' in *IHS*, I, 1938.

O'CURRY, E., *Lectures on the Manuscript Materials of Ancient Irish History*, Dublin, 1861.

O'DANACHAIR, C., 'The Luck of the House', *UFL*, 15, 1970.

O'DWYER, S., 'Three County Limerick Fairs' in Rynne, E. (ed.), *North Munster Studies*, 1967.

O'GRADY, S.O. (trans.), *Silva gadelica*, London, 1892.

Ó'HUIGINN, R., 'The Literature of the Laigin' in *Emania*, 7, 1990.

O'HÓGÁIN, D., 'Gearóid Iarla' in *Dawn*, vol. I, 1973.

O'RAHILLY, T.O., 'Aobh, Aoibheall', etc. in *Ériu*, XIV, 1946.

—, *EIHM*, Dublin, 1946.

O'REILLY, E., An Irish–English Dictionary, with a supplement by O'Donovan, J., Dublin, 1899.

Ó'RÍORDÁIN, S.P., *Antiquities of the Irish Countryside*, London, 1965.

—, 'Lough Gur Excavations, Great Stone Circle B', *PRIA*, 54c, 1951–2.

—, 'Neolithic and Bronze Age Houses on Knockadoon', *PRIA*, 55, 1952–3.

O'SULLIVAN, S., *The Folklore of Ireland*, London, 1974.

PLUMMER, C., *Bethada Náem Érenn* (Lives of the Irish Saints), 2 vols, Oxford, 1922.

—, 'Irish Litanies' in *Henry Bradshaw Society*, 62, 1924.

PUHVEL, J. (ed.), *Myth and Law Among the Indo-Europeans*, London, 1970.

RANK, O., *The Trauma of Birth*, New York, 1929; reprinted 1973.

—, *The Myth of the Birth of the Hero*, New York, 1952.

REES, A.D. and REES, B., *Celtic Heritage*, London, 1961.

ROGER OF WENDOVER, *Flores Historiarum*, trans. Giles, G.A., London, 1849.

ROLLESTON, T.W., *Myths and Legends of the Celtic Race*, London, 1985.

ROSS, A., *Pagan Celtic Britain*, London, 1967.

RYAN, REV. J., *Essays and Studies Presented to Professor Eoin MacNeill*, Dublin, 1940.

RYKWERT, J., *The Idea of a Town*, London, 1976.

'SEIGE OF HOWTH', trans. Stokes, W., in *RC*, VIII, 1887.

SIMMS, J.G., 'Connacht in the 18th Century' in *IHS*, II, 1959.

SKOMAL, S.N. and POLOMÉ, E.C. (ed.), *Proto-Indo-European, The Archaeology of a Linguistic Problem*, Washington, 1987.

SMYTH, A.P., *Celtic Leinster*, Blackrock, 1982.

SMYTH, D., *A Guide to Irish Mythology*, Blackrock, 1988.

SMYTH, D., and KENNEDY, G., *Places in Irish Mythology*, Killala, 1989.

SOMMERVILLE-LARGE, P., *Dublin*, Dublin, 1979.

STEVENSON, T.G. (ed. and trans.), *The Vision of Tundale*, Edinburgh, 1843.

STOKES, W., *The Lives of the Saints from the Book of Lismore*, Oxford, 1890.

STOKES, W., *The Tripartite Life of Patrick*, London, 1887.

STRICKER, B.H., *De Geboorte van Horus*, vol. I, Leiden, 1963.

STUTLEY, M. and J., *A Dictionary of Hinduism*, London, 1977.

Táin bó Cuailgne (The Tain . . .), trans. Kinsella, T., 1969.

TATLOCK, J.S.P., *The Legendary History of Britain*, London, 1950.

'The Burning of Finn's House', ed. Gwynn, E.J., in *Ériu*, I, 1904.

'The Destruction of Da Derga's Hostel', trans. Stokes, W., in *RC*, xxii, 1901.

'The Settling of The Manor of Tara', trans. Best, R., in *Ériu*, IV, 1910.

Tighernach's Annals, ed. Stokes, W., in *RC*, xxiii, 1902.

Tochmare Étaín (The Wooing of Étaín), trans. Bergin, O. and Best, R.I., in *Ériu*, xii, 1938.

Tóraidheacht Dhiarmada Agus Ghráinne (The Pursuit of Diarmid and Gráinne), ed. Sheaghdha, N.N., Dublin, 1967.

TOTLAND, J., *A Critical History of the Celtic Religion and Learning*, London, 1740.

VARRO, M.T., *De lingua latina*, trans. Kent, R.G., London, 1967.

—, *De re rustica*, trans, Hooper, W.D., London, 1934.

WEBB, E., *The Plays of Samuel Beckett*, London, 1972.

WENSINK, A.J., *The Ideas of the Western Semites concerning the Navel of the Earth*, Amsterdam, 1916.

WESTROPP, T.J., 'Brâzil and the Legendary Islands of the North Atlantic' in *PRIA*, 30c, 1912–14.

—, 'Dun Crot and the "Harps of Clíu" ', in *PRIA*, 35c, 1918–20.

—, 'The ancient sanctuaries of Knockainey and Clogher' in *PRIA*, 34c, 1917–19.

WHITTOW, J., *Geology and Scenery in Ireland*, London, 1974.

WILDE, LADY, *Ancient Legends, Mystic Charms and Superstitions of Ireland*, London, 1888.

WILDE, SIR W.R., 'Memoir of Gabriel Beranger' in *JRSAI*, 12, 1873.

WINDLE, B.C.A., 'On certain megalithic remains at Lough Gur' in *PRIA*, 30c, 1912–13.

WOODMAN, P.C., 'Problems in the Colonisation of Ireland' in *UJA*, 49, 1986.

—, 'The Post-glacial colonisation of Ireland' in D.Ó. Corráin, ed., *Irish Antiquity*, 93–110, Cork, 1981.

WOOD MARTIN, W.G., *Traces of the Elder Faiths of Ireland*, London, 1902.

WOODROFFE, J., *Shakti and Shakta*, Madras, 1914–16.

YEATS, W.B., *The Collected Poems*, 2nd edition, London, 1950.

—, *Mythologies*, London, 1959.

Glossary-index

Personages, deities and prominent features are indexed below. Page numbers in *italics* refer to captions

Manannán mac Lir: sea god, whose home was the Isle of Man. 69, 129, 216, 296

Manes: the Good Ones, infernal classical city gods. 135

Medb (Maev): goddess, and queen of Connacht, daughter of Crochen Croderg. 156, 168, 181, 225, 237–9, *183*

Mide: foster-son of Ériu; also the central, fifth province. 196–212

Midir: underworld god of Brí Léith (Ardagh, Co. Longford). 33, 101, 141, 233–4, 237–9, 240–2

Milesians, *alias* the Sons of Míl: Iron Age gods, and rivals of Tuatha Dé Danann. 123, 131, 201

Mórrígan (Morrigu); war goddess. 161

Nemed: leader of the mythical Nemedian invasion of Ireland. 181, 188

Nerthus: Germanic goddess. 84

Niet: war god of Grianan Ailech. 180

Oilioll Olum: King of Munster, and ravisher of Áine. 104

Oimelg (Imbolc): St Brigit's Eve and Day, 1st February; the Spring quarterday. 17, 103, 252–4; *18*

Oisín (Ossian): the blind poet son of Finn. 76, 93–4

Osiris: Egyptian harvest god, consort of Isis. 174

Partholón: king and leader of the Partholonian settlers of Ireland. 129, 178–81, 191, 215

Patrick: Patron saint of Ireland. 24–5, 29, 42, 44–5, 48, 50, 74, 100, 158, 168, 172, 200, 223; *20–1, 23, 27*

Samain: Hallowe'en; the 1st November quarterday, and traditional start of the New Year and of winter. 17, 42–3, 103, 141–3, 174, 178, 184–5, 188; *18*

Sheila-na-gig: statue of supernatural female displaying her vulva; from *Sighle na gCíoch*, 'Síle of the Breasts'. 182; *99*

Sinann: goddess of the river Shannon. 168, 170

Slighe Mhór: the great East-West Road, *see* Eiscir Riada.

síd (plural, *síde*): fairy hill or mound. 41, 47, 71, 69, 114, 135, 204, 230, 236–8, 240, 249–50; *65*

Sons of Míl: the Milesians. Iron Age gods, and rivals of the Tuatha Dé Danann. 123, 131, 201

súil: eye'; etymologically means 'sun'. 209

Tadhg: serpent of Lough Gur. 76

Táin bó Cualgne: the mythical cattle raid into Ulster from Connacht. 9, 97, 182

Tailtiu: harvest goddess of Teltown, Co. Meath. 223

Tea: goddess of Tara. 225

Tír na n'Óg: The Land of Youth. 41, 86–93

Tobar: lover of Delgnat at Inis Samer, the island below the falls at Ess Ruaid. 178–80, 181, 186

Tuan: nephew of Parthalón, sole survivor of the Partholonians, and fish lover of Nemain. 190–1

Tuatha Dé Danann; literally, the people of the Goddess Dana; a pre-Iron Age pantheon of deities; colloquially, the Fairies. 67–9, 95, 131, 160, 188

Tuathal Techmar: first-century AD king who enlarged Mide. 196, 225

Uainide: green god of Cnoc Áine. 68, 77–8, 219; *65*

Ugaine: ploughman god of Leinster. 121

Umbilicus Hiberniae: also Rock of the Cat (*Carraig a'chait*): *see* Aill na Mireann.

Uisnech (Uisneach), Co. Westmeath: synonymous with the hill of Mide, the mystical fifth province of Ireland. 15, 17, 196–214, 218, 220, 224, 228, 230, 237, 243–5, 255; *195, 199, 207*

Index

Personages and deities are separately indexed in the Glossary (above). Page numbers in *italics* refer to captions

269